MznLnx

Missing Links Exam Preps

Exam Prep for

Essentials of Investments

Bodie, Kane, & Marcus, 6th Edition

MznLnx

Rico
Publications

Exam Prep for Essentials of Investments
6th Edition
Bodie, Kane, & Marcus

Publisher: Raymond Houge

Assistant Editor: Michael Rouger

Text and Cover Designer: Lisa Buckner

Marketing Manager: Sara Swagger

Project Manager, Editorial Production: Jerry Emerson

Art Director: Vernon Lowerui

Product Manager: Dave Mason

Editorial Assitant: Rachel Guzmanji

Pedagogy: Debra Long

Cover Image: Jim Reed/Getty Images

Text and Cover Printer: City Printing, Inc.

Compositor: Media Mix, Inc.

For more information about our products, contact us at:

Dave.Mason@RicoPublications.com

For permission to use material from this text or

product, submit a request online to:

Dave.Mason@RicoPublications.com

Printed in the United States
ISBN:

Contents

Contents (Cont.)

TO THE STUDENT

COMPREHENSIVE

The *MznLnx* Exam Prep series is designed to help you pass your exams. Editors at MznLnx review your textbooks and then prepare these practice exams to help you master the textbook material. Unlike study guides, workbooks, and practice tests provided by the texbook publisher and textbook authors, *MznLnx* gives you **all** of the material in each chapter in exam form, not just samples, so you can be sure to nail your exam.

MECHANICAL

The MznLnx Exam Prep series creates exams that will help you learn the subject matter as well as test you on your understanding. Each question is designed to help you master the concept. Just working through the exams, you gain an understanding of the subject--its a simple mechanical process that produces success.

INTEGRATED STUDY GUIDE AND REVIEW

MznLnx is not just a set of exams designed to test you, its also a comprehensive review of the subject content. Each exam question is also a review of the concept, making sure that you will get the answer correct without having to go to other sources of material. You learn as you go! Its the easiest way to pass an exam.

HUMOR

Studying can be tedious and dry. MznLnx's instructional design includes moderate humor within the exam questions on occassion, to break the tedium and revitalize the brain

1. In finance, a _____ is a debt security, in which the authorized issuer owes the holders a debt and, depending on the terms of the _____, is obliged to pay interest (the coupon) and/or to repay the principal at a later date, termed maturity.

Thus a _____ is a loan: the issuer is the borrower, the _____ holder is the lender, and the coupon is the interest. _____s provide the borrower with external funds to finance long-term investments, or, in the case of government _____s, to finance current expenditure.

  a. Catastrophe bonds   b. Puttable bond
  c. Convertible bond   d. Bond

2. The _____ is a financial market where participants buy and sell debt securities, usually in the form of bonds. As of 2006, the size of the international _____ is an estimated $45 trillion, of which the size of the outstanding U.S. _____ debt was $25.2 trillion.

Nearly all of the $923 billion average daily trading volume in the U.S. _____ takes place between broker-dealers and large institutions in a decentralized, over-the-counter market.

  a. 4-4-5 Calendar   b. 529 plan
  c. Fixed income   d. Bond market

3. _____ are made by investors and investment managers.

Investors commonly perform investment analysis by making use of fundamental analysis, technical analysis and gut feel.

_____ are often supported by decision tools.

  a. Asset allocation   b. Investment decisions
  c. Investing online   d. Investment performance

4. In business and accounting, _____s are everything of value that is owned by a person or company. The balance sheet of a firm records the monetary value of the _____s owned by the firm. The two major _____ classes are tangible _____s and intangible _____s.

  a. Income   b. EBITDA
  c. Accounts payable   d. Asset

5. The _____ is the market for securities, where companies and governments can raise longterm funds. The _____ includes the stock market and the bond market. Financial regulators, such as the U.S. Securities and Exchange Commission, oversee the _____s in their designated countries to ensure that investors are protected against fraud.

  a. Capital market   b. Delta neutral
  c. Forward market   d. Spot rate

6.   The institution most often referenced by the word '_____' is a public or publicly traded _____, the shares of which are traded on a public stock exchange (e.g., the New York Stock Exchange or Nasdaq in the United States) where shares of stock of _____s are bought and sold by and to the general public. Most of the largest businesses in the world are publicly traded _____s. However, the majority of _____s are said to be closely held, privately held or close _____s, meaning that no ready market exists for the trading of shares.

  a. Depository Trust Company   b. Corporation
  c. Federal Home Loan Mortgage Corporation   d. Protect

7.   _____s are deposits denominated in United States dollars at banks outside the United States, and thus are not under the jurisdiction of the Federal Reserve. Consequently, such deposits are subject to much less regulation than similar deposits within the United States, allowing for higher margins. There is nothing 'European' about _____ deposits; a US dollar-denominated deposit in Tokyo or Caracas would likewise be deemed _____ deposits.

  a. Eurodollar   b. AAB
  c. ABN Amro   d. A Random Walk Down Wall Street

8.   _____ of a business involves analyzing its financial statements and health, its management and competitive advantages, and its competitors and markets. The term is used to distinguish such analysis from other types of investment analysis, such as quantitative analysis and technical analysis.

_____ is performed on historical and present data, but with the goal of making financial forecasts.

  a. Growth stocks   b. Fundamental analysis
  c. 4-4-5 Calendar   d. Stock valuation

9.   _____ is a branch of economics that deals with the performance, structure, and behavior of a national or regional economy as a whole. Along with microeconomics, _____ is one of the two most general fields in economics. Macroeconomists study aggregated indicators such as GDP, unemployment rates, and price indices to understand how the whole economy functions.

  a. Human capital   b. Behavioral finance
  c. Recession   d. Macroeconomics

10.   A _____ is a fungible, negotiable instrument representing financial value. They are broadly categorized into debt securities (such as banknotes, bonds and debentures), and equity securities; e.g., common stocks. The company or other entity issuing the _____ is called the issuer.

  a. Book entry   b. Securities lending
  c. Tracking stock   d. Security

11.   _____ is a security analysis discipline for forecasting the future direction of prices through the study of past market data, primarily price and volume. In its purest form, _____ considers only the actual price and volume behavior of the market or instrument. Technical analysts may employ models and trading rules based on price and volume transformations, such as the relative strength index, moving averages, regressions, inter-market and intra-market price correlations, cycles or, classically, through recognition of chart patterns.

  a. Point and figure   b. Technical analysis
  c. Support and resistance   d. Dow theory

12. _____ is a risk-adjusted measure of the so-called active return on an investment. It is the return in excess of the compensation for the risk borne, and thus commonly used to assess active managers' performances. Often, the return of a benchmark is subtracted in order to consider relative performance, which yields Jensen's _____.
   a. Amortization
   c. Option
   b. Alpha
   d. Annuity

13. In financial accounting, a _____ or statement of financial position is a summary of a person's or organization's balances. Assets, liabilities and ownership equity are listed as of a specific date, such as the end of its financial year. A _____ is often described as a snapshot of a company's financial condition.
   a. Financial statements
   c. Balance sheet
   b. Statement on Auditing Standards No. 70: Service Organizations
   d. Statement of retained earnings

14. _____ is a legal entity that develops, registers and sells securities for the purpose of financing its operations. _____s may be domestic or foreign governments, corporations or investment trusts. _____s are legally responsible for the obligations of the issue and for reporting financial conditions, material developments and any other operational activities as required by the regulations of their jurisdictions.
   a. Efficient-market hypothesis
   c. Initial margin
   b. Issuer
   d. Arbitrage

15. In the most general sense, a _____ is anything that is a hindrance, or puts individuals at a disadvantage.

Before we discuss the financial terms, we should note that a _____ can also have a much more important slang meaning.

This is best described in an example.

   a. McFadden Act
   c. Limited liability
   b. Covenant
   d. Liability

16. In finance, _____ is the process of estimating the potential market value of a financial asset or liability. they can be done on assets (for example, investments in marketable securities such as stocks, options, business enterprises, or intangible assets such as patents and trademarks) or on liabilities (e.g., Bonds issued by a company.) _____s are required in many contexts including investment analysis, capital budgeting, merger and acquisition transactions, financial reporting, taxable events to determine the proper tax liability, and in litigation.
   a. Share
   c. Procter ' Gamble
   b. Margin
   d. Valuation

17. _____ are dollar-denominated bonds, issued mostly by Latin American countries in the 1980s, named after U.S. Treasury Secretary Nicholas Brady.

_____ were created in March 1989 in order to convert bonds issued by mostly Latin American countries into a variety or 'menu' of new bonds after many of those countries defaulted on their debt in the 1980's. At that time, the market for sovereign debt was small and illiquid, and the standardization of emerging-market debt facilitated risk-spreading and trading.

a. Municipal bond
c. Coupon rate

b. Brady bonds
d. Nominal yield

18. A _____ s a time deposit, a financial product commonly offered to consumers by banks, thrift institutions, and credit unions.

They are similar to savings accounts in that they are insured and thus virtually risk-free; they are 'money in the bank'. They are different from savings accounts in that they have a specific, fixed term (often three months, six months, or one to five years), and, usually, a fixed interest rate.

a. Certificate of deposit
c. Time deposit

b. Reserve requirement
d. Variable rate mortgage

19. A _____ is a bond issued by a corporation. The term is usually applied to longer-term debt instruments, generally with a maturity date falling at least a year after their issue date. (The term 'commercial paper' is sometimes used for instruments with a shorter maturity.)

a. Serial bond
c. Brady bonds

b. Government bond
d. Corporate bond

20. _____ refers to any type of investment that yields a regular (or fixed) return.

For example, if you lend money to a borrower and the borrower has to pay interest once a month, you have been issued a fixed-income security. When a company does this, it is often called a bond or corporate bank debt (although preferred stock is also sometimes considered to be _____).

a. Fixed income
c. Bond market

b. 4-4-5 Calendar
d. 529 plan

21. _____ is a fee paid on borrowed assets. It is the price paid for the use of borrowed money , or, money earned by deposited funds . Assets that are sometimes lent with _____ include money, shares, consumer goods through hire purchase, major assets such as aircraft, and even entire factories in finance lease arrangements.

a. A Random Walk Down Wall Street
c. Interest

b. Insolvency
d. AAB

22. An _____ is the price a borrower pays for the use of money they do not own, and the return a lender receives for deferring the use of funds, by lending it to the borrower. _____s are normally expressed as a percentage rate over the period of one year.

_____s targets are also a vital tool of monetary policy and are used to control variables like investment, inflation, and unemployment.

a. A Random Walk Down Wall Street
c. ABN Amro

b. AAB
d. Interest rate

23.   In finance, the _____ is the global financial market for short-term borrowing and lending. It provides short-term liquidity funding for the global financial system. The _____ is where short-term obligations such as Treasury bills, commercial paper and bankers' acceptances are bought and sold.

   a. Debt-for-equity swap   b. Consumer debt

   c. Cramdown   d. Money market

24.   _____ mature in one year or less. Like zero-coupon bonds, they do not pay interest prior to maturity; instead they are sold at a discount of the par value to create a positive yield to maturity. Many regard _____ as the least risky investment available to U.S. investors.

   a. Treasury securities   b. 4-4-5 Calendar

   c. Treasury Inflation Protected Securities   d. Treasury bills

25.   _____ are government bonds issued by the United States Department of the Treasury through the Bureau of the Public Debt. They are the debt financing instruments of the U.S. Federal government, and they are often referred to simply as Treasuries or Treasurys. There are four types of marketable _____: Treasury bills, Treasury notes, Treasury bonds, and Treasury Inflation Protected Securities (TIPS.)

   a. Treasury Inflation-Protected Securities   b. 4-4-5 Calendar

   c. Treasury Inflation Protected Securities   d. Treasury securities

26.   The terms _____ , nominal _____, and effective _____ describe the interest rate for a whole year (annualized), rather than just a monthly fee/rate, as applied on a loan, mortgage, credit card, etc. Those terms have formal, legal definitions in some countries or legal jurisdictions, but in general:

      • The nominal _____ is the simple-interest rate (for a year.)

      • The effective _____ is the fee+compound interest rate (calculated across a year.)

The nominal _____ is calculated as: the rate, for a payment period, multiplied by the number of payment periods in a year. However, the exact legal definition of 'effective _____' can vary greatly in each jurisdiction, depending on the type of fees included, such as participation fees, loan origination fees, monthly service charges, or late fees. The effective _____ has been called the 'mathematically-true' interest rate for each year. The computation for the effective _____, as the fee+compound interest rate, can also vary depending on whether the up-front fees, such as origination or participation fees, are added to the entire amount, or treated as a short-term loan due in the first payment.

   a. Annual percentage rate   b. ABN Amro

   c. AAB   d. A Random Walk Down Wall Street

27.   In business, _____ is the total assets minus total outside liabilities of an individual or a company. For a company, this is called shareholders' equity and may be referred to as book value. _____ is stated as at a particular point in time.

   a. Moneylender   b. Restructuring

   c. Certified International Investment Analyst   d. Net worth

28.   A _____ is a financial contract between two parties, the buyer and the seller of this type of option. Often it is simply labeled a 'call'. The buyer of the option has the right, but not the obligation to buy an agreed quantity of a particular commodity or financial instrument (the underlying instrument) from the seller of the option at a certain time (the expiration date) for a certain price (the strike price.)

a. Bear spread   b. Bull spread

c. Bear call spread   d. Call option

29. _____ is a form of corporation equity ownership represented in the securities. It is dangerous in comparison to preferred shares and some other investment options, in that in the event of bankruptcy, _____ investors receive their funds after preferred stockholders, bondholders, creditors, etc. On the other hand, common shares on average perform better than preferred shares or bonds over time.

a. Stock split   b. Stop-limit order

c. Common stock   d. Stock market bubble

30. In finance, _____ occurs when a debtor has not met its legal obligations according to the debt contract, e.g. it has not made a scheduled payment, or has violated a loan covenant (condition) of the debt contract. _____ may occur if the debtor is either unwilling or unable to pay their debt. This can occur with all debt obligations including bonds, mortgages, loans, and promissory notes.

a. Credit crunch   b. Default

c. Vendor finance   d. Debt validation

31. _____ is the risk of loss due to a debtor's non-payment of a loan or other line of credit (either the principal or interest (coupon) or both)

Most lenders employ their own models (credit scorecards) to rank potential and existing customers according to risk, and then apply appropriate strategies. With products such as unsecured personal loans or mortgages, lenders charge a higher price for higher risk customers and vice versa. With revolving products such as credit cards and overdrafts, risk is controlled through careful setting of credit limits.

a. Market risk   b. Liquidity risk

c. Transaction risk   d. Credit risk

32. A _____ is a financial contract whose value is derived from the value of something else (known as the underlying.) The underlying on which a _____ is based can be an asset, weather conditions bonds or other forms of credit.

a. 529 plan   b. 7-Eleven

c. 4-4-5 Calendar   d. Derivative

33. In economics, a _____ is a mechanism that allows people to easily buy and sell (trade) financial securities (such as stocks and bonds), commodities (such as precious metals or agricultural goods), and other fungible items of value at low transaction costs and at prices that reflect the efficient-market hypothesis.

_____s have evolved significantly over several hundred years and are undergoing constant innovation to improve liquidity.

Both general markets (where many commodities are traded) and specialized markets (where only one commodity is traded) exist.

a. Secondary market

b. Cost of carry

c. Delta hedging

d. Financial market

34.   In finance, a _____ is a standardized contract, to buy or sell a specified commodity of standardized quality at a certain date in the future, at a market determined price (the futures price.)

The price is determined by the instantaneous equilibrium between the forces of supply and demand among competing buy and sell orders on the exchange at the time of the purchase or sale of the contract.

In many cases, the items may be such non-traditional 'commodities' as foreign currencies, commercial or government paper [e.g., bonds], or 'baskets' of corporate equity ['stock indices'] or other financial instruments.

a. Financial future

b. Repurchase agreement

c. Futures contract

d. Heston model

35.   In finance, a _____ (non-investment grade bond, speculative grade bond or junk bond) is a bond that is rated below investment grade at the time of purchase. These bonds have a higher risk of default or other adverse credit events, but typically pay higher yields than better quality bonds in order to make them attractive to investors.

a. High yield bond

b. Sharpe ratio

c. Volatility

d. Private equity

36.   An _____ is a contract written by a seller that conveys to the buyer the right -- but not the obligation -- to buy (in the case of a call _____) or to sell (in the case of a put _____) a particular asset, such as a piece of property such as, among others, a futures contract. In return for granting the _____, the seller collects a payment (the premium) from the buyer.

For example, buying a call _____ provides the right to buy a specified quantity of a security at a set strike price at some time on or before expiration, while buying a put _____ provides the right to sell.

a. AT'T Mobility LLC

b. Annuity

c. Amortization

d. Option

37.   _____ is the discipline of identifying, monitoring and limiting risks. In some cases the acceptable risk may be near zero. Risks can come from accidents, natural causes and disasters as well as deliberate attacks from an adversary.

a. 4-4-5 Calendar

b. Penny stock

c. FIFO

d. Risk management

38.   _____ (in a financial context) is the assumption of the risk of loss, in return for the uncertain possibility of a reward. Only if one may safely say that a particular position involves no risk may one say, strictly speaking, that such a position represents an 'investment.' Financial _____ involves the buying, holding, selling, and short-selling of stocks, bonds, commodities, currencies, collectibles, real estate, derivatives, or any valuable financial instrument to profit from fluctuations in its price as opposed to buying it for use or for income via methods such as dividends or interest. _____ represents one of four market roles in Western financial markets, distinct from hedging, long- or short-term investing, and arbitrage.

a. Central Securities Depository   b. Speculation

c. Market anomaly   d. Forward market

39.   In finance, a _____ is a derivative in which two counterparties agree to exchange one stream of cash flows against another stream. These streams are called the legs of the _____.

The cash flows are calculated over a notional principal amount, which is usually not exchanged between counterparties.

a. Volatility swap   b. Local volatility

c. Volatility arbitrage   d. Swap

40.   A _____ is an exchange of promises between two or more parties to do an act which is enforceable in a court of law. It is where an unqualified offer meets a qualified acceptance and the parties reach Consensus ad Idem. The parties must have the necessary capacity to _____ and the _____ must not be either trifling, indeterminate, impossible or illegal.

a. 7-Eleven   b. 529 plan

c. 4-4-5 Calendar   d. Contract

41.   A _____ is a variable associated with an increased risk of disease or infection. They are correlational and not necessarily causal, because correlation does not imply causation. For example, being young cannot be said to cause measles, but young people are more at risk as they are less likely to have developed immunity during a previous epidemic.

a. 4-4-5 Calendar   b. 7-Eleven

c. 529 plan   d. Risk factor

42.   In political science and economics, the _____ or agency dilemma treats the difficulties that arise under conditions of incomplete and asymmetric information when a principal hires an agent. Various mechanisms may be used to try to align the interests of the agent with those of the principal, such as piece rates/commissions, profit sharing, efficiency wages, performance measurement (including financial statements), the agent posting a bond, or fear of firing. The _____ is found in most employer/employee relationships, for example, when stockholders hire top executives of corporations.

a. Principal-agent problem   b. 529 plan

c. 7-Eleven   d. 4-4-5 Calendar

43.   The key date to remember for dividend paying stocks is the _____. The _____ is different from the record date. The _____ is typically two trading days before the record date.

In order to receive the upcoming dividend payment payout, you must already own or you must purchase the stock prior to the _____. It is important to note that in most countries, when you buy or sell any stock, there is a three trading-day settlement period on your order.

a. Index number   b. Insolvency

c. Asian Financial Crisis   d. Ex-dividend date

44.   An _____ is a company whose main business is holding securities of other companies purely for investment purposes. The _____ invests money on behalf of its shareholders who in turn share in the profits and losses.

a. Investment company   b. AAB

c. Unit investment trust   d. A Random Walk Down Wall Street

45. _____ is the risk that the value of an investment will decrease due to moves in market factors. The five standard _____ factors are:

- Equity risk, the risk that stock prices will change.
- Interest rate risk, the risk that interest rates will change.
- Currency risk, the risk that foreign exchange rates will change.
- Commodity risk, the risk that commodity prices (e.g. grains, metals) will change.

As with other forms of risk, _____ may be measured in a number of ways. Traditionally, this is done using a Value at Risk methodology. Value at risk is well established as a risk management technique, but it contains a number of limiting assumptions that constrain its accuracy.

a. Transaction risk   b. Currency risk

c. Tracking error   d. Market risk

46. _____ LLP, based in Chicago, was once one of the 'Big Five' accounting firms among PricewaterhouseCoopers, Deloitte Touche Tohmatsu, Ernst ' Young and KPMG, providing auditing, tax, and consulting services to large corporations. In 2002, the firm voluntarily surrendered its licenses to practice as Certified Public Accountants in the United States after being found guilty of criminal charges relating to the firm's handling of the auditing of Enron, the energy corporation, resulting in the loss of 85,000 jobs. Although the verdict was subsequently overturned by the Supreme Court of the United States, it has not returned as a viable business.

a. Information Systems Audit and Control Association   b. Institute of Financial Accountants

c. Accion USA   d. Arthur Andersen

47. _____ is the set of processes, customs, policies, laws and institutions affecting the way a corporation is directed, administered or controlled. _____ also includes the relationships among the many stakeholders involved and the goals for which the corporation is governed. The principal stakeholders are the shareholders, management and the board of directors.

a. Due diligence   b. Foreign Corrupt Practices Act

c. Corporate governance   d. Patent

48. The _____ is one of several stock market indices, created by nineteenth-century Wall Street Journal editor and Dow Jones ' Company co-founder Charles Dow. Dow compiled the index to gauge the performance of the industrial sector of the American stock market. It is the second-oldest U.S. market index, after the Dow Jones Transportation Average, which Dow also created.

a. 4-4-5 Calendar   b. 529 plan

c. 7-Eleven   d. Dow Jones Industrial Average

49. In business, a _____ is the purchase of one company (the target) by another (the acquirer or bidder). In the UK the term refers to the acquisition of a public company whose shares are listed on a stock exchange, in contrast to the acquisition of a private company.

Before a bidder makes an offer for another company, it usually first informs that company's board of directors.

a. 529 plan
b. Takeover
c. Stock swap
d. 4-4-5 Calendar

50. A _____ is the price of a single share of a no. of saleable stocks of the company. Once the stock is purchased, the owner becomes a shareholder of the company that issued the share.
a. Trading curb
b. Whisper numbers
c. Share price
d. Stock split

51. _____ is the provision of resources (such as granting a loan) by one party to another party where that second party does not reimburse the first party immediately, thereby generating a debt, and instead arranges either to repay or return those resources (or material(s) of equal value) at a later date. The first party is called a creditor, also known as a lender, while the second party is called a debtor, also known as a borrower.

Movements of financial capital are normally dependent on either _____ or equity transfers.

a. Clearing house
b. Comparable
c. Warrant
d. Credit

52. A _____ is a type of auction where the auctioneer begins with a high asking price which is lowered until some participant is willing to accept the auctioneer's price, or a predetermined reserve price (the seller's minimum acceptable price) is reached. The winning participant pays the last announced price. This is also known as a 'clock auction' or an open-outcry descending-price auction.
a. 529 plan
b. Dutch auction
c. 4-4-5 Calendar
d. 7-Eleven

53. The U.S. _____ is an independent agency of the United States government which holds primary responsibility for enforcing the federal securities laws and regulating the securities industry, the nation's stock and options exchanges, and other electronic securities markets. The SEC was created by section 4 of the SEC of 1934 (now codified as 15 U.S.C. §78d and commonly referred to as the 1934 Act.)
a. Securities and Exchange Commission
b. 4-4-5 Calendar
c. 7-Eleven
d. 529 plan

54. A _____, securities exchange or (in Europe) bourse is a corporation or mutual organization which provides 'trading' facilities for stock brokers and traders, to trade stocks and other securities. _____s also provide facilities for the issue and redemption of securities as well as other financial instruments and capital events including the payment of income and dividends. The securities traded on a _____ include: shares issued by companies, unit trusts and other pooled investment products and bonds.
a. 4-4-5 Calendar
b. 7-Eleven
c. Stock Exchange
d. 529 plan

55. A _____ is a private or public market for the trading of company stock and derivatives of company stock at an agreed price; these are securities listed on a stock exchange as well as those only traded privately.

The size of the world _____ is estimated at about $36.6 trillion US at the beginning of October 2008 . The world derivatives market has been estimated at about $480 trillion face or nominal value, 12 times the size of the entire world economy.

a. Andrew Tobias
c. Anton Gelonkin

b. Stock market
d. Adolph Coors

56. A _____ or bank is a financial institution whose primary activity is to act as a payment agent for customers and to borrow and lend money.

The first modern bank was founded in Italy in Genoa in 1406, its name was Banco di San Giorgio (Bank of St. George.)

Many other financial activities were added over time.

a. Banker
c. 4-4-5 Calendar

b. Black Sea Trade and Development Bank
d. Bought deal

57. In the global money market, _____ is an unsecured promissory note with a fixed maturity of one to 270 days. _____ is a money-market security issued (sold) by large banks and corporations to get money to meet short term debt obligations (for example, payroll), and is only backed by an issuing bank or corporation's promise to pay the face amount on the maturity date specified on the note. Since it is not backed by collateral, only firms with excellent credit ratings from a recognized rating agency will be able to sell their _____ at a reasonable price.

a. Book building
c. Trade-off theory

b. Commercial paper
d. Financial distress

58. _____, is when a company issues common stock or shares to the public for the first time. They are often issued by smaller, younger companies seeking capital to expand, but can also be done by large privately-owned companies looking to become publicly traded.

In an _____ the issuer may obtain the assistance of an underwriting firm, which helps it determine what type of security to issue (common or preferred), best offering price and time to bring it to market.

a. Insolvency
c. Interest

b. Initial public offering
d. Asian Financial Crisis

59. _____ is a term used to refer to how an investor distributes his or her investments among various classes of investment vehicles (e.g., stocks and bonds.)

A large part of financial planning is finding an _____ that is appropriate for a given person in terms of their appetite for and ability to shoulder risk. This can depend on various factors; see investor profile.

a. Investment performance
c. Investing online

b. Alternative investment
d. Asset allocation

60. Behavioral economics and _____ are closely related fields that have evolved to be a separate branch of economic and financial analysis which applies scientific research on human and social, cognitive and emotional factors to better understand economic decisions by, say, consumers, borrowers, investors, and how they affect market prices, returns and the allocation of resources.

The field is primarily concerned with the bounds of rationality (selfishness, self-control) of economic agents. Behavioral models typically integrate insights from psychology with neo-classical economic theory.

a. Market structure

b. Behavioral finance

c. Medium of exchange

d. Recession

61. _____ are organizations which pool large sums of money and invest those sums in companies. They include banks, insurance companies, retirement or pension funds, hedge funds and mutual funds. Their role in the economy is to act as highly specialized investors on behalf of others.

a. ABN Amro

b. Institutional investors

c. A Random Walk Down Wall Street

d. AAB

62. _____ is a life of security. It may also refer to the final payment date of a loan or other financial instrument, at which point all remaining interest and principal is due to be paid.

1, 3, 6 months _____ band can be calculated by using 30-day per month periods.

a. Primary market

b. Maturity

c. False billing

d. Replacement cost

63. _____, authored by professors Benjamin Graham and David Dodd of Columbia Business School, laid the intellectual foundation for what would later be called value investing. The work was first published in 1934, following unprecedented losses on Wall Street. In summing up lessons learned, Graham and Dodd chided Wall Street for its myopic focus on a company's reported earnings per share, and were particularly harsh on the favored 'earnings trends.' They encouraged investors to take an entirely different approach by gauging the rough value of the operating business that lay behind the security.

a. 4-4-5 Calendar

b. Stock valuation

c. Growth stocks

d. Security analysis

64. In finance, _____, also known as return on investment is the ratio of money gained or lost on an investment relative to the amount of money invested. The amount of money gained or lost may be referred to as interest, profit/loss, gain/loss, or net income/loss. The money invested may be referred to as the asset, capital, principal, or the cost basis of the investment.

a. Composiition of Creditors

b. Doctrine of the Proper Law

c. Stock or scrip dividends

d. Rate of return

65. _____ in finance is a risk management technique, related to hedging, that mixes a wide variety of investments within a portfolio. Because the fluctuations of a single security have less impact on a diverse portfolio, _____ minimizes the risk from any one investment.

A simple example of _____ is the following: On a particular island the entire economy consists of two companies: one that sells umbrellas and another that sells sunscreen.

a. 529 plan

b. 7-Eleven

c. 4-4-5 Calendar

d. Diversification

66. The _____ is the weighted-average most likely outcome in gambling, probability theory, economics or finance.

In gambling and probability theory, there is usually a discrete set of possible outcomes. In this case, _____ is a measure of the relative balance of win or loss weighted by their chances of occurring.

a. A Random Walk Down Wall Street

b. ABN Amro

c. Expected return

d. AAB

67. Depending on the nature of the investment, the type of _____ will vary.

A common concern with any investment is that you may lose the money you invest - your capital. This risk is therefore often referred to as 'capital risk.'

If the assets you invest in are held in another currency there is a risk that currency movements alone may affect the value.

a. A Random Walk Down Wall Street

b. ABN Amro

c. Investment risk

d. AAB

68. A _____ is a portfolio consisting of a weighted sum of every asset in the market, with weights in the proportions that they exist in the market (with the necessary assumption that these assets are infinitely divisible.)

Neha Tyagi's critique (1977) states that this is only a theoretical concept, as to create a _____ for investment purposes in practice would necessarily include every single possible available asset, including real estate, precious metals, stamp collections, jewelry, and anything with any worth, as the theoretical market being referred to would be the world market. As a result, proxies for the market are used in practice by investors.

a. Market price

b. Central Securities Depository

c. Delta neutral

d. Market portfolio

69. In statistics, _____ has two related meanings:

- the arithmetic _____
- the expected value of a random variable, which is also called the population _____.

It is sometimes stated that the '_____' is average. This is incorrect if '_____' is taken in the specific sense of 'arithmetic _____' as there are different types of averages: the _____, median, and mode. Other simple statistical analyses use measures of spread, such as range, interquartile range, or standard deviation. For a real-valued random variable X, the _____ is the expectation of X. Note that not every probability distribution has a defined _____; see the Cauchy distribution for an example.

a. Harmonic mean   b. Probability distribution
c. Sample size   d. Mean

70. _____ proposes how rational investors will use diversification to optimize their portfolios, and how a risky asset should be priced. The basic concepts of the theory are Markowitz diversification, the efficient frontier, capital asset pricing model, the alpha and beta coefficients, the Capital Market Line and the Securities Market Line.

_____ models an asset's return as a random variable, and models a portfolio as a weighted combination of assets so that the return of a portfolio is the weighted combination of the assets' returns.

a. Market value   b. Consumer basket
c. Modern portfolio theory   d. Payback period

71. The _____ is the relationship between the amount of return gained on an investment and the amount of risk undertaken in that investment. The more return sought, the more risk that must be undertaken.

There are various classes of possible investments, each with their own positions on the overall _____.

a. Blank endorsement   b. Post earnings announcement drift
c. Risk-return spectrum   d. Fiscal sponsorship

72. _____ refers to a portfolio management strategy where the manager makes specific investments with the goal of outperforming an investment benchmark index. Investors or mutual funds that do not aspire to create a return in excess of a benchmark index will often invest in an index fund that replicates as closely as possible the investment weighting and returns of that index; this is called passive management. _____ is the opposite of passive management, because in passive management the manager does not seek to outperform the benchmark index.

a. AAB   b. Active management
c. ABN Amro   d. A Random Walk Down Wall Street

73. A _____ is a situation that involves losing one quality or aspect of something in return for gaining another quality or aspect. It implies a decision to be made with full comprehension of both the upside and downside of a particular choice.

In economics the term is expressed as opportunity cost, referring the most preferred alternative given up.

a. Capital outflow   b. Total revenue
c. Break-even point   d. Trade-off

74. A _____ is an institution, firm or individual who mediates between two or more parties in a financial context. Typically the first party is a provider of a product or service and the second party is a consumer or customer.

In the U.S., a _____ is typically an institution that facilitates the channelling of funds between lenders and borrowers indirectly.

a. Net asset value   b. Mutual fund
c. Savings and loan association   d. Financial intermediary

75. In accounting, _____ or *Carrying value* is the value of an asset according to its balance sheet account balance. For assets, the value is based on the original cost of the asset less any depreciation, amortization or impairment costs made against the asset. A company's _____ is its total assets minus intangible assets and liabilities.
   a. Retained earnings
   c. Current liabilities
   b. Pro forma
   d. Book value

76. In finance, a _____ is the party in a loan agreement which receives money or other instrument from a lender and promises to repay the lender in a specified time.
   a. Borrower
   c. Cash credit
   b. Line of credit
   d. Debt management plan

77.

A _____ is a type of financial intermediary and a type of bank. Commercial banking is also known as business banking. It is a bank that provides checking accounts, savings accounts, and money market accounts and that accepts time deposits.

   a. 7-Eleven
   c. 4-4-5 Calendar
   b. Commercial bank
   d. 529 plan

78. A _____ is a cooperative financial institution that is owned and controlled by its members, and operated for the purpose of promoting thrift, providing credit at reasonable rates, and providing other financial services to its members. Many _____ s exist to further community development or sustainable international development on a local level. Worldwide, _____ systems vary significantly in terms of total system assets and average institution asset size since _____ s exist in a wide range of sizes, ranging from volunteer operations with a handful of members to institutions with several billion dollars in assets and hundreds of thousands of members.
   a. Credit union
   c. Fi-linx
   b. Corporate credit union
   d. Credit Union Service Organization

79. _____, in microeconomics, are the cost advantages that a business obtains due to expansion. _____ may be utilized by any size firm expanding its scale of operation.
   a. Articles of incorporation
   c. Uniform Commercial Code
   b. Employee Retirement Income Security Act
   d. Economies of scale

80. A _____ is a professionally managed type of collective investment scheme that pools money from many investors and invests it in stocks, bonds, short-term money market instruments, and/or other securities. The _____ will have a fund manager that trades the pooled money on a regular basis. Currently, the worldwide value of all _____ s totals more than $26 trillion.

Since 1940, there have been three basic types of investment companies in the United States: open-end funds, also known in the US as _____ s; unit investment trusts (UITs); and closed-end funds.

   a. Financial intermediary
   c. Net asset value
   b. Trust company
   d. Mutual fund

81.   An _____ represents the ownership in the shares of a foreign company trading on US financial markets. The stock
of many non-US companies trades on US exchanges through the use of _____s. _____s enable US investors to buy
shares in foreign companies without undertaking cross-border transactions.
   a. ABN Amro   b. A Random Walk Down Wall Street
   c. American Depository Receipt   d. AAB

82.   The _____ is that part of the capital markets that deals with the issuance of new securities. Companies,
governments or public sector institutions can obtain funding through the sale of a new stock or bond issue. This is typically done
through a syndicate of securities dealers.
   a. Sector rotation   b. Primary market
   c. Peer group analysis   d. Volatility clustering

83.   The _____ is the financial market where previously issued securities and financial instruments such as stock, bonds,
options, and futures are bought and sold. The term '_____' is also used refer to the market for any used goods or assets,
or an alternative use for an existing product or asset where the customer base is the second market

With primary issuances of securities or financial instruments, or the primary market, investors purchase these securities directly
from issuers such as corporations issuing shares in an IPO or private placement, or directly from the federal government in the
case of treasuries.

   a. Secondary market   b. Delta neutral
   c. Financial market   d. Performance attribution

84.   In business and finance, a _____ (also referred to as equity _____) of stock means a _____ of ownership
in a corporation (company.) In the plural, stocks is often used as a synonym for _____s especially in the United States, but
it is less commonly used that way outside of North America.

In the United Kingdom, South Africa, and Australia, stock can also refer to completely different financial instruments such as
government bonds or, less commonly, to all kinds of marketable securities.

   a. Margin   b. Procter ' Gamble
   c. Bucket shop   d. Share

85.   An _____ is a security whose value and income payments are derived from and collateralized (or 'backed') by a
specified pool of underlying assets. The pool of assets is typically a group of small and illiquid assets that are unable to be sold
individually. Pooling the assets allows them to be sold to general investors, a process called securitization, and allows the risk of
investing in the underlying assets to be diversified because each security will represent a fraction of the total value of the
diverse pool of underlying assets.
   a. ABN Amro   b. A Random Walk Down Wall Street
   c. Asset-backed security   d. AAB

86.   The _____ is a U.S. government-owned corporation within the Department of Housing and Urban Development

Ginnie Mae provides guarantees on mortgage-backed securities backed by federally insured or guaranteed loans, mainly loans issued by the Federal Housing Administration, Department of Veterans Affairs, Rural Housing Service, and Office of Public and Indian Housing. Ginnie Mae securities are the only MBS that are guaranteed by the United States government.

a. Jumbo mortgage

c. 4-4-5 Calendar

b. Graduated payment mortgage

d. Government National Mortgage Association

87.   A _____ is an asset-backed security whose cash flows are backed by the principal and interest payments of a set of mortgage loans. Payments are typically made monthly over the lifetime of the underlying loans.

a. Shared appreciation mortgage

c. Home equity line of credit

b. Conforming loan

d. Mortgage-backed security

88.   _____ is a structured finance process that involves pooling and repackaging of cash-flow-producing financial assets into securities, which are then sold to investors. The term '_____' is derived from the fact that the form of financial instruments used to obtain funds from the investors are securities. As a portfolio risk backed by amortizing cash flows - and unlike general corporate debt - the credit quality of securitized debt is non-stationary due to changes in volatility that are time- and structure-dependent.

a. Securitization

c. Reputational risk

b. Special journals

d. The Glass-Steagall Act of 1933

89.   The _____ is the over-the-counter financial market in contracts for future delivery, so called forward contracts. Forward contracts are personalized between parties. The _____ is a general term used to describe the informal market by which these contracts are entered into.

a. Delta hedging

c. Limits to arbitrage

b. Spot rate

d. Forward market

90.   The _____ (NYSE: FRE) is an insolvent government sponsored enterprise (GSE) of the United States federal government.

The _____ was created in 1970 to expand the secondary market for mortgages in the US. Along with other GSEs, Freddie Mac buys mortgages on the secondary market, pools them, and sells them as mortgage-backed securities to investors on the open market.

a. Governmental Accounting Standards Board

c. The Depository Trust ' Clearing Corporation

b. Public company

d. Federal Home Loan Mortgage Corporation

91.   The _____ (NYSE: FNM), commonly known as Fannie Mae, is a stockholder-owned corporation chartered by Congress in 1968 as a government sponsored enterprise (GSE), but founded in 1938 during the Great Depression. The corporation's purpose is to purchase and securitize mortgages in order to ensure that funds are consistently available to the institutions that lend money to home buyers.

On September 7, 2008, James Lockhart, director of the Federal Housing Finance Agency (FHFA), announced that Fannie Mae and Freddie Mac were being placed into conservatorship of the FHFA.

a. Federal National Mortgage Association

b. SPDR

c. General partnership

d. The Depository Trust ' Clearing Corporation

92.   An _____ is the term used in financial circles for a type of computer system that facilitates trading of financial products outside of stock exchanges. The primary products that are traded on an _____ are stocks and currencies. They came into existence in 1998 when the SEC authorized their creation.

a. Electronic communication network

b. Insider trading

c. Intellidex

d. Open outcry

93.   _____ has become the norm for individual investors and traders over the past decade with many, if not all brokers now offering online services with unique trading platforms.

In the past, investors had to call up their brokers and place an order on the phone. The broker would then enter the order in their system which was linked to trading floors and exchanges.

a. Asset allocation

b. Alternative investment

c. Investment decisions

d. Investing online

94.   _____ is typically a higher ranking stock than voting shares, and its terms are negotiated between the corporation and the investor.

_____ usually carry no voting rights, but may carry superior priority over common stock in the payment of dividends and upon liquidation. _____ may carry a dividend that is paid out prior to any dividends to common stock holders.

a. Follow-on offering

b. Second lien loan

c. Trade-off theory

d. Preferred stock

95.   In finance, a _____ is a type of bond that can be converted into shares of stock in the issuing company, usually at some pre-announced ratio. It is a hybrid security with debt- and equity-like features. Although it typically has a low coupon rate, the holder is compensated with the ability to convert the bond to common stock, usually at a substantial discount to the stock's market value.

a. Corporate bond

b. Bond fund

c. Gilts

d. Convertible bond

1. In finance, a _____ is a debt security, in which the authorized issuer owes the holders a debt and, depending on the terms of the _____, is obliged to pay interest (the coupon) and/or to repay the principal at a later date, termed maturity.

Thus a _____ is a loan: the issuer is the borrower, the _____ holder is the lender, and the coupon is the interest. _____s provide the borrower with external funds to finance long-term investments, or, in the case of government _____s, to finance current expenditure.

a. Puttable bond	b. Bond
c. Catastrophe bonds	d. Convertible bond

2. The _____ is a financial market where participants buy and sell debt securities, usually in the form of bonds. As of 2006, the size of the international _____ is an estimated $45 trillion, of which the size of the outstanding U.S. _____ debt was $25.2 trillion.

Nearly all of the $923 billion average daily trading volume in the U.S. _____ takes place between broker-dealers and large institutions in a decentralized, over-the-counter market.

a. Bond market	b. 529 plan
c. Fixed income	d. 4-4-5 Calendar

3. The _____ is the market for securities, where companies and governments can raise longterm funds. The _____ includes the stock market and the bond market. Financial regulators, such as the U.S. Securities and Exchange Commission, oversee the _____s in their designated countries to ensure that investors are protected against fraud.

a. Delta neutral	b. Capital market
c. Forward market	d. Spot rate

4. _____ is that which is owed; usually referencing assets owed, but the term can cover other obligations. In the case of assets, _____ is a means of using future purchasing power in the present before a summation has been earned. Some companies and corporations use _____ as a part of their overall corporate finance strategy.

a. Cross-collateralization	b. Partial Payment
c. Credit cycle	d. Debt

5. In finance, the _____ is the global financial market for short-term borrowing and lending. It provides short-term liquidity funding for the global financial system. The _____ is where short-term obligations such as Treasury bills, commercial paper and bankers' acceptances are bought and sold.

a. Debt-for-equity swap	b. Consumer debt
c. Cramdown	d. Money market

6. A _____ is a fungible, negotiable instrument representing financial value. They are broadly categorized into debt securities (such as banknotes, bonds and debentures), and equity securities; e.g., common stocks. The company or other entity issuing the _____ is called the issuer.

a. Securities lending	b. Book entry
c. Tracking stock	d. Security

7. _____ is a risk-adjusted measure of the so-called active return on an investment. It is the return in excess of the compensation for the risk borne, and thus commonly used to assess active managers' performances. Often, the return of a benchmark is subtracted in order to consider relative performance, which yields Jensen's _____.

   a. Option   b. Amortization

   c. Alpha   d. Annuity

8.   A _____ or bank is a financial institution whose primary activity is to act as a payment agent for customers and to borrow and lend money.

The first modern bank was founded in Italy in Genoa in 1406, its name was Banco di San Giorgio (Bank of St. George.)

Many other financial activities were added over time.

   a. 4-4-5 Calendar   b. Bought deal

   c. Banker   d. Black Sea Trade and Development Bank

9.   _____ or financing is to provide capital (funds), which means money for a project, a person, a business or any other private or public institutions.

Those funds can be allocated for either short term or long term purposes. The health fund is a new way of _____ private healthcare centers.

   a. Proxy fight   b. Synthetic CDO

   c. Funding   d. Product life cycle

10.   An _____ or index tracker is a collective investment scheme (usually a mutual fund or exchange-traded fund) that aims to replicate the movements of an index of a specific financial market regardless of market conditions.

Tracking can be achieved by trying to hold all of the securities in the index, in the same proportions as the index. Other methods include statistically sampling the market and holding 'representative' securities.

   a. Index fund   b. A Random Walk Down Wall Street

   c. Investment company   d. AAB

11.   A _____ is a professionally managed type of collective investment scheme that pools money from many investors and invests it in stocks, bonds, short-term money market instruments, and/or other securities. The _____ will have a fund manager that trades the pooled money on a regular basis. Currently, the worldwide value of all _____s totals more than $26 trillion.

Since 1940, there have been three basic types of investment companies in the United States: open-end funds, also known in the US as _____s; unit investment trusts (UITs); and closed-end funds.

   a. Financial intermediary   b. Mutual fund

   c. Trust company   d. Net asset value

12. _____ mature in one year or less. Like zero-coupon bonds, they do not pay interest prior to maturity; instead they are sold at a discount of the par value to create a positive yield to maturity. Many regard _____ as the least risky investment available to U.S. investors.

  a. 4-4-5 Calendar   b. Treasury bills

  c. Treasury securities   d. Treasury Inflation Protected Securities

13. An _____ represents the ownership in the shares of a foreign company trading on US financial markets. The stock of many non-US companies trades on US exchanges through the use of _____s. _____s enable US investors to buy shares in foreign companies without undertaking cross-border transactions.

  a. AAB   b. A Random Walk Down Wall Street

  c. ABN Amro   d. American Depository Receipt

14. _____ offer, asking price is a price a seller of a good is willing to accept for that particular good.

In bid and ask, the term _____ is used in contrast to the term bid price. The difference between the _____ and the bid price is called the spread.

  a. Interest rate parity   b. A Random Walk Down Wall Street

  c. AAB   d. Ask price

15. A _____ is the highest price that a buyer (i.e., bidder) is willing to pay for a good. It is usually referred to simply as the 'bid.'

In bid and ask, the _____ stands in contrast to the ask price or 'offer', and the difference between the two is called the bid/ask spread.

An unsolicited bid or offer is when a person or company receives a bid even though they are not looking to sell.

  a. Bid price   b. Political risk

  c. Settlement date   d. Mid price

16. _____ are government bonds issued by the United States Department of the Treasury through the Bureau of the Public Debt. They are the debt financing instruments of the U.S. Federal government, and they are often referred to simply as Treasuries or Treasurys. There are four types of marketable _____: Treasury bills, Treasury notes, Treasury bonds, and Treasury Inflation Protected Securities (TIPS.)

  a. Treasury Inflation-Protected Securities   b. 4-4-5 Calendar

  c. Treasury Inflation Protected Securities   d. Treasury securities

17. In finance, the term _____ describes the amount in cash that returns to the owners of a security. Normally it does not include the price variations, at the difference of the total return. _____ applies to various stated rates of return on stocks (common and preferred, and convertible), fixed income instruments (bonds, notes, bills, strips, zero coupon), and some other investment type insurance products (e.g. annuities.)

  a. Yield to maturity   b. Macaulay duration

  c. 4-4-5 Calendar   d. Yield

18.   A _____ s a time deposit, a financial product commonly offered to consumers by banks, thrift institutions, and credit unions.

They are similar to savings accounts in that they are insured and thus virtually risk-free; they are 'money in the bank'. They are different from savings accounts in that they have a specific, fixed term (often three months, six months, or one to five years), and, usually, a fixed interest rate.

a. Reserve requirement

b. Certificate of deposit

c. Variable rate mortgage

d. Time deposit

19.   In the global money market, _____ is an unsecured promissory note with a fixed maturity of one to 270 days. _____ is a money-market security issued (sold) by large banks and corporations to get money to meet short term debt obligations (for example, payroll), and is only backed by an issuing bank or corporation's promise to pay the face amount on the maturity date specified on the note. Since it is not backed by collateral, only firms with excellent credit ratings from a recognized rating agency will be able to sell their _____ at a reasonable price.

a. Financial distress

b. Book building

c. Trade-off theory

d. Commercial paper

20.   The institution most often referenced by the word '_____' is a public or publicly traded _____, the shares of which are traded on a public stock exchange (e.g., the New York Stock Exchange or Nasdaq in the United States) where shares of stock of _____ s are bought and sold by and to the general public. Most of the largest businesses in the world are publicly traded _____ s. However, the majority of _____ s are said to be closely held, privately held or close _____ s, meaning that no ready market exists for the trading of shares.

a. Depository Trust Company

b. Corporation

c. Federal Home Loan Mortgage Corporation

d. Protect

21.   Explicit _____ is a measure implemented in many countries to protect bank depositors, in full or in part, from losses caused by a bank's inability to pay its debts when due. _____ systems are one component of a financial system safety net that promotes financial stability.

a. Time deposit

b. Deposit Insurance

c. Banking panic

d. Reserve requirement

22.   _____ s are deposits denominated in United States dollars at banks outside the United States, and thus are not under the jurisdiction of the Federal Reserve. Consequently, such deposits are subject to much less regulation than similar deposits within the United States, allowing for higher margins. There is nothing 'European' about _____ deposits; a US dollar-denominated deposit in Tokyo or Caracas would likewise be deemed _____ deposits.

a. A Random Walk Down Wall Street

b. ABN Amro

c. Eurodollar

d. AAB

23.   The _____ is a United States government corporation created by the Glass-Steagall Act of 1933. It provides deposit insurance, which guarantees the safety of checking and savings deposits in member banks, currently up to $250,000 per depositor per bank. Insured deposits are backed by the full faith and credit of the United States.

a. Ford Foundation

b. NYSE Group

c. FASB

d. Federal Deposit Insurance Corporation

24.   A _____ is a money deposit at a banking institution that cannot be withdrawn for a certain 'term' or period of time. When the term is over it can be withdrawn or it can be held for another term. Generally speaking, the longer the term the better the yield on the money.

   a. Basel Accord   b. Private money

   c. Certificate of deposit   d. Time deposit

25.   In political science and economics, the _____ or agency dilemma treats the difficulties that arise under conditions of incomplete and asymmetric information when a principal hires an agent. Various mechanisms may be used to try to align the interests of the agent with those of the principal, such as piece rates/commissions, profit sharing, efficiency wages, performance measurement (including financial statements), the agent posting a bond, or fear of firing. The _____ is found in most employer/employee relationships, for example, when stockholders hire top executives of corporations.

   a. 4-4-5 Calendar   b. 529 plan

   c. 7-Eleven   d. Principal-agent problem

26.   In finance, a _____ is the party in a loan agreement which receives money or other instrument from a lender and promises to repay the lender in a specified time.

   a. Debt management plan   b. Borrower

   c. Cash credit   d. Line of credit

27.   _____ is the provision of resources (such as granting a loan) by one party to another party where that second party does not reimburse the first party immediately, thereby generating a debt, and instead arranges either to repay or return those resources (or material(s) of equal value) at a later date. The first party is called a creditor, also known as a lender, while the second party is called a debtor, also known as a borrower.

Movements of financial capital are normally dependent on either _____ or equity transfers.

   a. Clearing house   b. Warrant

   c. Comparable   d. Credit

28.   An _____ (or business indicator) is a statistic about the economy. _____s allow analysis of economic performance and predictions of future performance.

_____s include various indices, earnings reports, and economic summaries, such as unemployment, housing starts, Consumer Price Index (a measure for inflation), industrial production, bankruptcies, Gross Domestic Product, broadband internet penetration, retail sales, stock market prices, and money supply changes.

   a. AAB   b. Economic indicator

   c. A Random Walk Down Wall Street   d. ABN Amro

29.   The _____ is the over-the-counter financial market in contracts for future delivery, so called forward contracts. Forward contracts are personalized between parties. The _____ is a general term used to describe the informal market by which these contracts are entered into.

   a. Spot rate   b. Limits to arbitrage

   c. Delta hedging   d. Forward market

30.   A _____ is any credit facility extended to a business by a bank or financial institution. A _____ may take several forms such as cash credit, overdraft, demand loan, export packing credit, term loan, discounting or purchase of commercial bills etc. It is like an account that can readily be tapped into if the need arises or not touched at all and saved for emergencies.

   a. Debt-snowball method   b. Default Notice

   c. Cash credit   d. Line of credit

31.   In the United States, _____ are overnight borrowings by banks to maintain their bank reserves at the Federal Reserve. Banks keep reserves at Federal Reserve Banks to meet their reserve requirements and to clear financial transactions. Transactions in the _____ market enable depository institutions with reserve balances in excess of reserve requirements to lend reserves to institutions with reserve deficiencies.

   a. Federal funds rate   b. Regulation T

   c. 4-4-5 Calendar   d. Federal funds

32.   A _____ allows a borrower to use a financial security as collateral for a cash loan at a fixed rate of interest. In a repo, the borrower agrees to immediately sell a security to a lender and also agrees to buy the same security from the lender at a fixed price at some later date. A repo is equivalent to a cash transaction combined with a forward contract.

   a. Total return swap   b. Volatility arbitrage

   c. Contango   d. Repurchase agreement

33.   In financial accounting, the term _____ is most commonly used to describe any part of shareholders' equity, except for basic share capital. Sometimes, the term is used instead of the term provision; such a use, however, is inconsistent with the terminology suggested by International Accounting Standards Board. For more information about provisions, see provision (accounting.)

   a. Closing entries   b. Treasury stock

   c. FIFO and LIFO accounting   d. Reserve

34.   The _____ (or Euribor) is a daily reference rate based on the averaged interest rates at which banks offer to lend unsecured funds to other banks in the euro wholesale money market (or interbank market.)

Euribor rates are used as a reference rate for euro-denominated forward rate agreements, short term interest rate futures contracts and interest rate swaps, in very much the same way as LIBOR rates are commonly used for Sterling and US dollar-denominated instruments. They thus provide the basis for some of the world's most liquid and active interest rate markets.

   a. European Monetary System   b. Euro Interbank Offered Rate

   c. A Random Walk Down Wall Street   d. Exchange Rate Mechanism

35.   In economics, a _____ is a mechanism that allows people to easily buy and sell (trade) financial securities (such as stocks and bonds), commodities (such as precious metals or agricultural goods), and other fungible items of value at low transaction costs and at prices that reflect the efficient-market hypothesis.

_____s have evolved significantly over several hundred years and are undergoing constant innovation to improve liquidity.

Both general markets (where many commodities are traded) and specialized markets (where only one commodity is traded) exist.

a. Financial market   b. Secondary market
c. Cost of carry   d. Delta hedging

36. _____ refers to any type of investment that yields a regular (or fixed) return.

For example, if you lend money to a borrower and the borrower has to pay interest once a month, you have been issued a fixed-income security. When a company does this, it is often called a bond or corporate bank debt (although preferred stock is also sometimes considered to be _____).

a. 529 plan   b. Bond market
c. 4-4-5 Calendar   d. Fixed income

37.

In finance, the _____ can be the expected rate of return above the risk-free interest rate. When measuring risk, a common sense approach is to compare the risk-free return on T-bills and the very risky return on other investments. The difference between these two returns can be interpreted as a measure of the excess return on the average risky asset. This excess return is known as the _____.

a. Risk modeling   b. Risk adjusted return on capital
c. Risk premium   d. Risk aversion

38. A _____, securities exchange or (in Europe) bourse is a corporation or mutual organization which provides 'trading' facilities for stock brokers and traders, to trade stocks and other securities. _____s also provide facilities for the issue and redemption of securities as well as other financial instruments and capital events including the payment of income and dividends. The securities traded on a _____ include: shares issued by companies, unit trusts and other pooled investment products and bonds.

a. 7-Eleven   b. Stock exchange
c. 529 plan   d. 4-4-5 Calendar

39. In finance, _____ refers to Monday, October 19, 1987, when stock markets around the world crashed, shedding a huge value in a very short time. The crash began in Hong Kong, spread west through international time zones to Europe, hitting the United States after other markets had already declined by a significant margin. The Dow Jones Industrial Average (DJIA) dropped by 508 points to 1738.74 (22.61%).

a. 529 plan   b. 7-Eleven
c. 4-4-5 Calendar   d. Black Monday

40. _____ are dollar-denominated bonds, issued mostly by Latin American countries in the 1980s, named after U.S. Treasury Secretary Nicholas Brady.

_____ were created in March 1989 in order to convert bonds issued by mostly Latin American countries into a variety or 'menu' of new bonds after many of those countries defaulted on their debt in the 1980's. At that time, the market for sovereign debt was small and illiquid, and the standardization of emerging-market debt facilitated risk-spreading and trading.

a. Municipal bond
c. Nominal yield

b. Coupon rate
d. Brady bonds

41.   The coupon or _____ of a bond is the amount of interest paid per year expressed as a percentage of the face value of the bond.

For example if you hold $10,000 nominal of a bond described as a 4.5% loan stock, you will receive $450 in interest each year (probably in two installments of $225 each.)

Not all bonds have coupons.

a. Coupon rate
c. Revenue bonds

b. Puttable bond
d. Zero-coupon bond

42.   _____, in finance and accounting, means stated value or face value. From this comes the expressions at par (at the _____), over par (over _____) and under par (under _____.)

The term '_____' has several meanings depending on context and geography.

a. Sinking fund
c. Par value

b. Global Squeeze
d. FIDC

43.   An _____ is a security whose value and income payments are derived from and collateralized (or 'backed') by a specified pool of underlying assets. The pool of assets is typically a group of small and illiquid assets that are unable to be sold individually. Pooling the assets allows them to be sold to general investors, a process called securitization, and allows the risk of investing in the underlying assets to be diversified because each security will represent a fraction of the total value of the diverse pool of underlying assets.

a. ABN Amro
c. Asset-backed security

b. AAB
d. A Random Walk Down Wall Street

44.   A _____ is an international bond that is denominated in a currency not native to the country where it is issued. It can be categorised according to the currency in which it is issued. London is one of the centers of the _____ market, but _____s may be traded throughout the world - for example in Singapore or Tokyo.

a. Economic entity
c. Interest rate option

b. Education production function
d. Eurobond

45.   The _____ provide stable, on-demand, low-cost funding to American financial institutions for home mortgage loans, small business, rural, agricultural, and economic development lending. With their members, the _____ank System represents the largest collective source of home mortgage and community credit in the United States. The banks do not provide loans directly to individuals, only to other banks.

a. 7-Eleven

b. Federal Home Loan Banks

c. 529 plan

d. 4-4-5 Calendar

46.   The _____ (NYSE: FRE) is an insolvent government sponsored enterprise (GSE) of the United States federal government.

The _____ was created in 1970 to expand the secondary market for mortgages in the US. Along with other GSEs, Freddie Mac buys mortgages on the secondary market, pools them, and sells them as mortgage-backed securities to investors on the open market.

a. Governmental Accounting Standards Board

b. Public company

c. The Depository Trust ' Clearing Corporation

d. Federal Home Loan Mortgage Corporation

47.   The _____ (NYSE: FNM), commonly known as Fannie Mae, is a stockholder-owned corporation chartered by Congress in 1968 as a government sponsored enterprise (GSE), but founded in 1938 during the Great Depression. The corporation's purpose is to purchase and securitize mortgages in order to ensure that funds are consistently available to the institutions that lend money to home buyers.

On September 7, 2008, James Lockhart, director of the Federal Housing Finance Agency (FHFA), announced that Fannie Mae and Freddie Mac were being placed into conservatorship of the FHFA.

a. The Depository Trust ' Clearing Corporation

b. SPDR

c. General partnership

d. Federal National Mortgage Association

48.   The _____ is a U.S. government-owned corporation within the Department of Housing and Urban Development

Ginnie Mae provides guarantees on mortgage-backed securities backed by federally insured or guaranteed loans, mainly loans issued by the Federal Housing Administration, Department of Veterans Affairs, Rural Housing Service, and Office of Public and Indian Housing. Ginnie Mae securities are the only MBS that are guaranteed by the United States government.

a. Graduated payment mortgage

b. Jumbo mortgage

c. 4-4-5 Calendar

d. Government National Mortgage Association

49.   _____ is a measure of the ability of a debtor to pay their debts as and when they fall due. It is usually expressed as a ratio or a percentage of current liabilities.

For a corporation with a published balance sheet there are various ratios used to calculate a measure of liquidity.

a. Operating leverage

b. Operating profit margin

c. Invested capital

d. Accounting liquidity

50.   A _____ is an asset-backed security whose cash flows are backed by the principal and interest payments of a set of mortgage loans. Payments are typically made monthly over the lifetime of the underlying loans.

a. Shared appreciation mortgage

b. Conforming loan

c. Mortgage-backed security

d. Home equity line of credit

51. _____ is a business, economics or investment term that refers to an asset's ability to be easily converted through an act of buying or selling without causing a significant movement in the price and with minimum loss of value. Money, or cash on hand, is the most liquid asset. An act of exchange of a less liquid asset with a more liquid asset is called liquidation.

a. 529 plan

b. 7-Eleven

c. 4-4-5 Calendar

d. Market Liquidity

52. The _____ is one of the measures of national income and input for a given country's economy. _____ is defined as the total cost of all finished goods and services produced within the country in a stipulated period of time (usually a 365-day year.) It is sometimes regarded as the sum of profits added at every level of production (the intermediate stages) of all final goods and services produced within a country in a stipulated timeframe, and it is rarely given a monetary value.

a. Recession

b. Macroeconomics

c. Behavioral finance

d. Gross domestic product

53. A _____ is a legal pledge in United States municipal finance, in which an entity pledges its full faith and credit to repay its debt, typically a _____ bond.

a. Financial Institutions Reform Recovery and Enforcement Act

b. General obligation

c. Letter of credit

d. Covenant

54. In the United States, a _____ is a bond issued by a city or other local government, or their agencies. Potential issuers of these bonds include cities, counties, redevelopment agencies, school districts, publicly owned airports and seaports, and any other governmental entity (or group of governments) below the state level. They may be general obligations of the issuer or secured by specified revenues.

a. Premium bond

b. Puttable bond

c. Senior debt

d. Municipal bond

55. In finance, _____, also known as return on investment is the ratio of money gained or lost on an investment relative to the amount of money invested. The amount of money gained or lost may be referred to as interest, profit/loss, gain/loss, or net income/loss. The money invested may be referred to as the asset, capital, principal, or the cost basis of the investment.

a. Stock or scrip dividends

b. Composiition of Creditors

c. Doctrine of the Proper Law

d. Rate of return

56. In business, _____ is income that a company receives from its normal business activities, usually from the sale of goods and services to customers. Some companies also receive _____ from interest, dividends or royalties paid to them by other companies. _____ may refer to business income in general, or it may refer to the amount, in a monetary unit, received during a period of time, as in 'Last year, Company X had _____ of $32 million.'

In many countries, including the UK, _____ is referred to as turnover.

a. Revenue

b. Furniture, Fixtures and Equipment

c. Matching principle

d. Bottom line

57. _____ are bonds issued by governments, authorities, or public benefit corporations that are guaranteed by the revenue flow of the issuing agency.

The Supreme Court decision of Pollock versus Farmer's Loan and Trust Company of 1895 initiated a wave or series of innovations for the financial services community in both tax-treatment and regulation from government. This specific case, according to a leading investment bank's research, resulted in the 'intergovernmental tax immunity doctrine,' ultimately leading to 'tax-free status.' Municipal bonds are generally exempt from federal tax on their interest payments (not capital gains.)

a. Callable bond

b. Gilts

c. Private activity bond

d. Revenue bonds

58. A _____ is a collective investment scheme that invests in bonds and other debt securities. _____s yield monthly dividends that include interest payments on the fund's underlying securities plus any capital appreciation in the prices of the portfolio's bonds. _____s tend to pay higher dividends than CDs and money market accounts, and they generally pay out dividends more frequently and regularly than individual bonds.

a. Bond fund

b. Private activity bond

c. Premium bond

d. Gilts

59. _____ are the divisions at which tax rates change in a progressive tax system (or an explicitly regressive tax system, although this is much rarer.) Essentially, they are the cutoff values for taxable income -- income past a certain point will be taxed at a higher rate.

Imagine that there are three _____: 10%, 20%, and 30%.

a. Tax holiday

b. Payroll tax

c. Tax brackets

d. Capital gains tax

60. A _____ is a unit that is equal to 1/100th of a percentage point. It is frequently used to express percentage point changes of less than 1%. It avoids the ambiguity between relative and absolute discussions about rates.

a. Bond market

b. Basis point

c. 529 plan

d. 4-4-5 Calendar

61. _____ is a type of bond that allows the issuer of the bond to retain the privilege of redeeming the bond at some point before the bond reaches the date of maturity. In other words, on the call dates, the issuer has the right, but not the obligation, to buy back the bonds from the bond holders at the call price. Technically speaking, the bonds are not really bought and held by the issuer but cancelled immediately.

a. Callable bond

b. Bond fund

c. Gilts

d. Coupon rate

62. In finance, a _____ is a type of bond that can be converted into shares of stock in the issuing company, usually at some pre-announced ratio. It is a hybrid security with debt- and equity-like features. Although it typically has a low coupon rate, the holder is compensated with the ability to convert the bond to common stock, usually at a substantial discount to the stock's market value.

a. Bond fund   b. Gilts

c. Corporate bond   d. Convertible bond

63.   A _____ is a bond issued by a corporation. The term is usually applied to longer-term debt instruments, generally with a maturity date falling at least a year after their issue date. (The term 'commercial paper' is sometimes used for instruments with a shorter maturity.)

a. Government bond   b. Brady bonds

c. Serial bond   d. Corporate bond

64.   In finance, _____ occurs when a debtor has not met its legal obligations according to the debt contract, e.g. it has not made a scheduled payment, or has violated a loan covenant (condition) of the debt contract. _____ may occur if the debtor is either unwilling or unable to pay their debt. This can occur with all debt obligations including bonds, mortgages, loans, and promissory notes.

a. Credit crunch   b. Default

c. Vendor finance   d. Debt validation

65.   _____ is the risk of loss due to a debtor's non-payment of a loan or other line of credit (either the principal or interest (coupon) or both)

Most lenders employ their own models (credit scorecards) to rank potential and existing customers according to risk, and then apply appropriate strategies. With products such as unsecured personal loans or mortgages, lenders charge a higher price for higher risk customers and vice versa. With revolving products such as credit cards and overdrafts, risk is controlled through careful setting of credit limits.

a. Transaction risk   b. Market risk

c. Liquidity risk   d. Credit risk

66.   An _____ is a mortgage loan where the interest rate on the note is periodically adjusted based on a variety of indices. Among the most common indices are the rates on 1-year constant-maturity Treasury (CMT) securities, the Cost of Funds Index (COFI), and the London Interbank Offered Rate (LIBOR.) A few lenders use their own cost of funds as an index, rather than using other indices.

a. ABN Amro   b. AAB

c. A Random Walk Down Wall Street   d. Adjustable rate mortgage

67.   _____ is a form of corporation equity ownership represented in the securities. It is dangerous in comparison to preferred shares and some other investment options, in that in the event of bankruptcy, _____ investors receive their funds after preferred stockholders, bondholders, creditors, etc. On the other hand, common shares on average perform better than preferred shares or bonds over time.

a. Common stock   b. Stock market bubble

c. Stop-limit order   d. Stock split

68.   _____ is commonly used in corporations for voting by members or shareholders, because it allows members who have confidence in the judgment of other members to vote for them and allows the assembly to have a quorum of votes when it is difficult for all members to attend, or there are too many members for all of them to conveniently meet and deliberate.

a. 529 plan	b. 4-4-5 Calendar
c. 7-Eleven	d. Proxy voting

69.   In business, a _____ is the purchase of one company (the target) by another (the acquirer or bidder). In the UK the term refers to the acquisition of a public company whose shares are listed on a stock exchange, in contrast to the acquisition of a private company.

Before a bidder makes an offer for another company, it usually first informs that company's board of directors.

a. 4-4-5 Calendar	b. Takeover
c. 529 plan	d. Stock swap

70.   In the most general sense, a _____ is anything that is a hindrance, or puts individuals at a disadvantage.

Before we discuss the financial terms, we should note that a _____ can also have a much more important slang meaning.

This is best described in an example.

a. McFadden Act	b. Covenant
c. Limited liability	d. Liability

71.   In business and finance, a _____ (also referred to as equity _____) of stock means a _____ of ownership in a corporation (company.) In the plural, stocks is often used as a synonym for _____s especially in the United States, but it is less commonly used that way outside of North America.

In the United Kingdom, South Africa, and Australia, stock can also refer to completely different financial instruments such as government bonds or, less commonly, to all kinds of marketable securities.

a. Procter ' Gamble	b. Margin
c. Bucket shop	d. Share

72.   A _____ is a profit that results from investments into a capital asset, such as stocks, bonds or real estate, which exceeds the purchase price. It is the difference between a higher selling price and a lower purchase price, resulting in a financial gain for the seller. Conversely, a capital loss arises if the proceeds from the sale of a capital asset are less than the purchase price.

a. Capital gain	b. Capital gains tax
c. Payroll tax	d. Tax brackets

73.   A _____ is a payment made by a corporation to its shareholder members. When a corporation earns a profit or surplus, that money can be put to two uses: it can either be re-invested in the business (called retained earnings), or it can be paid to the shareholders as a _____. Many corporations retain a portion of their earnings and pay the remainder as a _____.

a. Dividend	b. Dividend yield
c. Dividend puzzle	d. Special dividend

74. The _____ on a company stock is the company's annual dividend payments divided by its market cap, or the dividend per share divided by the price per share. It is often expressed as a percentage.

Dividend payments on preferred shares are stipulated by the prospectus.

   a. Dividend imputation   b. Special dividend

   c. Dividend reinvestment plan   d. Dividend yield

75. The _____ is a stock exchange based in New York City, New York. It is the largest stock exchange in the world by dollar value of its listed companies securities. As of October 2008, the combined capitalization of all domestic _____ listed companies was $10.1 trillion.

   a. 4-4-5 Calendar   b. 529 plan

   c. 7-Eleven   d. New York Stock Exchange

76. _____ is typically a higher ranking stock than voting shares, and its terms are negotiated between the corporation and the investor.

_____ usually carry no voting rights, but may carry superior priority over common stock in the payment of dividends and upon liquidation. _____ may carry a dividend that is paid out prior to any dividends to common stock holders.

   a. Second lien loan   b. Trade-off theory

   c. Follow-on offering   d. Preferred stock

77. A _____ is a private or public market for the trading of company stock and derivatives of company stock at an agreed price; these are securities listed on a stock exchange as well as those only traded privately.

The size of the world _____ is estimated at about $36.6 trillion US at the beginning of October 2008 . The world derivatives market has been estimated at about $480 trillion face or nominal value, 12 times the size of the entire world economy.

   a. Anton Gelonkin   b. Adolph Coors

   c. Andrew Tobias   d. Stock market

78. In finance, the Acid-test or _____ or liquid ratio measures the ability of a company to use its near cash or quick assets to immediately extinguish or retire its current liabilities. Quick assets include those current assets that presumably can be quickly converted to cash at close to their book values.

Generally, the acid test ratio should be 1:1 or better, however this varies widely by industry.

   a. Net assets   b. Financial ratio

   c. P/E ratio   d. Quick ratio

79. The _____ is one of several stock market indices, created by nineteenth-century Wall Street Journal editor and Dow Jones ' Company co-founder Charles Dow. Dow compiled the index to gauge the performance of the industrial sector of the American stock market. It is the second-oldest U.S. market index, after the Dow Jones Transportation Average, which Dow also created.

    a. 529 plan   b. Dow Jones Industrial Average
    c. 4-4-5 Calendar   d. 7-Eleven

80. A _____ is a method of measuring a section of the stock market. Many indices are cited by news or financial services firms and are used to benchmark the performance of portfolios such as mutual funds.

    a. Stock market index   b. Stop order
    c. Program trading   d. Trading curb

81. _____ are those dividends paid out in form of additional stock shares of the issuing corporation or other corporation They are usually issued in proportion to shares owned (for example for every 100 shares of stock owned, 5% stock dividend will yield 5 extra shares). If this payment involves the issue of new shares, this is very similar to a stock split in that it increases the total number of shares while lowering the price of each share and does not change the market capitalization or the total value of the shares held

    a. Stock or scrip dividends   b. Database auditing
    c. Time-based currency   d. The Hong Kong Securities Institute

82. A _____ index is a stock market index where each constituent makes up a fraction of the index that is proportional to its price. For a stock market index this implies that stocks are included in proportions based on their quoted prices. A stock trading at $100 will thus be making up 10 times more of the total index compared to a stock trading at $10.

    a. Golden parachute   b. Price-weighted
    c. Trade finance   d. Product life cycle

83. A _____ or stock divide increases or decreases the number of shares in a public company. The price is adjusted such that the before and after market capitalization of the company remains the same and dilution does not occur. Options and warrants are included.

    a. Stop price   b. Stop order
    c. Contract for difference   d. Stock split

84. In economics, _____ is a measure of the relative satisfaction from or desirability of consumption of various goods and services. Given this measure, one may speak meaningfully of increasing or decreasing _____, and thereby explain economic behavior in terms of attempts to increase one's _____. For illustrative purposes, changes in _____ are sometimes expressed in units called utils.

    a. Utility function   b. AAB
    c. Utility   d. A Random Walk Down Wall Street

85. _____ is the price at which an asset would trade in a competitive Walrasian auction setting. _____ is often used interchangeably with open _____, fair value or fair _____, although these terms have distinct definitions in different standards, and may differ in some circumstances.

International Valuation Standards defines _____ as 'the estimated amount for which a property should exchange on the date of valuation between a willing buyer and a willing seller in an arm'e;s-length transaction after proper marketing wherein the parties had each acted knowledgeably, prudently, and without compulsion.'

_____ is a concept distinct from market price, which is 'e;the price at which one can transact'e;, while _____ is 'e;the true underlying value'e; according to theoretical standards.

a. Market value	b. T-Model
c. Wrap account	d. Debt restructuring

86.   The _____ is an American stock exchange. It is the largest electronic screen-based equity securities trading market in the United States. With approximately 3,200 companies, it has more trading volume per day than any other stock exchange in the world.

a. 529 plan	b. 7-Eleven
c. 4-4-5 Calendar	d. NASDAQ

87.   In the United States, the Financial Industry Regulatory Authority (FINRA) is a self-regulatory organization (SRO) under the Securities Exchange Act of 1934, successor to the _____, Inc.

FINRA is responsible for regulatory oversight of all securities firms that do business with the public; professional training, testing and licensing of registered persons; arbitration and mediation; market regulation by contract for The NASDAQ Stock Market, Inc., the American Stock Exchange LLC, and the International Securities Exchange, LLC; and industry utilities, such as Trade Reporting Facilities and other over-the-counter operations.

a. 529 plan	b. 4-4-5 Calendar
c. 7-Eleven	d. National Association of Securities Dealers

88.   A _____ is a financial contract whose value is derived from the value of something else (known as the underlying.) The underlying on which a _____ is based can be an asset, weather conditions bonds or other forms of credit.

a. Derivative	b. 4-4-5 Calendar
c. 7-Eleven	d. 529 plan

89.   In finance, a _____ is a standardized contract, to buy or sell a specified commodity of standardized quality at a certain date in the future, at a market determined price (the futures price.)

The price is determined by the instantaneous equilibrium between the forces of supply and demand among competing buy and sell orders on the exchange at the time of the purchase or sale of the contract.

In many cases, the items may be such non-traditional 'commodities' as foreign currencies, commercial or government paper [e.g., bonds], or 'baskets' of corporate equity ['stock indices'] or other financial instruments.

a. Financial future	b. Repurchase agreement
c. Futures contract	d. Heston model

90.   An _____ is a contract written by a seller that conveys to the buyer the right -- but not the obligation -- to buy (in the case of a call _____) or to sell (in the case of a put _____) a particular asset, such as a piece of property such as, among others, a futures contract. In return for granting the _____, the seller collects a payment (the premium) from the buyer.

For example, buying a call _____ provides the right to buy a specified quantity of a security at a set strike price at some time on or before expiration, while buying a put _____ provides the right to sell.

a. AT'T Mobility LLC
c. Annuity

b. Amortization
d. Option

91. In business and accounting, _____s are everything of value that is owned by a person or company. The balance sheet of a firm records the monetary value of the _____s owned by the firm. The two major _____ classes are tangible _____s and intangible _____s.

a. Income
c. EBITDA

b. Accounts payable
d. Asset

92. A _____ is a listing of bonds or fixed income instruments and a statistic reflecting the composite value of its components. It is used as a tool to represent the characteristics of its component fixed income instruments. They differ from stock market indices in their complexity.

a. 4-4-5 Calendar
c. 7-Eleven

b. 529 plan
d. Bond market index

93. A _____ is a financial contract between two parties, the buyer and the seller of this type of option. Often it is simply labeled a 'call'. The buyer of the option has the right, but not the obligation to buy an agreed quantity of a particular commodity or financial instrument (the underlying instrument) from the seller of the option at a certain time (the expiration date) for a certain price (the strike price.)

a. Bear spread
c. Bear call spread

b. Bull spread
d. Call option

94. In options, the _____ is a key variable in a derivatives contract between two parties. Where the contract requires delivery of the underlying instrument, the trade will be at the _____, regardless of the spot price (market price) of the underlying instrument at that time.

Definition - The fixed price at which the owner of an option can purchase, in the case of a call in the case of a put, the underlying security or commodity.

a. Swaption
c. Moneyness

b. Naked put
d. Strike price

95. A _____ is a financial contract between two parties, the seller (writer) and the buyer of the option. The put allows its buyer the right but not the obligation to sell a commodity or financial instrument (the underlying instrument) to the writer (seller) of the option at a certain time for a certain price (the strike price.) The writer (seller) has the obligation to purchase the underlying asset at that strike price, if the buyer exercises the option.

a. Debit spread
c. Bear spread

b. Put option
d. Bear call spread

96.   A _____ is an exchange of promises between two or more parties to do an act which is enforceable in a court of law. It is where an unqualified offer meets a qualified acceptance and the parties reach Consensus ad Idem. The parties must have the necessary capacity to _____ and the _____ must not be either trifling, indeterminate, impossible or illegal.

  a. Contract

                        b. 529 plan

  c. 4-4-5 Calendar

                        d. 7-Eleven

97.   In finance, _____ (or gearing) is borrowing money to supplement existing funds for investment in such a way that the potential positive or negative outcome is magnified and/or enhanced. It generally refers to using borrowed funds, or debt, so as to attempt to increase the returns to equity. Deleveraging is the action of reducing borrowings.

  a. Pension fund

                        b. Limited partnership

  c. Leverage

                        d. Financial endowment

98.   An _____ is defined as 'a promise which meets the requirements for the formation of a contract and limits the promisor's power to revoke an offer.' Restatement (Second) of Contracts Â§ 25 (1981.)

Quite simply, an _____ is a type of contract that protects an offeree from an offeror's ability to revoke the contract.

Consideration for the _____ is still required as it is still a form of contract.

  a. ABN Amro

                        b. AAB

  c. A Random Walk Down Wall Street

                        d. Option contract

99.   In finance, a _____ in a security, such as a stock or a bond means the holder of the position owns the security and will profit if the price of the security goes up.

Similarly, a _____ in a futures contract or similar derivative, means the holder of the position will profit if the price of the underlying security goes up. Going long is the more conventional practice of investing and is contrasted with going short

- Short (finance)

  a. Long position

                        b. Delta hedging

  c. Central Securities Depository

                        d. Forward market

100.   Days to Cover (DTC) is a numerical term that describes the relationship between the amount of shares in a given equity that have been short sold and the number of days of typical trading that it would require to 'cover' all _____ outstanding. For example, if there are ten million shares of XYZ Inc. that are currently short sold and the average daily volume of XYZ shares traded each day is one million, it would require ten days of trading for all _____ to be covered (10 million / 1 million.)

  a. Guaranteed investment contracts

                        b. Stock or scrip dividends

  c. Cash budget

                        d. Short positions

101. In finance, the _____ is the difference between the quoted rates of return on two different investments, usually of different credit quality.

It is a compound of yield and spread.

The '_____ of X over Y' is simply the percentage return on investment (ROI) from financial instrument X minus the percentage return on investment from financial instrument Y (per annum.)

a. Debtor-in-possession financing

b. Portfolio insurance

c. Duty of loyalty

d. Yield spread

1. _____s are deposits denominated in United States dollars at banks outside the United States, and thus are not under the jurisdiction of the Federal Reserve. Consequently, such deposits are subject to much less regulation than similar deposits within the United States, allowing for higher margins. There is nothing 'European' about _____ deposits; a US dollar-denominated deposit in Tokyo or Caracas would likewise be deemed _____ deposits.
   a. A Random Walk Down Wall Street   b. AAB
   c. ABN Amro   d. Eurodollar

2. _____, is when a company issues common stock or shares to the public for the first time. They are often issued by smaller, younger companies seeking capital to expand, but can also be done by large privately-owned companies looking to become publicly traded.

In an _____ the issuer may obtain the assistance of an underwriting firm, which helps it determine what type of security to issue (common or preferred), best offering price and time to bring it to market.

   a. Asian Financial Crisis   b. Interest
   c. Insolvency   d. Initial public offering

3. The _____ is that part of the capital markets that deals with the issuance of new securities. Companies, governments or public sector institutions can obtain funding through the sale of a new stock or bond issue. This is typically done through a syndicate of securities dealers.
   a. Peer group analysis   b. Primary market
   c. Volatility clustering   d. Sector rotation

4. In the United States, a _____ is an offering of securities that are not registered with the Securities and Exchange Commission (SEC.) Such offerings exploit an exemption offered by the Securities Act of 1933 that comes with several restrictions, including a prohibition against general solicitation. This exemption allows companies to avoid quarterly reporting requirements and many of the legal liabilities associated with the Sarbanes-Oxley Act.
   a. 7-Eleven   b. 529 plan
   c. Private placement   d. 4-4-5 Calendar

5. The _____ is the financial market where previously issued securities and financial instruments such as stock, bonds, options, and futures are bought and sold. The term '_____' is also used refer to the market for any used goods or assets, or an alternative use for an existing product or asset where the customer base is the second market

With primary issuances of securities or financial instruments, or the primary market, investors purchase these securities directly from issuers such as corporations issuing shares in an IPO or private placement, or directly from the federal government in the case of treasuries.

   a. Performance attribution   b. Financial market
   c. Delta neutral   d. Secondary market

6. A _____ is a fungible, negotiable instrument representing financial value. They are broadly categorized into debt securities (such as banknotes, bonds and debentures), and equity securities; e.g., common stocks. The company or other entity issuing the _____ is called the issuer.
   a. Tracking stock   b. Book entry
   c. Security   d. Securities lending

7.   Unemployment occurs when a person is available to work and currently seeking work, but the person is without work. The prevalence of unemployment is usually measured using the _____, which is defined as the percentage of those in the labor force who are unemployed. The _____ is also used in economic studies and economic indexes such as the United States' Conference Board's Index of Leading Indicators as a measure of the state of the macroeconomics.

a. ABN Amro

b. A Random Walk Down Wall Street

c. Unemployment rate

d. AAB

8.   A _____ or bank is a financial institution whose primary activity is to act as a payment agent for customers and to borrow and lend money.

The first modern bank was founded in Italy in Genoa in 1406, its name was Banco di San Giorgio (Bank of St. George.)

Many other financial activities were added over time.

a. Bought deal

b. 4-4-5 Calendar

c. Black Sea Trade and Development Bank

d. Banker

9.   In the global money market, _____ is an unsecured promissory note with a fixed maturity of one to 270 days. _____ is a money-market security issued (sold) by large banks and corporations to get money to meet short term debt obligations (for example, payroll), and is only backed by an issuing bank or corporation's promise to pay the face amount on the maturity date specified on the note. Since it is not backed by collateral, only firms with excellent credit ratings from a recognized rating agency will be able to sell their _____ at a reasonable price.

a. Trade-off theory

b. Financial distress

c. Book building

d. Commercial paper

10.   In the _____ contract the underwriter guarantees the sale of the issued stock at the agreed-upon price. For the issuer, it is the safest but the most expensive type of the contracts, since the underwriter takes the risk of sale.

In the best efforts contract the underwriter agrees to sell as many shares as possible at the agreed-upon price.

a. Firm commitment

b. Special purpose entity

c. Participating preferred stock

d. Rights issue

11.   _____ is an arrangement with the U.S. Securities and Exchange Commission that allows a single registration document to be filed that permits the issuance of multiple securities.

_____ is a registration of a new issue which can be prepared up to two years in advance, so that the issue can be offered quickly as soon as funds are needed or market conditions are favorable.

For example, current market conditions in the housing market are not favorable for a specific firm to issue a public offering.

a. Shelf registration

b. Bought deal

c. Black Sea Trade and Development Bank

d. 4-4-5 Calendar

12. _____, adopted pursuant to the U.S. Securities Act of 1933, as amended (the 'Securities Act') provides a safe harbor from the registration requirements of the Securities Act of 1933 for certain private resales of restricted securities to QIBs (qualified institutional buyers), which generally are large institutional investors with over $100 million in investable assets. When a broker or dealer is selling securities in reliance on _____, it is subject to the condition that it may not make offers to persons other than those it reasonably believes to be QIBs.

Since its adoption, _____ has greatly increased the liquidity of the securities affected.

a. Prudent man rule
c. SIPC

b. Securities Investor Protection Corporation
d. Rule 144A

13. Behavioral economics and _____ are closely related fields that have evolved to be a separate branch of economic and financial analysis which applies scientific research on human and social, cognitive and emotional factors to better understand economic decisions by, say, consumers, borrowers, investors, and how they affect market prices, returns and the allocation of resources.

The field is primarily concerned with the bounds of rationality (selfishness, self-control) of economic agents. Behavioral models typically integrate insights from psychology with neo-classical economic theory.

a. Recession
c. Medium of exchange

b. Market structure
d. Behavioral finance

14. _____ is basically the process of generating a book of investor demand for the shares during an IPO for efficient price discovery. Usually, the issuer appoints a major investment bank to act as a book runner.

_____ is a common practice in developed countries and has recently been making inroads into emerging markets as well, including India.

a. Preferred stock
c. Gross profit margin

b. Gross profit
d. Book building

15. A _____ is a type of auction where the auctioneer begins with a high asking price which is lowered until some participant is willing to accept the auctioneer's price, or a predetermined reserve price (the seller's minimum acceptable price) is reached. The winning participant pays the last announced price. This is also known as a 'clock auction' or an open-outcry descending-price auction.
a. 529 plan
c. 4-4-5 Calendar

b. 7-Eleven
d. Dutch auction

16. _____ are organizations which pool large sums of money and invest those sums in companies. They include banks, insurance companies, retirement or pension funds, hedge funds and mutual funds. Their role in the economy is to act as highly specialized investors on behalf of others.
a. A Random Walk Down Wall Street
c. ABN Amro

b. AAB
d. Institutional investors

17. In finance, a _____ is a debt security, in which the authorized issuer owes the holders a debt and, depending on the terms of the _____, is obliged to pay interest (the coupon) and/or to repay the principal at a later date, termed maturity.

Thus a _____ is a loan: the issuer is the borrower, the _____ holder is the lender, and the coupon is the interest. _____s provide the borrower with external funds to finance long-term investments, or, in the case of government _____s, to finance current expenditure.

a. Puttable bond

b. Catastrophe bonds

c. Convertible bond

d. Bond

18. In business, a _____ is the purchase of one company (the target) by another (the acquirer or bidder). In the UK the term refers to the acquisition of a public company whose shares are listed on a stock exchange, in contrast to the acquisition of a private company.

Before a bidder makes an offer for another company, it usually first informs that company's board of directors.

a. 4-4-5 Calendar

b. 529 plan

c. Stock swap

d. Takeover

19. In economics, business, and accounting, a _____ is the value of money that has been used up to produce something, and hence is not available for use anymore. In business, the _____ may be one of acquisition, in which case the amount of money expended to acquire it is counted as _____. In this case, money is the input that is gone in order to acquire the thing.

a. Marginal cost

b. Cost

c. Sliding scale fees

d. Fixed costs

20. In economic models, the _____ time frame assumes no fixed factors of production. Firms can enter or leave the marketplace, and the cost (and availability) of land, labor, raw materials, and capital goods can be assumed to vary. In contrast, in the short-run time frame, certain factors are assumed to be fixed, because there is not sufficient time for them to change.

a. Long-run

b. 529 plan

c. Short-run

d. 4-4-5 Calendar

21. A _____ is a professionally managed type of collective investment scheme that pools money from many investors and invests it in stocks, bonds, short-term money market instruments, and/or other securities. The _____ will have a fund manager that trades the pooled money on a regular basis. Currently, the worldwide value of all _____s totals more than $26 trillion.

Since 1940, there have been three basic types of investment companies in the United States: open-end funds, also known in the US as _____s; unit investment trusts (UITs); and closed-end funds.

a. Net asset value

b. Trust company

c. Financial intermediary

d. Mutual fund

22. _____ mature in one year or less. Like zero-coupon bonds, they do not pay interest prior to maturity; instead they are sold at a discount of the par value to create a positive yield to maturity. Many regard _____ as the least risky investment available to U.S. investors.

    a. Treasury Inflation Protected Securities   b. Treasury securities

    c. 4-4-5 Calendar   d. Treasury bills

23. An _____ represents the ownership in the shares of a foreign company trading on US financial markets. The stock of many non-US companies trades on US exchanges through the use of _____s. _____s enable US investors to buy shares in foreign companies without undertaking cross-border transactions.

    a. ABN Amro   b. AAB

    c. A Random Walk Down Wall Street   d. American Depository Receipt

24. _____ offer, asking price is a price a seller of a good is willing to accept for that particular good.

In bid and ask, the term _____ is used in contrast to the term bid price. The difference between the _____ and the bid price is called the spread.

    a. Ask price   b. AAB

    c. Interest rate parity   d. A Random Walk Down Wall Street

25. A _____ is the highest price that a buyer (i.e., bidder) is willing to pay for a good. It is usually referred to simply as the 'bid.'

In bid and ask, the _____ stands in contrast to the ask price or 'offer', and the difference between the two is called the bid/ask spread.

An unsolicited bid or offer is when a person or company receives a bid even though they are not looking to sell.

    a. Bid price   b. Settlement date

    c. Political risk   d. Mid price

26. A _____ is a buy or sell order to be executed by the broker immediately at current market prices. As long as there are willing sellers and buyers, _____s are filled.

A _____ is the simplest of the order types.

    a. Block premium   b. Stockholder

    c. Market order   d. Trading curb

27. The _____ is an American stock exchange. It is the largest electronic screen-based equity securities trading market in the United States. With approximately 3,200 companies, it has more trading volume per day than any other stock exchange in the world.

    a. 7-Eleven   b. 529 plan

    c. 4-4-5 Calendar   d. NASDAQ

28. The _____ is a stock exchange based in New York City, New York. It is the largest stock exchange in the world by dollar value of its listed companies securities. As of October 2008, the combined capitalization of all domestic _____ listed companies was $10.1 trillion.

a. 7-Eleven
b. 4-4-5 Calendar
c. 529 plan
d. New York Stock Exchange

29. A _____, securities exchange or (in Europe) bourse is a corporation or mutual organization which provides 'trading' facilities for stock brokers and traders, to trade stocks and other securities. _____s also provide facilities for the issue and redemption of securities as well as other financial instruments and capital events including the payment of income and dividends. The securities traded on a _____ include: shares issued by companies, unit trusts and other pooled investment products and bonds.

a. 529 plan
b. 4-4-5 Calendar
c. 7-Eleven
d. Stock Exchange

30. A _____ is an order to buy (or sell) a security once the price of the security has climbed above (or dropped below) a specified stop price. When the specified stop price is reached, the _____ is entered as a market order (no limit.)

With a _____, the customer does not have to actively monitor how a stock is performing.

a. Wash sale
b. Stock split
c. Share price
d. Stop order

31. The institution most often referenced by the word '_____' is a public or publicly traded _____, the shares of which are traded on a public stock exchange (e.g., the New York Stock Exchange or Nasdaq in the United States) where shares of stock of _____s are bought and sold by and to the general public. Most of the largest businesses in the world are publicly traded _____s. However, the majority of _____s are said to be closely held, privately held or close _____s, meaning that no ready market exists for the trading of shares.

a. Corporation
b. Depository Trust Company
c. Protect
d. Federal Home Loan Mortgage Corporation

32. In economics, a _____ is a mechanism that allows people to easily buy and sell (trade) financial securities (such as stocks and bonds), commodities (such as precious metals or agricultural goods), and other fungible items of value at low transaction costs and at prices that reflect the efficient-market hypothesis.

_____s have evolved significantly over several hundred years and are undergoing constant innovation to improve liquidity.

Both general markets (where many commodities are traded) and specialized markets (where only one commodity is traded) exist.

a. Cost of carry
b. Delta hedging
c. Financial market
d. Secondary market

33. A _____ is an order to buy a security at no more (or sell at no less) than a specific price. This gives the customer some control over the price at which the trade is executed, but may prevent the order from being executed ('filled'.)

A buy _____ can only be executed by the broker at the limit price or lower.

a. Block premium   b. Common stock

c. Commercial mortgage-backed securities   d. Limit order

34. In finance, _____ or 'shorting' is the practice of selling a financial instrument that the seller does not own at the time of the sale. _____ is done with intent of later purchasing the financial instrument at a lower price. Short-sellers attempt to profit from an expected decline in the price of a financial instrument.

a. 529 plan   b. Short selling

c. Short ratio   d. 4-4-5 Calendar

35. A _____ is the price of a single share of a no. of saleable stocks of the company. Once the stock is purchased, the owner becomes a shareholder of the company that issued the share.

a. Whisper numbers   b. Stock split

c. Trading curb   d. Share price

36. The _____ is a financial market where participants buy and sell debt securities, usually in the form of bonds. As of 2006, the size of the international _____ is an estimated $45 trillion, of which the size of the outstanding U.S. _____ debt was $25.2 trillion.

Nearly all of the $923 billion average daily trading volume in the U.S. _____ takes place between broker-dealers and large institutions in a decentralized, over-the-counter market.

a. 4-4-5 Calendar   b. Fixed income

c. 529 plan   d. Bond market

37. In finance, _____ is the process of estimating the potential market value of a financial asset or liability. they can be done on assets (for example, investments in marketable securities such as stocks, options, business enterprises, or intangible assets such as patents and trademarks) or on liabilities (e.g., Bonds issued by a company.) _____s are required in many contexts including investment analysis, capital budgeting, merger and acquisition transactions, financial reporting, taxable events to determine the proper tax liability, and in litigation.

a. Valuation   b. Margin

c. Procter ' Gamble   d. Share

38. An _____ is the term used in financial circles for a type of computer system that facilitates trading of financial products outside of stock exchanges. The primary products that are traded on an _____ are stocks and currencies. They came into existence in 1998 when the SEC authorized their creation.

a. Open outcry   b. Electronic communication network

c. Insider trading   d. Intellidex

39. _____ is a measure of the ability of a debtor to pay their debts as and when they fall due. It is usually expressed as a ratio or a percentage of current liabilities.

For a corporation with a published balance sheet there are various ratios used to calculate a measure of liquidity.

a. Operating leverage

c. Operating profit margin

b. Invested capital

d. Accounting liquidity

40. _____ is a business, economics or investment term that refers to an asset's ability to be easily converted through an act of buying or selling without causing a significant movement in the price and with minimum loss of value. Money, or cash on hand, is the most liquid asset. An act of exchange of a less liquid asset with a more liquid asset is called liquidation.

a. 7-Eleven

c. Market Liquidity

b. 4-4-5 Calendar

d. 529 plan

41. A _____ is a private or public market for the trading of company stock and derivatives of company stock at an agreed price; these are securities listed on a stock exchange as well as those only traded privately.

The size of the world _____ is estimated at about $36.6 trillion US at the beginning of October 2008 . The world derivatives market has been estimated at about $480 trillion face or nominal value, 12 times the size of the entire world economy.

a. Stock market

c. Anton Gelonkin

b. Adolph Coors

d. Andrew Tobias

42. _____ N.V. is a pan-European stock exchange based in Paris and with subsidiaries in Belgium, France, Netherlands, Luxembourg, Portugal and the United Kingdom. In addition to equities and derivatives markets, the _____ group provides clearing and information services. As of 31 January 2006, markets run by _____ had a market capitalization of US$2.9 trillion, making it the 5th largest exchange on the planet.

a. AAB

c. A Random Walk Down Wall Street

b. ABN Amro

d. Euronext

43. A _____ is a firm that quotes both a buy and a sell price in a financial instrument or commodity, hoping to make a profit on the bid/offer spread, or turn.

In foreign exchange trading, where most deals are conducted over-the-counter and are, therefore, completely virtual, the _____ sells to and buys from its clients. Hence, the client's loss and the spread is the _____ firm's profit, which gets thus compensated for the effort of providing liquidity in a competitive market.

a. 4-4-5 Calendar

c. 7-Eleven

b. 529 plan

d. Market maker

44. In the United States, the Financial Industry Regulatory Authority (FINRA) is a self-regulatory organization (SRO) under the Securities Exchange Act of 1934, successor to the _____, Inc.

FINRA is responsible for regulatory oversight of all securities firms that do business with the public; professional training, testing and licensing of registered persons; arbitration and mediation; market regulation by contract for The NASDAQ Stock Market, Inc., the American Stock Exchange LLC, and the International Securities Exchange, LLC; and industry utilities, such as Trade Reporting Facilities and other over-the-counter operations.

a. 4-4-5 Calendar   b. 7-Eleven
c. National Association of Securities Dealers   d. 529 plan

45.   The _____ is an electronic quotation system in the United States that displays real-time quotes, last-sale prices, and volume information for many over-the-counter (OTC) equity securities that are not listed on the NASDAQ stock exchange or a national securities exchange. Broker-dealers who subscribe to the system can use the _____ to look up prices or enter quotes for OTC securities.

a. AT'T Inc.   b. OTC Bulletin Board
c. Insolvency   d. Internal control

46.   A _____ is a member of an exchange who is an employee of a member firm and executes orders, as agent, on the floor of the exchange for clients. The _____ receives an order via teletype machine from his firm's trading department and then proceeds to the appropriate trading post on the exchange floor. There he joins other brokers and the specialist in the security being bought or sold and executes the trade at the best competitive price available.

a. Floor broker   b. Business valuation standards
c. Case-Shiller Home Price Indices   d. Multivariate normal distribution

47.   An _____ is an investment vehicle traded on stock exchanges, much like stocks. An ETF holds assets such as stocks or bonds and trades at approximately the same price as the net asset value of its underlying assets over the course of the trading day. Most ETFs track an index, such as the Dow Jones Industrial Average or the S'P 500.

a. ABN Amro   b. AAB
c. A Random Walk Down Wall Street   d. Exchange-traded fund

48.   A _____ is a term used in the United States to describe stock exchanges that operates outside of the country's main financial center in New York City. A _____ operates in the trading of listed and over-the-counter (OTC) equities under the SEC's Unlisted Trading Priviliges (UTP) rule.

Regional exchanges currently registered with the SEC include:

- Boston Stock Exchange (BSE or BSX)
- CBOE Stock Exchange (CBSX)
- Chicago Stock Exchange (CHX)
- National Stock Exchange (NSX)
- Philadelphia Stock Exchange (PHLX), the nation's first stock exchange
- Pacific Stock Exchange (PSE)

The Boston and Philadelphia Stock Exchanges were both acquired by NASDAQ in 2007, and the Pacific Exchange acquired in 2006 by the New York Stock Exchange, thus ending their identities as separate stock exchanges.

There used to be many more such exchanges in the United States.

a. 529 plan   b. 4-4-5 Calendar
c. 7-Eleven   d. Regional stock exchange

49.   In business and finance, a _____ (also referred to as equity _____) of stock means a _____ of ownership in a corporation (company.) In the plural, stocks is often used as a synonym for _____s especially in the United States, but it is less commonly used that way outside of North America.

In the United Kingdom, South Africa, and Australia, stock can also refer to completely different financial instruments such as government bonds or, less commonly, to all kinds of marketable securities.

a. Margin   b. Share
c. Procter ' Gamble   d. Bucket shop

50.   A _____ is a financial services company that provides clearing and settlement services for financial transactions, usually on a futures exchange, and often acts as central counterparty (the payor actually pays the _____, which then pays the payee). A _____ may also offer novation, the substitution of a new contract or debt for an old, or other credit enhancement services to its members.

The term is also used for banks like Suffolk Bank that acted as a restraint on the over-issuance of private bank notes.

a. Clearing house   b. Warrant
c. Bucket shop   d. Valuation

51.   The _____ is one of several stock market indices, created by nineteenth-century Wall Street Journal editor and Dow Jones ' Company co-founder Charles Dow. Dow compiled the index to gauge the performance of the industrial sector of the American stock market. It is the second-oldest U.S. market index, after the Dow Jones Transportation Average, which Dow also created.

a. 7-Eleven   b. 529 plan
c. 4-4-5 Calendar   d. Dow Jones Industrial Average

52.   _____ is a risk-adjusted measure of the so-called active return on an investment. It is the return in excess of the compensation for the risk borne, and thus commonly used to assess active managers' performances. Often, the return of a benchmark is subtracted in order to consider relative performance, which yields Jensen's _____.

a. Alpha   b. Annuity
c. Option   d. Amortization

53.   A '_____' is a 'Charge' that is paid to obtain the right to delay a payment. Essentially, the payer purchases the right to make a given payment in the future instead of in the Present. The '_____', or 'Charge' that must be paid to delay the payment, is simply the difference between what the payment amount would be if it were paid in the present and what the payment amount would be paid if it were paid in the future.

a. Risk modeling   b. Value at risk
c. Discount   d. Risk aversion

54.   A _____ is a payment made by a corporation to its shareholder members. When a corporation earns a profit or surplus, that money can be put to two uses: it can either be re-invested in the business (called retained earnings), or it can be paid to the shareholders as a _____. Many corporations retain a portion of their earnings and pay the remainder as a _____.

a. Special dividend   b. Dividend yield
c. Dividend puzzle   d. Dividend

55.   The _____ is overseen by the _____ Association.

Tape C contains over-the-counter stocks listed on the NASDAQ National Market or NASDAQ Small Cap Market, and is overseen by the OTC/UTP Operating Committee.

a. Consolidated Tape   b. Liquidating dividend
c. Peer group analysis   d. January effect

56.   _____ arises from situations in which a party interested in trading an asset cannot do it because nobody in the market wants to trade that asset. _____ becomes particularly important to parties who are about to hold or currently hold an asset, since it affects their ability to trade.

Manifestation of _____ is very different from a drop of price to zero.

a. Currency risk   b. Liquidity risk
c. Tracking error   d. Credit risk

57.   A _____ is a futures contract on a short term interest rate (STIR.) Contracts vary, but are often defined on an interest rate index such as 3-month sterling or US dollar LIBOR.

They are traded across a wide range of currencies, including the G12 country currencies and many others.

a. Dual currency deposit   b. Real estate derivatives
c. Notional amount   d. Financial Future

58.   In finance, a _____ is a standardized contract, to buy or sell a specified commodity of standardized quality at a certain date in the future, at a market determined price (the futures price.)

The price is determined by the instantaneous equilibrium between the forces of supply and demand among competing buy and sell orders on the exchange at the time of the purchase or sale of the contract.

In many cases, the items may be such non-traditional 'commodities' as foreign currencies, commercial or government paper [e.g., bonds], or 'baskets' of corporate equity ['stock indices'] or other financial instruments.

a. Repurchase agreement   b. Financial future
c. Heston model   d. Futures contract

59.   A _____ is a central financial exchange where people can trade standardized futures contracts; that is, a contract to buy specific quantities of a commodity or financial instrument at a specified price with delivery set at a specified time in the future.

Though the origins of futures trading can supposedly be traced to Ancient Greek or Phoenician times, the first modern organized _____ began in 1710 at the Dojima Rice Exchange in Osaka, Japan.

The United States followed in the early 1800s.

a. 529 plan

b. 4-4-5 Calendar

c. Futures Exchange

d. 7-Eleven

60. The _____ started life on September 30, 1982, to take advantage of the removal of currency controls in the UK in 1979. The exchange modelled itself after the Chicago Board of Trade and the Chicago Mercantile Exchange. It initially offered futures contracts and options linked to short term interest rates.

a. 529 plan

b. 4-4-5 Calendar

c. 7-Eleven

d. London International Financial Futures Exchange

61. _____ or amalgamation is the act of merging many things into one. In business, it often refers to the mergers or acquisitions of many smaller companies into much larger ones. The financial accounting term of _____ refers to the aggregated financial statements of a group company as consolidated account.

a. Retained earnings

b. Write-off

c. Cost of goods sold

d. Consolidation

62. _____, in bookkeeping, refers to assets, liabilities, income, and expenses recorded on individual pages of the so called book of final entry or ledger. Changes in _____ value are made by chronologically posting debit (DR) and credit (CR) entries to its page. Examples of _____s are cash, _____s receivable, mortgages, loans, land and buildings, common stock, sales, services provided, wages, and payroll overhead.

a. Option

b. Accretion

c. Alpha

d. Account

63. _____ is a form of corporation equity ownership represented in the securities. It is dangerous in comparison to preferred shares and some other investment options, in that in the event of bankruptcy, _____ investors receive their funds after preferred stockholders, bondholders, creditors, etc. On the other hand, common shares on average perform better than preferred shares or bonds over time.

a. Common stock

b. Stock market bubble

c. Stop-limit order

d. Stock split

64. _____ has become the norm for individual investors and traders over the past decade with many, if not all brokers now offering online services with unique trading platforms.

In the past, investors had to call up their brokers and place an order on the phone. The broker would then enter the order in their system which was linked to trading floors and exchanges.

a. Alternative investment

b. Asset allocation

c. Investing online

d. Investment decisions

65. _____ is buying securities with cash borrowed from a broker, using other securities as collateral. This has the effect of magnifying any profit or loss made on the securities. The securities serve as collateral for the loan.

a. Triple witching hour
b. Margin buying
c. Risk-neutral measure
d. SPI 200 futures contract

66.   In finance, a _____ is collateral that the holder of a position in securities, options, or futures contracts has to deposit to cover the credit risk of his counterparty (most often his broker.) This risk can arise if the holder has done any of the following:

- borrowed cash from the counterparty to buy securities or options,
- sold securities or options short, or
- entered into a futures contract.

The collateral can be in the form of cash or securities, and it is deposited in a _____ account. On U.S. futures exchanges, '_____' was formally called performance bond.

_____ buying is buying securities with cash borrowed from a broker, using other securities as collateral.

a. Share
b. Procter ' Gamble
c. Credit
d. Margin

67.   The variation margin or _____ is not collateral, but a daily offsetting of profits and losses. Futures are marked-to-market every day, so the current price is compared to the previous day's price. The profit or loss on the day of a position is then paid to or debited from the holder by the futures exchange.
a. SPI 200 futures contract
b. Delivery month
c. Total return swap
d. Maintenance margin

68.   The _____ is the amount required to be collateralized in order to open a position. Thereafter, the amount required to be kept in collateral until the position is closed is the maintenance requirement. The maintenance requirement is the minimum amount to be collateralized in order to keep an open position.
a. ABN Amro
b. AAB
c. Initial margin requirement
d. A Random Walk Down Wall Street

69.   _____ is the balance of the amounts of cash being received and paid by a business during a defined period of time, sometimes tied to a specific project. Measurement of _____ can be used

- to evaluate the state or performance of a business or project.
- to determine problems with liquidity. Being profitable does not necessarily mean being liquid. A company can fail because of a shortage of cash, even while profitable.
- to generate project rate of returns. The time of _____s into and out of projects are used as inputs to financial models such as internal rate of return, and net present value.
- to examine income or growth of a business when it is believed that accrual accounting concepts do not represent economic realities. Alternately, _____ can be used to 'validate' the net income generated by accrual accounting.

_____ as a generic term may be used differently depending on context, and certain _____ definitions may be adapted by analysts and users for their own uses. Common terms include operating _____ and free _____.

_____s can be classified into:

1. Operational _____s: Cash received or expended as a result of the company's core business activities.
2. Investment _____s: Cash received or expended through capital expenditure, investments or acquisitions.
3. Financing _____s: Cash received or expended as a result of financial activities, such as interests and dividends.

All three together - the net _____ - are necessary to reconcile the beginning cash balance to the ending cash balance. Loan draw downs or equity injections, that is just shifting of capital but no expenditure as such, are not considered in the net _____.

a. Corporate finance

b. Shareholder value

c. Real option

d. Cash flow

70. _____ or financing is to provide capital (funds), which means money for a project, a person, a business or any other private or public institutions.

Those funds can be allocated for either short term or long term purposes. The health fund is a new way of _____ private healthcare centers.

a. Funding

b. Product life cycle

c. Proxy fight

d. Synthetic CDO

71. Days to Cover (DTC) is a numerical term that describes the relationship between the amount of shares in a given equity that have been short sold and the number of days of typical trading that it would require to 'cover' all _____ outstanding. For example, if there are ten million shares of XYZ Inc. that are currently short sold and the average daily volume of XYZ shares traded each day is one million, it would require ten days of trading for all _____ to be covered (10 million / 1 million.)

a. Guaranteed investment contracts

b. Short positions

c. Stock or scrip dividends

d. Cash budget

72. In the original and simplified sense, _____ were things of value, of uniform quality, that were produced in large quantities by many different producers; the items from each different producer are considered equivalent. It is the contract and this underlying standard that define the commodity, not any quality inherent in the product.

_____ exchanges include:

- Chicago Board of Trade
- Kansas City Board of Trade
- Euronext.liffe
- Kuala Lumpur Futures Exchange
- Bhatinda Om ' Oil Exchange
- London Metal Exchange
- New York Mercantile Exchange
- Multi Commodity Exchange
- Dalian Commodity Exchange

Markets for trading _____ can be very efficient, particularly if the division into pools matches demand segments. These markets will quickly respond to changes in supply and demand to find an equilibrium price and quantity.

a. 529 plan   b. 7-Eleven
c. 4-4-5 Calendar   d. Commodities

73.   _____ are formal records of a business' financial activities.

_____ provide an overview of a business' financial condition in both short and long term. There are four basic _____:

1. **Balance sheet**: also referred to as statement of financial position or condition, reports on a company's assets, liabilities, and net equity as of a given point in time.
2. **Income statement**: also referred to as Profit and Loss statement (or a 'P'L'), reports on a company's income, expenses, and profits over a period of time.
3. **Statement of retained earnings**: explains the changes in a company's retained earnings over the reporting period.
4. **Statement of cash flows**: reports on a company's cash flow activities, particularly its operating, investing and financing activities.

a. Financial statements   b. Notes to the Financial Statements

c. Statement of retained earnings   d. Statement on Auditing Standards No. 70: Service Organizations

74.   Congress enacted the _____, in the aftermath of the stock market crash of 1929 and during the ensuing Great Depression. It requires that any offer or sale of securities using the means and instrumentalities of interstate commerce be registered pursuant to the 1933 Act, unless an exemption from registration exists under the law.

a. 7-Eleven   b. 529 plan
c. 4-4-5 Calendar   d. Securities Act of 1933

75. The _____ of 1934 is a law governing the secondary trading of securities (stocks, bonds, and debentures) in the United States of America. The Act, 48 Stat. 881 (enacted June 6, 1934), codified at 15 U.S.C. §§ 78a et seq., was a sweeping piece of legislation. The Act and related statutes form the basis of regulation of the financial markets and their participants in the United States.

    a. 529 plan

    b. 4-4-5 Calendar

    c. 7-Eleven

    d. Securities Exchange Act

76. A _____ is a state law in the United States that regulates the offering and sale of securities to protect the public from fraud. Though the specific provisions of these laws vary among states, they all require the registration of all securities offerings and sales, as well as of stock brokers and brokerage firms. Each state's _____ is administered by its appropriate regulatory agency, and most also provide private causes of action for private investors who have been injured by securities fraud.

    a. Patent

    b. Bundesrechnungshof

    c. Court of Audit of Belgium

    d. Blue sky law

77. The _____ is headquartered in the United States of America at Charlottesville, Virginia with offices in Hong Kong and London. Formerly known as the Association for Investment Management and Research (AIMR), the Institute awards the Chartered Financial Analyst (CFA) designation.

In 1925, an organization of investment analysts founded the Investment Analyst Society of Chicago.

    a. CFA Institute

    b. Credit card balance transfer

    c. Payback period

    d. Financial rand

78. _____ is an international professional designation offered by the _____ Institute (formerly known as AIMR) to financial analysts who complete a series of three examinations. In order to become a '_____ Charterholder' candidates must pass all three six-hour exams, possess a bachelor's degree (or equivalent, as assessed by the _____ institute) and have 48 months of work experience in an investment decision-making position. _____ charterholders are also obligated to adhere to a strict Code of Ethics and Standards governing their professional conduct.

    a. 529 plan

    b. 7-Eleven

    c. Chartered Financial Analyst

    d. 4-4-5 Calendar

79. Explicit _____ is a measure implemented in many countries to protect bank depositors, in full or in part, from losses caused by a bank's inability to pay its debts when due. _____ systems are one component of a financial system safety net that promotes financial stability.

    a. Reserve requirement

    b. Deposit Insurance

    c. Banking panic

    d. Time deposit

80. The _____ is a United States government corporation created by the Glass-Steagall Act of 1933. It provides deposit insurance, which guarantees the safety of checking and savings deposits in member banks, currently up to $250,000 per depositor per bank. Insured deposits are backed by the full faith and credit of the United States.

    a. Ford Foundation

    b. NYSE Group

    c. Federal Deposit Insurance Corporation

    d. FASB

81. A _____, securities analyst, research analyst, equity analyst, or investment analyst is a person who performs financial analysis for external or internal clients as a core part of the job.

An analyst studies companies and other entities to arrive at the estimate of their financial value. It is normally done by analyzing financial reports, aided by follow-up interviews with company representatives and industry experts.

a. Stockbroker

b. Purchasing manager

c. Financial Analyst

d. Portfolio manager

82.　The term _____ usually refers to a company that is permitted to offer its registered securities for sale to the general public, typically through a stock exchange, or occasionally a company whose stock is traded over the counter via market makers who use non-exchange quotation services.

The term '_____' may also refer to a company owned by the government.

a. Corporation

b. Public Company

c. First Prudential Markets

d. General partnership

83.　The _____ (sometimes called 'Peekaboo') is a private-sector, non-profit corporation created by the Sarbanes-Oxley Act, a 2002 United States federal law, to oversee the auditors of public companies. Its stated purpose is to 'protect the interests of investors and further the public interest in the preparation of informative, fair, and independent audit reports'. Although a private entity, the _____ has many government-like regulatory functions, making it in some ways similar to the private Self Regulatory Organizations (SROs) that regulate stock markets and other aspects of the financial markets in the United States.

a. Financial Crimes Enforcement Network

b. World Trade Organization

c. Gamelan Council

d. Public Company Accounting Oversight Board

84.　The _____ of 2002 (Pub.L. 107-204, 116 Stat. 745, enacted July 30, 2002), also known as the Public Company Accounting Reform and Investor Protection Act of 2002 and commonly called Sarbanes-Oxley, Sarbox or SOX, is a United States federal law enacted on July 30, 2002 in response to a number of major corporate and accounting scandals including those affecting Enron, Tyco International, Adelphia, Peregrine Systems and WorldCom.

a. Sarbanes-Oxley Act

b. Blue sky law

c. Foreign Corrupt Practices Act

d. Duty of loyalty

85.　The _____ of 1970 codified at 15 U.S.C. Â§ 78aaa through 15 U.S.C. Â§ 78lll, established the Securities Investor Protection Corporation (SIPC). Most brokers and dealers registered under the Securities Exchange Act of 1934 are required to be members of the SIPC.

The SIPC maintains a fund that is intended to protect investors against the misappropriation of their funds and of most types of securities in the event of the failure of their broker.

a. Fiduciary

b. McFadden Act

c. Quiet period

d. Securities Investor Protection Act

86.　The _____ is a federally mandated non-profit corporation in the United States that protects securities investors from harm if a broker-dealer company fails. Investors are not insured for any potential loss while invested in the market.

Congress created _____ in 1970 through the Securities Investor Protection Act (15 U.S.C.

a. Rule 144A

c. SIPC

b. Prudent man rule

d. Securities Investor Protection Corporation

87. The _____ is a model statute designed to guide each state in drafting its state securities law. It was created by the National Conference of Commissioners on Uniform State Laws (NCCUSL.)

The purpose of the _____ is to provide model legislation that can be adopted by a state to deal with securities fraud at the state level, supplementing enforcement and regulation efforts of the U.S. Securities and Exchange Commission (SEC.)

a. External risks

c. Uniform Securities Act

b. Economies of scale

d. Employee Retirement Income Security Act

88. _____ is the set of processes, customs, policies, laws and institutions affecting the way a corporation is directed, administered or controlled. _____ also includes the relationships among the many stakeholders involved and the goals for which the corporation is governed. The principal stakeholders are the shareholders, management and the board of directors.

a. Patent

c. Due diligence

b. Corporate governance

d. Foreign Corrupt Practices Act

89. A _____ is a point at which a stock market will stop trading for a period of time in response to substantial drops in value.

On the New York Stock Exchange, one type of _____ is referred to as a 'circuit breaker.' These limits were put in place after Black Monday in order to reduce market volatility and massive panic sell-offs, giving traders time to reconsider their transactions.

At the start of each quarter, the NYSE sets three circuit breaker levels at levels of 10%, 20%, and 30% of the average closing price of the Dow Jones Industrial Average for the month preceding the start of the quarter, rounded to the nearest 50-point interval.

a. Common stock

c. Stock market index

b. Stock repurchase

d. Trading curb

90. _____ is the trading of a corporation's stock or other securities (e.g. bonds or stock options) by individuals with potential access to non-public information about the company. In most countries, trading by corporate insiders such as officers, key employees, directors, and large shareholders may be legal, if this trading is done in a way that does not take advantage of non-public information. However, the term is frequently used to refer to a practice in which an insider or a related party trades based on material non-public information obtained during the performance of the insider's duties at the corporation, or otherwise in breach of a fiduciary duty or other relationship of trust and confidence or where the non-public information was misappropriated from the company.

a. Insider trading

c. Equity investment

b. Open outcry

d. Intellidex

91.   The _____ generally prohibits short selling of securities except on an uptick. The rule was defined by U.S. Securities and Exchange Commission (SEC) which summarized it: 'Rule 10a-1(a)(1) provided that, subject to certain exceptions, a listed security may be sold short (A) at a price above the price at which the immediately preceding sale was effected (plus tick), or (B) at the last sale price if it is higher than the last different price (zero-plus tick.) Short sales were not permitted on minus ticks or zero-minus ticks, subject to narrow exceptions.'

The rule went into effect in 1938 and was removed when Rule 201 Regulation SHO became effective in 2007.

a. ABN Amro   b. AAB
c. A Random Walk Down Wall Street   d. Uptick rule

92.   The U.S. Securities and Exchange Commission's (SEC's) Regulation Fair Disclosure, also commonly referred to as _____ was an SEC ruling implemented in October 2000 (.) It mandated that all publicly traded companies must disclose material information to all investors at the same time.

The regulation sought to stamp out selective disclosure, in which some investors (often large institutional investors) received market moving information before others (often smaller, individual investors.)

a. Revenue recognition   b. Regulation FD
c. Commodity Pool Operator   d. Regulation Fair Disclosure

93.   In economics and finance, _____ is the practice of taking advantage of a price differential between two or more markets: striking a combination of matching deals that capitalize upon the imbalance, the profit being the difference between the market prices. When used by academics, an _____ is a transaction that involves no negative cash flow at any probabilistic or temporal state and a positive cash flow in at least one state; in simple terms, a risk-free profit.
a. Efficient-market hypothesis   b. Initial margin
c. Issuer   d. Arbitrage

94.   In finance, _____ refers to Monday, October 19, 1987, when stock markets around the world crashed, shedding a huge value in a very short time. The crash began in Hong Kong, spread west through international time zones to Europe, hitting the United States after other markets had already declined by a significant margin. The Dow Jones Industrial Average (DJIA) dropped by 508 points to 1738.74 (22.61%).
a. Black Monday   b. 7-Eleven
c. 4-4-5 Calendar   d. 529 plan

95.   _____ most frequently refers to the standard deviation of the continuously compounded returns of a financial instrument with a specific time horizon. It is often used to quantify the risk of the instrument over that time period. _____ is typically expressed in annualized terms, and it may either be an absolute number ($5) or a fraction of the mean (5%).
a. Currency swap   b. Portfolio insurance
c. Volatility   d. Seasoned equity offering

1.   In business and accounting, _____s are everything of value that is owned by a person or company. The balance sheet of a firm records the monetary value of the _____s owned by the firm. The two major _____ classes are tangible _____s and intangible _____s.

   a. Income
                           b. Asset

   c. Accounts payable
                d. EBITDA

2.   _____ is a term used to refer to how an investor distributes his or her investments among various classes of investment vehicles (e.g., stocks and bonds.)

A large part of financial planning is finding an _____ that is appropriate for a given person in terms of their appetite for and ability to shoulder risk. This can depend on various factors; see investor profile.

   a. Asset allocation
                b. Investing online

   c. Investment performance
          d. Alternative investment

3.   Behavioral economics and _____ are closely related fields that have evolved to be a separate branch of economic and financial analysis which applies scientific research on human and social, cognitive and emotional factors to better understand economic decisions by, say, consumers, borrowers, investors, and how they affect market prices, returns and the allocation of resources.

The field is primarily concerned with the bounds of rationality (selfishness, self-control) of economic agents. Behavioral models typically integrate insights from psychology with neo-classical economic theory.

   a. Medium of exchange
             b. Behavioral finance

   c. Market structure
              d. Recession

4.   A _____ is an institution, firm or individual who mediates between two or more parties in a financial context. Typically the first party is a provider of a product or service and the second party is a consumer or customer.

In the U.S., a _____ is typically an institution that facilitates the channelling of funds between lenders and borrowers indirectly.

   a. Savings and loan association
       b. Financial intermediary

   c. Net asset value
              d. Mutual fund

5.   In economics, a _____ is a mechanism that allows people to easily buy and sell (trade) financial securities (such as stocks and bonds), commodities (such as precious metals or agricultural goods), and other fungible items of value at low transaction costs and at prices that reflect the efficient-market hypothesis.

_____s have evolved significantly over several hundred years and are undergoing constant innovation to improve liquidity.

Both general markets (where many commodities are traded) and specialized markets (where only one commodity is traded) exist.

a. Delta hedging   b. Secondary market

c. Cost of carry   d. Financial market

6. _____ are organizations which pool large sums of money and invest those sums in companies. They include banks, insurance companies, retirement or pension funds, hedge funds and mutual funds. Their role in the economy is to act as highly specialized investors on behalf of others.

a. AAB   b. A Random Walk Down Wall Street

c. ABN Amro   d. Institutional investors

7. An _____ is a company whose main business is holding securities of other companies purely for investment purposes. The _____ invests money on behalf of its shareholders who in turn share in the profits and losses.

a. Investment company   b. Unit investment trust

c. AAB   d. A Random Walk Down Wall Street

8. In financial accounting, a _____ or statement of financial position is a summary of a person's or organization's balances. Assets, liabilities and ownership equity are listed as of a specific date, such as the end of its financial year. A _____ is often described as a snapshot of a company's financial condition.

a. Statement of retained earnings   b. Balance sheet

c. Statement on Auditing Standards No. 70: Service Organizations   d. Financial statements

9. In finance, a _____ is a debt security, in which the authorized issuer owes the holders a debt and, depending on the terms of the _____, is obliged to pay interest (the coupon) and/or to repay the principal at a later date, termed maturity.

Thus a _____ is a loan: the issuer is the borrower, the _____ holder is the lender, and the coupon is the interest. _____ s provide the borrower with external funds to finance long-term investments, or, in the case of government _____ s, to finance current expenditure.

a. Bond   b. Catastrophe bonds

c. Puttable bond   d. Convertible bond

10. The _____ is a financial market where participants buy and sell debt securities, usually in the form of bonds. As of 2006, the size of the international _____ is an estimated $45 trillion, of which the size of the outstanding U.S. _____ debt was $25.2 trillion.

Nearly all of the $923 billion average daily trading volume in the U.S. _____ takes place between broker-dealers and large institutions in a decentralized, over-the-counter market.

a. 529 plan   b. Bond market

c. 4-4-5 Calendar   d. Fixed income

11. The _____ is one of several stock market indices, created by nineteenth-century Wall Street Journal editor and Dow Jones ' Company co-founder Charles Dow. Dow compiled the index to gauge the performance of the industrial sector of the American stock market. It is the second-oldest U.S. market index, after the Dow Jones Transportation Average, which Dow also created.

a. 7-Eleven

b. 529 plan

c. 4-4-5 Calendar

d. Dow Jones Industrial Average

12. _____ is a term used to describe the value of an entity's assets less the value of its liabilities. The term is commonly used in relation to collective investment schemes. It may also be used as a synonym for the book value of a firm.

a. Financial intermediary

b. Passive management

c. Retail broker

d. Net asset value

13. In economics and related disciplines, a _____ is a cost incurred in making an economic exchange. For example, most people, when buying or selling a stock, must pay a commission to their broker; that commission is a _____ of doing the stock deal. Or consider buying a banana from a store; to purchase the banana, your costs will be not only the price of the banana itself, but also the energy and effort it requires to find out which of the various banana products you prefer, where to get them and at what price, the cost of traveling from your house to the store and back, the time waiting in line, and the effort of the paying itself; the costs above and beyond the cost of the banana are the _____s.

a. Variable costs

b. Marginal cost

c. Fixed costs

d. Transaction cost

14. A _____ is a US investment company offering a fixed (unmanaged) portfolio of securities having a definite life. _____s are assembled by a sponsor and sold through brokers to investors.

A _____ portfolio may contain one of several different types of securities.

a. A Random Walk Down Wall Street

b. AAB

c. Investment company

d. Unit investment trust

15. In economics, business, and accounting, a _____ is the value of money that has been used up to produce something, and hence is not available for use anymore. In business, the _____ may be one of acquisition, in which case the amount of money expended to acquire it is counted as _____. In this case, money is the input that is gone in order to acquire the thing.

a. Fixed costs

b. Marginal cost

c. Sliding scale fees

d. Cost

16. A _____, is a collective investment scheme with a limited number of shares.

New shares are rarely issued after the fund is launched; shares are not normally redeemable for cash or securities until the fund liquidates. Typically an investor can acquire shares in a _____ by buying shares on a secondary market from a broker, market maker, or other investor as opposed to an open-end fund where all transactions eventually involve the fund company creating new shares on the fly (in exchange for either cash or securities) or redeeming shares (for cash or securities.)

a. Closed-end fund

b. Stock fund

c. Money market funds

d. Mutual fund fees and expenses

17.   The institution most often referenced by the word '_____' is a public or publicly traded _____, the shares of which are traded on a public stock exchange (e.g., the New York Stock Exchange or Nasdaq in the United States) where shares of stock of _____s are bought and sold by and to the general public. Most of the largest businesses in the world are publicly traded _____s. However, the majority of _____s are said to be closely held, privately held or close _____s, meaning that no ready market exists for the trading of shares.

a. Corporation   b. Federal Home Loan Mortgage Corporation
c. Depository Trust Company   d. Protect

18.   The _____ is an American stock exchange. It is the largest electronic screen-based equity securities trading market in the United States. With approximately 3,200 companies, it has more trading volume per day than any other stock exchange in the world.

a. NASDAQ   b. 4-4-5 Calendar
c. 7-Eleven   d. 529 plan

19.   A '_____' is a 'Charge' that is paid to obtain the right to delay a payment. Essentially, the payer purchases the right to make a given payment in the future instead of in the Present. The '_____', or 'Charge' that must be paid to delay the payment, is simply the difference between what the payment amount would be if it were paid in the present and what the payment amount would be paid if it were paid in the future.

a. Discount   b. Risk aversion
c. Risk modeling   d. Value at risk

20.   In finance, a _____ is a position established in one market in an attempt to offset exposure to the price risk of an equal but opposite obligation or position in another market -- usually, but not always, in the context of one's commercial activity. Hedging is a strategy designed to minimize exposure to such business risks as a sharp contraction in demand for one's inventory, while still allowing the business to profit from producing and maintaining that inventory. A typical hedger might be a farmer with 2000 acres of unharvested wheat in the ground, who would rather tend his crop without the distraction of uncertain prices.

a. 7-Eleven   b. Hedge
c. 4-4-5 Calendar   d. 529 plan

21.   A _____ is a private investment fund open to a limited range of investors that is permitted by regulators to undertake a wider range of activities than other investment funds and also pays a performance fee to its investment manager. Each fund will have its own strategy which determines the type of investments and the methods of investment it undertakes. _____s as a class invest in a broad range of investments extending over shares, debt, commodities and beyond.

a. 7-Eleven   b. Hedge fund
c. 4-4-5 Calendar   d. 529 plan

22.   A _____ or _____ is a tax designation for a corporation investing in real estate that reduces or eliminates corporate income taxes. In return, _____s are required to distribute 95% of their income, which may be taxable in the hands of the investors. The _____ structure was designed to provide a similar structure for investment in real estate as mutual funds provide for investment in stocks.

a. Real estate investing   b. Real estate investment trust
c. Liquidation value   d. Tenancy

23.   In finance, _____ (or gearing) is borrowing money to supplement existing funds for investment in such a way that the potential positive or negative outcome is magnified and/or enhanced. It generally refers to using borrowed funds, or debt, so as to attempt to increase the returns to equity. Deleveraging is the action of reducing borrowings.

a. Financial endowment   b. Leverage
c. Pension fund   d. Limited partnership

24.   An investment strategy or portfolio is considered _____ if it seeks to entirely avoid some form of market risk, typically by hedging. In order to evaluate market neutrality, it is first necessary to specify the risk being avoided. For example, convertible arbitrage attempts to fully hedge fluctuations in the price of the underlying common stock.

a. Black-Litterman model   b. Flight-to-quality
c. Credit event   d. Market neutral

25.   A _____ is an asset-backed security whose cash flows are backed by the principal and interest payments of a set of mortgage loans. Payments are typically made monthly over the lifetime of the underlying loans.

a. Home equity line of credit   b. Shared appreciation mortgage
c. Conforming loan   d. Mortgage-backed security

26.   A _____ is a professionally managed type of collective investment scheme that pools money from many investors and invests it in stocks, bonds, short-term money market instruments, and/or other securities. The _____ will have a fund manager that trades the pooled money on a regular basis. Currently, the worldwide value of all _____s totals more than $26 trillion.

Since 1940, there have been three basic types of investment companies in the United States: open-end funds, also known in the US as _____s; unit investment trusts (UITs); and closed-end funds.

a. Trust company   b. Financial intermediary
c. Net asset value   d. Mutual fund

27.   An _____ is a contract written by a seller that conveys to the buyer the right -- but not the obligation -- to buy (in the case of a call _____) or to sell (in the case of a put _____) a particular asset, such as a piece of property such as, among others, a futures contract. In return for granting the _____, the seller collects a payment (the premium) from the buyer.

For example, buying a call _____ provides the right to buy a specified quantity of a security at a set strike price at some time on or before expiration, while buying a put _____ provides the right to sell.

a. AT'T Mobility LLC   b. Annuity
c. Amortization   d. Option

28.   A _____ is a tax designation for a corporation investing in real estate that reduces or eliminates corporate income taxes. In return, _____s are required to distribute 95% of their income, which may be taxable in the hands of the investors. The _____ structure was designed to provide a similar structure for investment in real estate as mutual funds provide for investment in stocks.

a. Real Estate Investment Trust   b. Real estate investing
c. Liquidation value   d. REIT

29. A _____ is a fungible, negotiable instrument representing financial value. They are broadly categorized into debt securities (such as banknotes, bonds and debentures), and equity securities; e.g., common stocks. The company or other entity issuing the _____ is called the issuer.

a. Book entry

b. Securities lending

c. Tracking stock

d. Security

30. _____ is a risk-adjusted measure of the so-called active return on an investment. It is the return in excess of the compensation for the risk borne, and thus commonly used to assess active managers' performances. Often, the return of a benchmark is subtracted in order to consider relative performance, which yields Jensen's _____.

a. Option

b. Annuity

c. Amortization

d. Alpha

31. A _____ or bank is a financial institution whose primary activity is to act as a payment agent for customers and to borrow and lend money.

The first modern bank was founded in Italy in Genoa in 1406, its name was Banco di San Giorgio (Bank of St. George.)

Many other financial activities were added over time.

a. 4-4-5 Calendar

b. Bought deal

c. Banker

d. Black Sea Trade and Development Bank

32. In finance, _____ is the process of estimating the potential market value of a financial asset or liability. they can be done on assets (for example, investments in marketable securities such as stocks, options, business enterprises, or intangible assets such as patents and trademarks) or on liabilities (e.g., Bonds issued by a company.) _____s are required in many contexts including investment analysis, capital budgeting, merger and acquisition transactions, financial reporting, taxable events to determine the proper tax liability, and in litigation.

a. Share

b. Margin

c. Procter ' Gamble

d. Valuation

33. A _____ or equity fund is a fund that invests in Equities more commonly known as stocks. Such funds are typically held either in stock or cash, as opposed to Bonds, notes, or other securities. This may be a mutual fund or exchange-traded fund.

a. Money market funds

b. Closed-end fund

c. Mutual fund fees and expenses

d. Stock fund

34. A '_____' (FoF) is an investment fund that uses an investment strategy of holding a portfolio of other investment funds rather than investing directly in shares, bonds or other securities. This type of investing is often referred to as multi-manager investment.

There are different types of '_____', each investing in a different type of collective investment scheme (typically one type per FoF), eg.

a. Leverage

b. Limited liability company

c. Pension fund

d. Fund of funds

35. _____, refers to consumption opportunity gained by an entity within a specified time frame, which is generally expressed in monetary terms. However, for households and individuals, '_____ is the sum of all the wages, salaries, profits, interests payments, rents and other forms of earnings received... in a given period of time.' For firms, _____ generally refers to net-profit: what remains of revenue after expenses have been subtracted.

a. OIBDA

b. Annual report

c. Accrual

d. Income

36. In finance, the _____ is the global financial market for short-term borrowing and lending. It provides short-term liquidity funding for the global financial system. The _____ is where short-term obligations such as Treasury bills, commercial paper and bankers' acceptances are bought and sold.

a. Money market

b. Consumer debt

c. Cramdown

d. Debt-for-equity swap

37. Money funds (or _____, money market mutual funds) are mutual funds that invest in short-term debt instruments.

_____, also known as principal stability funds, seek to limit exposure to losses due to credit, market and liquidity risks. _____, in the United States, are regulated by the Securities and Exchange Commission's (SEC) Investment Company Act of 1940.

a. Money market funds

b. Stock fund

c. Closed-end fund

d. Mutual fund fees and expenses

38. A _____ is a payment made by a corporation to its shareholder members. When a corporation earns a profit or surplus, that money can be put to two uses: it can either be re-invested in the business (called retained earnings), or it can be paid to the shareholders as a _____. Many corporations retain a portion of their earnings and pay the remainder as a _____.

a. Dividend

b. Dividend puzzle

c. Dividend yield

d. Special dividend

39. An _____ or index tracker is a collective investment scheme (usually a mutual fund or exchange-traded fund) that aims to replicate the movements of an index of a specific financial market regardless of market conditions.

Tracking can be achieved by trying to hold all of the securities in the index, in the same proportions as the index. Other methods include statistically sampling the market and holding 'representative' securities.

a. A Random Walk Down Wall Street

b. AAB

c. Investment company

d. Index fund

40. An _____ is any government regulation or law that encourages or discourages foreign investment in the local economy, e.g. currency exchange limits.

As globalization integrates the economies of neighboring and of trading states, they are typically forced to trade off such rules as part of a common tax, tariff and trade regime, e.g. as defined by a free trade pact. _____ favoring local investors over global ones is typically discouraged in such pacts, and the idea of a separate _____ rapidly becomes a fiction or fantasy, as real decisions reflect the real need for nations to compete for investment, even from their own local investors.

a. AAB   b. A Random Walk Down Wall Street
c. ABN Amro   d. Investment policy

41.   A _____ is a collective investment scheme that invests in bonds and other debt securities. _____s yield monthly dividends that include interest payments on the fund's underlying securities plus any capital appreciation in the prices of the portfolio's bonds. _____s tend to pay higher dividends than CDs and money market accounts, and they generally pay out dividends more frequently and regularly than individual bonds.

a. Private activity bond   b. Premium bond
c. Gilts   d. Bond fund

42.   _____ refers to any type of investment that yields a regular (or fixed) return.

For example, if you lend money to a borrower and the borrower has to pay interest once a month, you have been issued a fixed-income security. When a company does this, it is often called a bond or corporate bank debt (although preferred stock is also sometimes considered to be _____).

a. Fixed income   b. 529 plan
c. 4-4-5 Calendar   d. Bond market

43.   In finance, a _____ (non-investment grade bond, speculative grade bond or junk bond) is a bond that is rated below investment grade at the time of purchase. These bonds have a higher risk of default or other adverse credit events, but typically pay higher yields than better quality bonds in order to make them attractive to investors.

a. High yield bond   b. Private equity
c. Volatility   d. Sharpe ratio

44.   In the United States, a _____ is a bond issued by a city or other local government, or their agencies. Potential issuers of these bonds include cities, counties, redevelopment agencies, school districts, publicly owned airports and seaports, and any other governmental entity (or group of governments) below the state level. They may be general obligations of the issuer or secured by specified revenues.

a. Senior debt   b. Premium bond
c. Puttable bond   d. Municipal bond

45.   In business, _____ is income that a company receives from its normal business activities, usually from the sale of goods and services to customers. Some companies also receive _____ from interest, dividends or royalties paid to them by other companies. _____ may refer to business income in general, or it may refer to the amount, in a monetary unit, received during a period of time, as in 'Last year, Company X had _____ of $32 million.'

In many countries, including the UK, _____ is referred to as turnover.

a. Bottom line

b. Furniture, Fixtures and Equipment

c. Matching principle

d. Revenue

46.   In business, _____ refers to the sharing of profits and losses among different groups. One form shares between the general partner(s) and limited partners in a limited partnership. Another form shares with a company's employees, and another between companies in a business alliance.

a. Revenue sharing

b. 7-Eleven

c. 4-4-5 Calendar

d. 529 plan

47.   The U.S. _____ is an independent agency of the United States government which holds primary responsibility for enforcing the federal securities laws and regulating the securities industry, the nation's stock and options exchanges, and other electronic securities markets. The SEC was created by section 4 of the SEC of 1934 (now codified as 15 U.S.C. Â§ 78d and commonly referred to as the 1934 Act.)

a. Securities and Exchange Commission

b. 4-4-5 Calendar

c. 529 plan

d. 7-Eleven

48.   Unemployment occurs when a person is available to work and currently seeking work, but the person is without work. The prevalence of unemployment is usually measured using the _____, which is defined as the percentage of those in the labor force who are unemployed. The _____ is also used in economic studies and economic indexes such as the United States' Conference Board's Index of Leading Indicators as a measure of the state of the macroeconomics.

a. Unemployment rate

b. A Random Walk Down Wall Street

c. ABN Amro

d. AAB

49.   _____ is a fee paid on borrowed assets. It is the price paid for the use of borrowed money , or, money earned by deposited funds . Assets that are sometimes lent with _____ include money, shares, consumer goods through hire purchase, major assets such as aircraft, and even entire factories in finance lease arrangements.

a. Interest

b. A Random Walk Down Wall Street

c. Insolvency

d. AAB

50.   _____, adopted pursuant to the U.S. Securities Act of 1933, as amended (the 'Securities Act') provides a safe harbor from the registration requirements of the Securities Act of 1933 for certain private resales of restricted securities to QIBs (qualified institutional buyers), which generally are large institutional investors with over $100 million in investable assets. When a broker or dealer is selling securities in reliance on _____, it is subject to the condition that it may not make offers to persons other than those it reasonably believes to be QIBs.

Since its adoption, _____ has greatly increased the liquidity of the securities affected.

a. Prudent man rule

b. Securities Investor Protection Corporation

c. SIPC

d. Rule 144A

51.   _____ also known as Deferred Sales Charge, is a fee paid when shares are sold. This fee typically goes to the brokers that sell the fund's shares. The amount of this type of load will depend on how long the investor holds his or her shares and typically decreases to zero if the investor holds his or her shares long enough.

a. Back-end load

b. Closed-end fund

c. Mutual fund fees and expenses

d. Money market funds

52.   An _____, operating expenditure, operational expense, operational expenditure or OPEX is an on-going cost for running a product, business, or system. Its counterpart, a capital expenditure (CAPEX), is the cost of developing or providing non-consumable parts for the product or system. For example, the purchase of a photocopier is the CAPEX, and the annual paper and toner cost is the OPEX.

a. ABN Amro

b. A Random Walk Down Wall Street

c. AAB

d. Operating expense

53.   In finance, _____, also known as return on investment is the ratio of money gained or lost on an investment relative to the amount of money invested. The amount of money gained or lost may be referred to as interest, profit/loss, gain/loss, or net income/loss. The money invested may be referred to as the asset, capital, principal, or the cost basis of the investment.

a. Rate of return

b. Stock or scrip dividends

c. Doctrine of the Proper Law

d. Composiition of Creditors

54.   _____ is the provision of resources (such as granting a loan) by one party to another party where that second party does not reimburse the first party immediately, thereby generating a debt, and instead arranges either to repay or return those resources (or material(s) of equal value) at a later date. The first party is called a creditor, also known as a lender, while the second party is called a debtor, also known as a borrower.

Movements of financial capital are normally dependent on either _____ or equity transfers.

a. Clearing house

b. Comparable

c. Warrant

d. Credit

55.   _____ is trading executed after the standard local national exchanges have closed. This is distinct from after-hours trading, as they have in context specific meanings, the former may be illegal while the latter is legal.

In the mutual fund context, _____ involves placing orders for mutual fund shares after the close of the stock market, 4:00 p.m for the New York Stock Exchange, but still getting that day's closing price, rather than the next day's opening price.

a. Certificate in Investment Performance Measurement

b. Divestment

c. Late trading

d. Tactical asset allocation

56.   _____ is the strategy of making buy or sell decisions of financial assets (often stocks) by attempting to predict future market price movements. The prediction may be based on an outlook of market or economic conditions resulting from technical or fundamental analysis. This is an investment strategy based on the outlook for an aggregate market, rather than for a particular financial asset.

a. Divestment

b. Market timing

c. Late trading

d. Portable alpha

57. _____, also called fair price (in a commonplace conflation of the two distinct concepts), is a concept used in finance and economics, defined as a rational and unbiased estimate of the potential market price of a good, service, or asset, taking into account such objective factors as:

- acquisition/production/distribution costs, replacement costs, or costs of close substitutes
- actual utility at a given level of development of social productive capability
- supply vs. demand

and subjective factors such as

- risk characteristics
- cost of capital
- individually perceived utility

In accounting, _____ is used as an estimate of the market value of an asset (or liability) for which a market price cannot be determined (usually because there is no established market for the asset.) Under GAAP (FAS 157), _____ is the amount at which the asset could be bought or sold in a current transaction between willing parties, or transferred to an equivalent party, other than in a liquidation sale. This is used for assets whose carrying value is based on mark-to-market valuations; for assets carried at historical cost, the _____ of the asset is not used. One example of where _____ is an issue is a College kitchen with a cost of $2 million which was built 5 years ago.

a. 7-Eleven
c. 4-4-5 Calendar

b. Fair value
d. 529 plan

58. In economics and finance, _____ is the practice of taking advantage of a price differential between two or more markets: striking a combination of matching deals that capitalize upon the imbalance, the profit being the difference between the market prices. When used by academics, an _____ is a transaction that involves no negative cash flow at any probabilistic or temporal state and a positive cash flow in at least one state; in simple terms, a risk-free profit.

a. Issuer
c. Arbitrage

b. Efficient-market hypothesis
d. Initial margin

59. A _____ is a profit that results from investments into a capital asset, such as stocks, bonds or real estate, which exceeds the purchase price. It is the difference between a higher selling price and a lower purchase price, resulting in a financial gain for the seller. Conversely, a capital loss arises if the proceeds from the sale of a capital asset are less than the purchase price.

a. Capital gains tax
c. Payroll tax

b. Capital gain
d. Tax brackets

60. An _____ is a tax levied on the financial income of people, corporations, or other legal entities. Various _____ systems exist, with varying degrees of tax incidence. Income taxation can be progressive, proportional, or regressive.

a. AAB
c. ABN Amro

b. A Random Walk Down Wall Street
d. Income Tax

61. An _____ is an investment vehicle traded on stock exchanges, much like stocks. An ETF holds assets such as stocks or bonds and trades at approximately the same price as the net asset value of its underlying assets over the course of the trading day. Most ETFs track an index, such as the Dow Jones Industrial Average or the S'P 500.

a. AAB

b. A Random Walk Down Wall Street

c. Exchange-traded fund

d. ABN Amro

62. In business and finance, a _____ (also referred to as equity _____) of stock means a _____ of ownership in a corporation (company.) In the plural, stocks is often used as a synonym for _____s especially in the United States, but it is less commonly used that way outside of North America.

In the United Kingdom, South Africa, and Australia, stock can also refer to completely different financial instruments such as government bonds or, less commonly, to all kinds of marketable securities.

a. Bucket shop

b. Margin

c. Procter ' Gamble

d. Share

63. A _____, securities exchange or (in Europe) bourse is a corporation or mutual organization which provides 'trading' facilities for stock brokers and traders, to trade stocks and other securities. _____s also provide facilities for the issue and redemption of securities as well as other financial instruments and capital events including the payment of income and dividends. The securities traded on a _____ include: shares issued by companies, unit trusts and other pooled investment products and bonds.

a. 529 plan

b. 7-Eleven

c. 4-4-5 Calendar

d. Stock Exchange

64. A _____ is a private or public market for the trading of company stock and derivatives of company stock at an agreed price; these are securities listed on a stock exchange as well as those only traded privately.

The size of the world _____ is estimated at about $36.6 trillion US at the beginning of October 2008 . The world derivatives market has been estimated at about $480 trillion face or nominal value, 12 times the size of the entire world economy.

a. Stock Market

b. Adolph Coors

c. Anton Gelonkin

d. Andrew Tobias

65. _____ are units of families of exchange-traded funds (ETFs) managed by Barclays Global Investors. The first _____ were known as WEBS but were since rebranded.

Each _____ fund tracks a bond or stock market index.

a. IShares

b. AAB

c. ABN Amro

d. A Random Walk Down Wall Street

66. In finance, _____ are stocks that appreciate in value and yield a high return on equity (ROE.) Analysts compute ROE by taking the company's net income and dividing it by the company's equity. To be classified as a growth stock, analysts expect to see at least 15 percent return on equity.

a. Security Analysis

b. Stock valuation

c. 4-4-5 Calendar

d. Growth stocks

67.　The _____ is the national association of U.S. investment companies. _____ encourages adherence to high ethical standards, promotes public understanding of funds and investing, and advances the interests of investment funds and their shareholders, directors, and advisers.

As of July 1, 2008, _____ membership included 9,067 mutual funds, 675 closed-end funds, 625 exchange-traded funds (ETFs), and three sponsors of unit investment trust (UITs.)

a. AAB

b. A Random Walk Down Wall Street

c. ABN Amro

d. Investment Company Institute

68.　The key date to remember for dividend paying stocks is the _____. The _____ is different from the record date. The _____ is typically two trading days before the record date.

In order to receive the upcoming dividend payment payout, you must already own or you must purchase the stock prior to the _____. It is important to note that in most countries, when you buy or sell any stock, there is a three trading-day settlement period on your order.

a. Ex-dividend date

b. Index number

c. Asian Financial Crisis

d. Insolvency

69.　_____ in finance is a risk management technique, related to hedging, that mixes a wide variety of investments within a portfolio. Because the fluctuations of a single security have less impact on a diverse portfolio, _____ minimizes the risk from any one investment.

A simple example of _____ is the following: On a particular island the entire economy consists of two companies: one that sells umbrellas and another that sells sunscreen.

a. 7-Eleven

b. Diversification

c. 4-4-5 Calendar

d. 529 plan

70.　A _____ is a portfolio consisting of a weighted sum of every asset in the market, with weights in the proportions that they exist in the market (with the necessary assumption that these assets are infinitely divisible.)

Neha Tyagi's critique (1977) states that this is only a theoretical concept, as to create a _____ for investment purposes in practice would necessarily include every single possible available asset, including real estate, precious metals, stamp collections, jewelry, and anything with any worth, as the theoretical market being referred to would be the world market. As a result, proxies for the market are used in practice by investors.

a. Market price

b. Central Securities Depository

c. Market portfolio

d. Delta neutral

71.   _____ proposes how rational investors will use diversification to optimize their portfolios, and how a risky asset should be priced. The basic concepts of the theory are Markowitz diversification, the efficient frontier, capital asset pricing model, the alpha and beta coefficients, the Capital Market Line and the Securities Market Line.

_____ models an asset's return as a random variable, and models a portfolio as a weighted combination of assets so that the return of a portfolio is the weighted combination of the assets' returns.

a. Consumer basket   b. Payback period
c. Market value   d. Modern portfolio theory

1. The _____ is one of several stock market indices, created by nineteenth-century Wall Street Journal editor and Dow Jones ' Company co-founder Charles Dow. Dow compiled the index to gauge the performance of the industrial sector of the American stock market. It is the second-oldest U.S. market index, after the Dow Jones Transportation Average, which Dow also created.
   a. 7-Eleven
   b. 529 plan
   c. 4-4-5 Calendar
   d. Dow Jones Industrial Average

2. The _____ is the weighted-average most likely outcome in gambling, probability theory, economics or finance.

   In gambling and probability theory, there is usually a discrete set of possible outcomes. In this case, _____ is a measure of the relative balance of win or loss weighted by their chances of occurring.

   a. AAB
   b. ABN Amro
   c. A Random Walk Down Wall Street
   d. Expected return

3. In finance, _____, also known as return on investment is the ratio of money gained or lost on an investment relative to the amount of money invested. The amount of money gained or lost may be referred to as interest, profit/loss, gain/loss, or net income/loss. The money invested may be referred to as the asset, capital, principal, or the cost basis of the investment.
   a. Rate of return
   b. Doctrine of the Proper Law
   c. Stock or scrip dividends
   d. Composiition of Creditors

4. In business and accounting, _____s are everything of value that is owned by a person or company. The balance sheet of a firm records the monetary value of the _____s owned by the firm. The two major _____ classes are tangible _____s and intangible _____s.
   a. EBITDA
   b. Income
   c. Accounts payable
   d. Asset

5. _____ is the balance of the amounts of cash being received and paid by a business during a defined period of time, sometimes tied to a specific project. Measurement of _____ can be used

   - to evaluate the state or performance of a business or project.
   - to determine problems with liquidity. Being profitable does not necessarily mean being liquid. A company can fail because of a shortage of cash, even while profitable.
   - to generate project rate of returns. The time of _____s into and out of projects are used as inputs to financial models such as internal rate of return, and net present value.
   - to examine income or growth of a business when it is believed that accrual accounting concepts do not represent economic realities. Alternately, _____ can be used to 'validate' the net income generated by accrual accounting.

   _____ as a generic term may be used differently depending on context, and certain _____ definitions may be adapted by analysts and users for their own uses. Common terms include operating _____ and free _____.

_____s can be classified into:

1. Operational _____s: Cash received or expended as a result of the company's core business activities.
2. Investment _____s: Cash received or expended through capital expenditure, investments or acquisitions.
3. Financing _____s: Cash received or expended as a result of financial activities, such as interests and dividends.

All three together - the net _____ - are necessary to reconcile the beginning cash balance to the ending cash balance. Loan draw downs or equity injections, that is just shifting of capital but no expenditure as such, are not considered in the net _____.

a. Real option

b. Shareholder value

c. Corporate finance

d. Cash flow

6.   A _____ is a payment made by a corporation to its shareholder members. When a corporation earns a profit or surplus, that money can be put to two uses: it can either be re-invested in the business (called retained earnings), or it can be paid to the shareholders as a _____. Many corporations retain a portion of their earnings and pay the remainder as a _____.

a. Dividend puzzle

b. Dividend

c. Dividend yield

d. Special dividend

7.   The _____ on a company stock is the company's annual dividend payments divided by its market cap, or the dividend per share divided by the price per share. It is often expressed as a percentage.

Dividend payments on preferred shares are stipulated by the prospectus.

a. Special dividend

b. Dividend reinvestment plan

c. Dividend yield

d. Dividend imputation

8.   In law, _____ refers to the process by which a company (or part of a company) is brought to an end, and the assets and property of the company redistributed. _____ can also be referred to as winding-up or dissolution, although dissolution technically refers to the last stage of _____. The process of _____ also arises when customs, an authority or agency in a country responsible for collecting and safeguarding customs duties, determines the final computation or ascertainment of the duties or drawback accruing on an entry.

a. 4-4-5 Calendar

b. Debt settlement

c. Liquidation

d. 529 plan

9.   _____ is the likely price of an asset when it is allowed insufficient time to sell on the open market, thereby reducing its exposure to potential buyers. _____ is typically lower than fair market value. Unlike cash or securities, certain illiquid assets, like real estate, often require a period of several months in order to obtain their fair market value in a sale, and will generally sell for a significantly lower price if a sale is forced to occur in a shorter time period.

a. Real estate investing

b. Tenancy

c. REIT

d. Liquidation value

10. _____ or financing is to provide capital (funds), which means money for a project, a person, a business or any other private or public institutions.

Those funds can be allocated for either short term or long term purposes. The health fund is a new way of _____ private healthcare centers.

a. Funding   b. Proxy fight

c. Product life cycle   d. Synthetic CDO

11. An _____ or index tracker is a collective investment scheme (usually a mutual fund or exchange-traded fund) that aims to replicate the movements of an index of a specific financial market regardless of market conditions.

Tracking can be achieved by trying to hold all of the securities in the index, in the same proportions as the index. Other methods include statistically sampling the market and holding 'representative' securities.

a. Investment company   b. A Random Walk Down Wall Street

c. AAB   d. Index fund

12. A _____ is a professionally managed type of collective investment scheme that pools money from many investors and invests it in stocks, bonds, short-term money market instruments, and/or other securities. The _____ will have a fund manager that trades the pooled money on a regular basis. Currently, the worldwide value of all _____s totals more than $26 trillion.

Since 1940, there have been three basic types of investment companies in the United States: open-end funds, also known in the US as _____s; unit investment trusts (UITs); and closed-end funds.

a. Financial intermediary   b. Net asset value

c. Trust company   d. Mutual fund

13. In finance, the term _____ describes the amount in cash that returns to the owners of a security. Normally it does not include the price variations, at the difference of the total return. _____ applies to various stated rates of return on stocks (common and preferred, and convertible), fixed income instruments (bonds, notes, bills, strips, zero coupon), and some other investment type insurance products (e.g. annuities.)

a. Macaulay duration   b. 4-4-5 Calendar

c. Yield to maturity   d. Yield

14. The _____ is a capital budgeting metric used by firms to decide whether they should make investments. It is an indicator of the efficiency or quality of an investment, as opposed to net present value (NPV), which indicates value or magnitude.

The IRR is the annualized effective compounded return rate which can be earned on the invested capital, i.e., the yield on the investment.

a. A Random Walk Down Wall Street   b. AAB

c. ABN Amro   d. Internal rate of return

15.   The terms _____ , nominal _____, and effective _____ describe the interest rate for a whole year (annualized), rather than just a monthly fee/rate, as applied on a loan, mortgage, credit card, etc. Those terms have formal, legal definitions in some countries or legal jurisdictions, but in general:

- The nominal _____ is the simple-interest rate (for a year.)
- The effective _____ is the fee+compound interest rate (calculated across a year.)

The nominal _____ is calculated as: the rate, for a payment period, multiplied by the number of payment periods in a year. However, the exact legal definition of 'effective _____' can vary greatly in each jurisdiction, depending on the type of fees included, such as participation fees, loan origination fees, monthly service charges, or late fees. The effective _____ has been called the 'mathematically-true' interest rate for each year. The computation for the effective _____, as the fee+compound interest rate, can also vary depending on whether the up-front fees, such as origination or participation fees, are added to the entire amount, or treated as a short-term loan due in the first payment.

a. Annual percentage rate   b. A Random Walk Down Wall Street
c. ABN Amro   d. AAB

16.   In finance, a _____ is a debt security, in which the authorized issuer owes the holders a debt and, depending on the terms of the _____, is obliged to pay interest (the coupon) and/or to repay the principal at a later date, termed maturity.

Thus a _____ is a loan: the issuer is the borrower, the _____ holder is the lender, and the coupon is the interest. _____s provide the borrower with external funds to finance long-term investments, or, in the case of government _____s, to finance current expenditure.

a. Bond   b. Catastrophe bonds
c. Puttable bond   d. Convertible bond

17.   The _____, effective annual interest rate, Annual Equivalent Rate (AER) or simply effective rate is the interest rate on a loan or financial product restated from the nominal interest rate as an interest rate with annual compound interest. It is used to compare the annual interest between loans with different compounding terms (daily, monthly, annually, or other.)

The _____ differs in two important respects from the annual percentage rate (APR):

1.   the _____ generally does not incorporate one-time charges such as front-end fees;
2.   the _____ is (generally) not defined by legal or regulatory authorities (as APR is in many jurisdictions.)

By contrast, the 'effective APR' is used as a legal term, where front-fees and other costs can be included, as defined by local law.

Annual Percentage Yield or effective annual yield is the analogous concept used for savings or investment products, such as a certificate of deposit.

a. Effective interest rate   b. AAB

c. ABN Amro   d. A Random Walk Down Wall Street

18. _____ is a fee paid on borrowed assets. It is the price paid for the use of borrowed money , or, money earned by deposited funds . Assets that are sometimes lent with _____ include money, shares, consumer goods through hire purchase, major assets such as aircraft, and even entire factories in finance lease arrangements.

a. A Random Walk Down Wall Street   b. Interest

c. Insolvency   d. AAB

19. An _____ is the price a borrower pays for the use of money they do not own, and the return a lender receives for deferring the use of funds, by lending it to the borrower. _____s are normally expressed as a percentage rate over the period of one year.

_____s targets are also a vital tool of monetary policy and are used to control variables like investment, inflation, and unemployment.

a. Interest rate   b. ABN Amro

c. AAB   d. A Random Walk Down Wall Street

20. Depending on the nature of the investment, the type of _____ will vary.

A common concern with any investment is that you may lose the money you invest - your capital. This risk is therefore often referred to as 'capital risk.'

If the assets you invest in are held in another currency there is a risk that currency movements alone may affect the value.

a. ABN Amro   b. AAB

c. A Random Walk Down Wall Street   d. Investment risk

21. In statistics, _____ has two related meanings:

- the arithmetic _____
- the expected value of a random variable, which is also called the population _____.

It is sometimes stated that the '_____' is average. This is incorrect if '_____' is taken in the specific sense of 'arithmetic _____' as there are different types of averages: the _____, median, and mode. Other simple statistical analyses use measures of spread, such as range, interquartile range, or standard deviation. For a real-valued random variable X, the _____ is the expectation of X. Note that not every probability distribution has a defined _____; see the Cauchy distribution for an example.

a. Harmonic mean   b. Probability distribution

c. Mean   d. Sample size

22.   In probability theory and statistics, a _____ identifies either the probability of each value of an unidentified random variable (when the variable is discrete), or the probability of the value falling within a particular interval (when the variable is continuous.) The _____ describes the range of possible values that a random variable can attain and the probability that the value of the random variable is within any (measurable) subset of that range. The Normal distribution, often called the 'bell curve'

When the random variable takes values in the set of real numbers, the _____ is completely described by the cumulative distribution function, whose value at each real x is the probability that the random variable is smaller than or equal to x.

   a. P-value
   c. Standard deviation

   b. Probability distribution
   d. Correlation

23.   _____ is a process of analyzing possible future events by considering alternative possible outcomes (scenarios.) The analysis is designed to allow improved decision-making by allowing consideration of outcomes and their implications.

For example, in economics and finance, a financial institution might attempt to forecast several possible scenarios for the economy (e.g. rapid growth, moderate growth, slow growth) and it might also attempt to forecast financial market returns (for bonds, stocks and cash) in each of those scenarios.

   a. 529 plan
   c. Detection Risk

   b. 4-4-5 Calendar
   d. Scenario analysis

24.   _____ is a concept in economics, finance, and psychology related to the behaviour of consumers and investors under uncertainty. _____ is the reluctance of a person to accept a bargain with an uncertain payoff rather than another bargain with a more certain, but possibly lower, expected payoff.

The inverse of a person's _____ is sometimes called their risk tolerance

   a. Risk adjusted return on capital
   c. Risk aversion

   b. Risk premium
   d. Discount factor

25.

In finance, the _____ can be the expected rate of return above the risk-free interest rate. When measuring risk, a common sense approach is to compare the risk-free return on T-bills and the very risky return on other investments. The difference between these two returns can be interpreted as a measure of the excess return on the average risky asset. This excess return is known as the _____.

   a. Risk premium
   c. Risk adjusted return on capital

   b. Risk modeling
   d. Risk aversion

26.   The _____ is an important family of continuous probability distributions, applicable in many fields. Each member of the family may be defined by two parameters, location and scale: the mean and variance respectively. The standard _____ is the _____ with a mean of zero and a variance of one

a. Random variables

b. Probability distribution

c. Normal distribution

d. Correlation

27.   In probability and statistics, the _____ of a collection of numbers is a measure of the dispersion of the numbers from their expected (mean) value. It can apply to a probability distribution, a random variable, a population or a data set. The _____ is usually denoted with the letter σ (lowercase sigma.)

a. Kurtosis

b. Mean

c. Sample size

d. Standard deviation

28.   _____ mature in one year or less. Like zero-coupon bonds, they do not pay interest prior to maturity; instead they are sold at a discount of the par value to create a positive yield to maturity. Many regard _____ as the least risky investment available to U.S. investors.

a. Treasury Inflation Protected Securities

b. Treasury securities

c. Treasury bills

d. 4-4-5 Calendar

29.   In probability theory and statistics, the _____ of a random variable, probability distribution averaging the squared distance of its possible values from the expected value (mean.) Whereas the mean is a way to describe the location of a distribution, the _____ is a way to capture its scale or degree of being spread out. The unit of _____ is the square of the unit of the original variable.

a. Semivariance

b. Monte Carlo methods

c. Harmonic mean

d. Variance

30.   _____ is a risk-adjusted measure of the so-called active return on an investment. It is the return in excess of the compensation for the risk borne, and thus commonly used to assess active managers' performances. Often, the return of a benchmark is subtracted in order to consider relative performance, which yields Jensen's _____.

a. Annuity

b. Amortization

c. Option

d. Alpha

31.   The _____ is the relationship between the amount of return gained on an investment and the amount of risk undertaken in that investment. The more return sought, the more risk that must be undertaken.

There are various classes of possible investments, each with their own positions on the overall _____.

a. Risk-return spectrum

b. Post earnings announcement drift

c. Blank endorsement

d. Fiscal sponsorship

32.   _____ (in a financial context) is the assumption of the risk of loss, in return for the uncertain possibility of a reward. Only if one may safely say that a particular position involves no risk may one say, strictly speaking, that such a position represents an 'investment.' Financial _____ involves the buying, holding, selling, and short-selling of stocks, bonds, commodities, currencies, collectibles, real estate, derivatives, or any valuable financial instrument to profit from fluctuations in its price as opposed to buying it for use or for income via methods such as dividends or interest. _____ represents one of four market roles in Western financial markets, distinct from hedging, long- or short-term investing, and arbitrage.

a. Market anomaly

b. Central Securities Depository

c. Forward market

d. Speculation

33.   A _____ is a situation that involves losing one quality or aspect of something in return for gaining another quality or aspect. It implies a decision to be made with full comprehension of both the upside and downside of a particular choice.

In economics the term is expressed as opportunity cost, referring the most preferred alternative given up.

a. Total revenue

b. Capital outflow

c. Break-even point

d. Trade-off

34.   _____s are deposits denominated in United States dollars at banks outside the United States, and thus are not under the jurisdiction of the Federal Reserve. Consequently, such deposits are subject to much less regulation than similar deposits within the United States, allowing for higher margins. There is nothing 'European' about _____ deposits; a US dollar-denominated deposit in Tokyo or Caracas would likewise be deemed _____ deposits.

a. A Random Walk Down Wall Street

b. ABN Amro

c. Eurodollar

d. AAB

35.   In economics, _____ is a rise in the general level of prices of goods and services in an economy over a period of time. The term '_____' once referred to increases in the money supply (monetary _____); however, economic debates about the relationship between money supply and price levels have led to its primary use today in describing price _____. _____ can also be described as a decline in the real value of money--a loss of purchasing power in the medium of exchange which is also the monetary unit of account.

a. ABN Amro

b. A Random Walk Down Wall Street

c. AAB

d. Inflation

36.   A _____, securities exchange or (in Europe) bourse is a corporation or mutual organization which provides 'trading' facilities for stock brokers and traders, to trade stocks and other securities. _____s also provide facilities for the issue and redemption of securities as well as other financial instruments and capital events including the payment of income and dividends. The securities traded on a _____ include: shares issued by companies, unit trusts and other pooled investment products and bonds.

a. 4-4-5 Calendar

b. Stock exchange

c. 7-Eleven

d. 529 plan

37.   The _____ is the market for securities, where companies and governments can raise longterm funds. The _____ includes the stock market and the bond market. Financial regulators, such as the U.S. Securities and Exchange Commission, oversee the _____s in their designated countries to ensure that investors are protected against fraud.

a. Delta neutral

b. Forward market

c. Spot rate

d. Capital market

38.   _____ proposes how rational investors will use diversification to optimize their portfolios, and how a risky asset should be priced. The basic concepts of the theory are Markowitz diversification, the efficient frontier, capital asset pricing model, the alpha and beta coefficients, the Capital Market Line and the Securities Market Line.

_____ models an asset's return as a random variable, and models a portfolio as a weighted combination of assets so that the return of a portfolio is the weighted combination of the assets' returns.

a. Payback period   b. Modern portfolio theory
c. Market value   d. Consumer basket

39.   In statistics, a _____ is a tabulation of the values that one or more variables take in a sample.

Univariate _____s are often presented as lists ordered by quantity showing the number of times each value appears. For example, if 100 people rate a five-point Likert scale assessing their agreement with a statement on a scale on which 1 denotes strong agreement and 5 strong disagreement, the _____ of their responses might look like:

This simple tabulation has two drawbacks.

a. Variance   b. Random variables
c. Covariance   d. Frequency distribution

40.   The _____, in mathematics, is a type of mean or average, which indicates the central tendency or typical value of a set of numbers. It is similar to the arithmetic mean, which is what most people think of with the word 'average,' except that instead of adding the set of numbers and then dividing the sum by the count of numbers in the set, n, the numbers are multiplied and then the nth root of the resulting product is taken.

For instance, the _____ of two numbers, say 2 and 8, is just the square root (i.e., the second root) of their product, 16, which is 4.

a. Standard deviation   b. Statistics
c. Kurtosis   d. Geometric mean

41.   In economic models, the _____ time frame assumes no fixed factors of production. Firms can enter or leave the marketplace, and the cost (and availability) of land, labor, raw materials, and capital goods can be assumed to vary. In contrast, in the short-run time frame, certain factors are assumed to be fixed, because there is not sufficient time for them to change.
a. Short-run   b. Long-run
c. 4-4-5 Calendar   d. 529 plan

42.   A _____ is a bond issued by a national government denominated in the country's own currency. Bonds issued by national governments in foreign currencies are normally referred to as sovereign bonds. The first ever _____ was issued by the British government in 1693 to raise money to fund a war against France.
a. Municipal bond   b. Zero-coupon bond
c. Government bond   d. Collateralized debt obligations

43.   In business and finance, a _____ (also referred to as equity _____) of stock means a _____ of ownership in a corporation (company.) In the plural, stocks is often used as a synonym for _____s especially in the United States, but it is less commonly used that way outside of North America.

In the United Kingdom, South Africa, and Australia, stock can also refer to completely different financial instruments such as government bonds or, less commonly, to all kinds of marketable securities.

a. Procter ' Gamble   b. Share
c. Bucket shop   d. Margin

44.   A _____ is a measure of the average price of consumer goods and services purchased by households. The _____ can be used to index (i.e., adjust for the effects of inflation) wages, salaries, pensions, or regulated or contracted prices. The _____ is, along with the population census and the National Income and Product Accounts, one of the most closely watched national economic statistics.
   a. Divisia index   b. 4-4-5 Calendar
   c. Consumer price index   d. 529 plan

45.   A _____ is a normalized average (typically a weighted average) of prices for a given class of goods or services in a given region, during a given interval of time. It is a statistic designed to help to compare how these prices, taken as a whole, differ between time periods or geographical locations.
   a. Price index   b. Discounts and allowances
   c. Price discrimination   d. Transfer pricing

46.   In finance and economics _____ refers to the rate of interest before adjustment for inflation (in contrast with the real interest rate); or, for interest balls stated' without adjustment for the full effect of compounding (also referred to as the nominal annual rate.) An interest rate is called nominal if the frequency of compounding (e.g. a month) is not identical to the basic time unit (normally a year.)

The real interest rate includes compensation for the lender's lost value due to inflation, whereas the _____ excludes inflation.

   a. Nominal interest rate   b. SIBOR
   c. Cash accumulation equation   d. Shanghai Interbank Offered Rate

47.   _____ refers to a business or organization attempting to acquire goods or services to accomplish the goals of the enterprise. Though there are several organizations that attempt to set standards in the _____ process, processes can vary greatly between organizations. Typically the word '_____' is not used interchangeably with the word 'procurement', since procurement typically includes Expediting, Supplier Quality, and Traffic and Logistics (T'L) in addition to _____.
   a. 7-Eleven   b. 529 plan
   c. 4-4-5 Calendar   d. Purchasing

48.   _____ is the value of goods/services compared to the amount paid with a currency. Currency can be either a commodity money, like gold or silver, or fiat currency like US dollars which are the world reserve currency. As Adam Smith noted, having money gives one the ability to 'command' others' labor, so _____ to some extent is power over other people, to the extent that they are willing to trade their labor or goods for money or currency.
   a. 4-4-5 Calendar   b. 529 plan
   c. 7-Eleven   d. Purchasing power

49.   The '_____' is approximately the nominal interest rate minus the inflation rate Since the inflation rate over the course of a loan is not known initially, volatility in inflation represents a risk to both the lender and the borrower.

In economics and finance, an individual who lends money for repayment at a later point in time expects to be compensated for the time value of money, or not having the use of that money while it is lent.

a. 7-Eleven

c. 529 plan

b. 4-4-5 Calendar

d. Real interest rate

50. _____ is a term used to refer to how an investor distributes his or her investments among various classes of investment vehicles (e.g., stocks and bonds.)

A large part of financial planning is finding an _____ that is appropriate for a given person in terms of their appetite for and ability to shoulder risk. This can depend on various factors; see investor profile.

a. Investing online

c. Alternative investment

b. Investment performance

d. Asset allocation

51. The _____ in financial mathematics and economics estimates the relationship between nominal and real interest rates under inflation. It is named after Irving Fisher who was famous for his works on the theory of interest. In finance, the _____ is primarily used in YTM calculations of bonds or IRR calculations of investments.

Letting *r* denote the real interest rate, *i* denote the nominal interest rate, and let >π denote the inflation rate, the _____ is:

>

a. Binomial options pricing model

c. Fisher equation

b. Treynor-Black model

d. Discount rate

52. The institution most often referenced by the word '_____' is a public or publicly traded _____, the shares of which are traded on a public stock exchange (e.g., the New York Stock Exchange or Nasdaq in the United States) where shares of stock of _____s are bought and sold by and to the general public. Most of the largest businesses in the world are publicly traded _____s. However, the majority of _____s are said to be closely held, privately held or close _____s, meaning that no ready market exists for the trading of shares.

a. Protect

c. Depository Trust Company

b. Federal Home Loan Mortgage Corporation

d. Corporation

53. In finance, the _____ is the global financial market for short-term borrowing and lending. It provides short-term liquidity funding for the global financial system. The _____ is where short-term obligations such as Treasury bills, commercial paper and bankers' acceptances are bought and sold.

a. Consumer debt

c. Money market

b. Debt-for-equity swap

d. Cramdown

54. Money funds (or _____, money market mutual funds) are mutual funds that invest in short-term debt instruments.

_____, also known as principal stability funds, seek to limit exposure to losses due to credit, market and liquidity risks.

_____, in the United States, are regulated by the Securities and Exchange Commission's (SEC) Investment Company Act of 1940.

a. Closed-end fund   b. Stock fund

c. Money market funds   d. Mutual fund fees and expenses

55. _____ are government bonds issued by the United States Department of the Treasury through the Bureau of the Public Debt. They are the debt financing instruments of the U.S. Federal government, and they are often referred to simply as Treasuries or Treasurys. There are four types of marketable _____: Treasury bills, Treasury notes, Treasury bonds, and Treasury Inflation Protected Securities (TIPS.)

a. Treasury Inflation-Protected Securities   b. Treasury Inflation Protected Securities

c. 4-4-5 Calendar   d. Treasury securities

56. The _____ or redemption yield is the yield promised to the bondholder on the assumption that the bond or other fixed-interest security such as gilts will be held to maturity, that all coupon and principal payments will be made and coupon payments are reinvested at the bond's promised yield at the same rate as invested. It is a measure of the return of the bond. This technique in theory allows investors to calculate the fair value of different financial instruments.

a. Yield   b. Macaulay duration

c. 4-4-5 Calendar   d. Yield to maturity

57. A _____ s a time deposit, a financial product commonly offered to consumers by banks, thrift institutions, and credit unions.

They are similar to savings accounts in that they are insured and thus virtually risk-free; they are 'money in the bank'. They are different from savings accounts in that they have a specific, fixed term (often three months, six months, or one to five years), and, usually, a fixed interest rate.

a. Variable rate mortgage   b. Time deposit

c. Reserve requirement   d. Certificate of deposit

58. _____ is a life of security. It may also refer to the final payment date of a loan or other financial instrument, at which point all remaining interest and principal is due to be paid.

1, 3, 6 months _____ band can be calculated by using 30-day per month periods.

a. False billing   b. Primary market

c. Maturity   d. Replacement cost

59. A _____ is a fungible, negotiable instrument representing financial value. They are broadly categorized into debt securities (such as banknotes, bonds and debentures), and equity securities; e.g., common stocks. The company or other entity issuing the _____ is called the issuer.

a. Tracking stock   b. Securities lending

c. Book entry   d. Security

60. _____ is a graph created by investors to measure the risk of risky and risk-free assets. The graph displays to the investors on the return they can make by taking on a certain level of risk. It is also known as a 'reward-to-variability ratio'.

a. Divestment   b. Portfolio investment

c. Capital allocation line   d. Dollar cost averaging

61. In finance, the Acid-test or _____ or liquid ratio measures the ability of a company to use its near cash or quick assets to immediately extinguish or retire its current liabilities. Quick assets include those current assets that presumably can be quickly converted to cash at close to their book values.

Generally, the acid test ratio should be 1:1 or better, however this varies widely by industry.

a. Financial ratio
c. P/E ratio

b. Net assets
d. Quick ratio

62. In finance, _____ occurs when a debtor has not met its legal obligations according to the debt contract, e.g. it has not made a scheduled payment, or has violated a loan covenant (condition) of the debt contract. _____ may occur if the debtor is either unwilling or unable to pay their debt. This can occur with all debt obligations including bonds, mortgages, loans, and promissory notes.

a. Vendor finance
c. Default

b. Credit crunch
d. Debt validation

63. _____ is the risk of loss due to a debtor's non-payment of a loan or other line of credit (either the principal or interest (coupon) or both)

Most lenders employ their own models (credit scorecards) to rank potential and existing customers according to risk, and then apply appropriate strategies. With products such as unsecured personal loans or mortgages, lenders charge a higher price for higher risk customers and vice versa. With revolving products such as credit cards and overdrafts, risk is controlled through careful setting of credit limits.

a. Credit risk
c. Liquidity risk

b. Transaction risk
d. Market risk

64. Behavioral economics and _____ are closely related fields that have evolved to be a separate branch of economic and financial analysis which applies scientific research on human and social, cognitive and emotional factors to better understand economic decisions by, say, consumers, borrowers, investors, and how they affect market prices, returns and the allocation of resources.

The field is primarily concerned with the bounds of rationality (selfishness, self-control) of economic agents. Behavioral models typically integrate insights from psychology with neo-classical economic theory.

a. Market structure
c. Recession

b. Medium of exchange
d. Behavioral finance

65. _____ are organizations which pool large sums of money and invest those sums in companies. They include banks, insurance companies, retirement or pension funds, hedge funds and mutual funds. Their role in the economy is to act as highly specialized investors on behalf of others.

a. AAB   b. Institutional investors
c. A Random Walk Down Wall Street   d. ABN Amro

66.   In finance, _____ (or gearing) is borrowing money to supplement existing funds for investment in such a way that the potential positive or negative outcome is magnified and/or enhanced. It generally refers to using borrowed funds, or debt, so as to attempt to increase the returns to equity. Deleveraging is the action of reducing borrowings.
a. Limited partnership   b. Financial endowment
c. Pension fund   d. Leverage

67.   A _____ is a portfolio consisting of a weighted sum of every asset in the market, with weights in the proportions that they exist in the market (with the necessary assumption that these assets are infinitely divisible.)

Neha Tyagi's critique (1977) states that this is only a theoretical concept, as to create a _____ for investment purposes in practice would necessarily include every single possible available asset, including real estate, precious metals, stamp collections, jewelry, and anything with any worth, as the theoretical market being referred to would be the world market. As a result, proxies for the market are used in practice by investors.

a. Market price   b. Delta neutral
c. Central Securities Depository   d. Market portfolio

68.   _____ is a form of corporation equity ownership represented in the securities. It is dangerous in comparison to preferred shares and some other investment options, in that in the event of bankruptcy, _____ investors receive their funds after preferred stockholders, bondholders, creditors, etc. On the other hand, common shares on average perform better than preferred shares or bonds over time.
a. Stock split   b. Stock market bubble
c. Stop-limit order   d. Common stock

69.   _____ is a term coined in 1985 by economists Rajnish Mehra and Edward C. Prescott. It is based on the observation that in order to reconcile the much higher return on equity stock compared to government bonds in the United States, individuals must have implausibly high risk aversion according to standard economics models. Similar situations prevail in many other industrialized countries.
a. The equity premium puzzle   b. Perth Leadership Outcome Model
c. Loss aversion   d. Quantitative behavioral finance

70.   _____ is the task of determining how a business will afford to achieve its strategic goals and objectives. Usually, a company creates a Financial Plan immediately after the vision and objectives have been set. The Financial Plan describes each of the activities, resources, equipment and materials that are needed to achieve these objectives, as well as the timeframes involved.
a. Performance measurement   b. Management by exception
c. Corporate Transparency   d. Financial Planning

71.   _____ refers to a portfolio management strategy where the manager makes specific investments with the goal of outperforming an investment benchmark index. Investors or mutual funds that do not aspire to create a return in excess of a benchmark index will often invest in an index fund that replicates as closely as possible the investment weighting and returns of that index; this is called passive management. _____ is the opposite of passive management, because in passive management the manager does not seek to outperform the benchmark index.

a. AAB   b. Active management

c. ABN Amro   d. A Random Walk Down Wall Street

72.   In economics, business, and accounting, a _____ is the value of money that has been used up to produce something, and hence is not available for use anymore. In business, the _____ may be one of acquisition, in which case the amount of money expended to acquire it is counted as _____. In this case, money is the input that is gone in order to acquire the thing.

  a. Marginal cost   b. Fixed costs

  c. Sliding scale fees   d. Cost

73.   In financial accounting, the term _____ is most commonly used to describe any part of shareholders' equity, except for basic share capital. Sometimes, the term is used instead of the term provision; such a use, however, is inconsistent with the terminology suggested by International Accounting Standards Board. For more information about provisions, see provision (accounting.)

  a. Closing entries   b. FIFO and LIFO accounting

  c. Reserve   d. Treasury stock

74.   A _____, reserve bank, or monetary authority is the entity responsible for the monetary policy of a country or of a group of member states. It is a bank that can lend money to other banks in times of need. Its primary responsibility is to maintain the stability of the national currency and money supply, but more active duties include controlling subsidized-loan interest rates, and acting as a lender of last resort to the banking sector during times of financial crisis (private banks often being integral to the national financial system.)

  a. 4-4-5 Calendar   b. 529 plan

  c. 7-Eleven   d. Central bank

1. In business and accounting, _____s are everything of value that is owned by a person or company. The balance sheet of a firm records the monetary value of the _____s owned by the firm. The two major _____ classes are tangible _____s and intangible _____s.
    a. EBITDA
    b. Income
    c. Accounts payable
    d. Asset

2. _____ is a term used to refer to how an investor distributes his or her investments among various classes of investment vehicles (e.g., stocks and bonds.)

    A large part of financial planning is finding an _____ that is appropriate for a given person in terms of their appetite for and ability to shoulder risk. This can depend on various factors; see investor profile.

    a. Investment performance
    b. Alternative investment
    c. Investing online
    d. Asset allocation

3. The institution most often referenced by the word '_____' is a public or publicly traded _____, the shares of which are traded on a public stock exchange (e.g., the New York Stock Exchange or Nasdaq in the United States) where shares of stock of _____s are bought and sold by and to the general public. Most of the largest businesses in the world are publicly traded _____s. However, the majority of _____s are said to be closely held, privately held or close _____s, meaning that no ready market exists for the trading of shares.
    a. Depository Trust Company
    b. Protect
    c. Federal Home Loan Mortgage Corporation
    d. Corporation

4. _____ is a branch of economics that deals with the performance, structure, and behavior of a national or regional economy as a whole. Along with microeconomics, _____ is one of the two most general fields in economics. Macroeconomists study aggregated indicators such as GDP, unemployment rates, and price indices to understand how the whole economy functions.
    a. Recession
    b. Macroeconomics
    c. Human capital
    d. Behavioral finance

5. _____ in finance is a risk management technique, related to hedging, that mixes a wide variety of investments within a portfolio. Because the fluctuations of a single security have less impact on a diverse portfolio, _____ minimizes the risk from any one investment.

    A simple example of _____ is the following: On a particular island the entire economy consists of two companies: one that sells umbrellas and another that sells sunscreen.

    a. 4-4-5 Calendar
    b. 7-Eleven
    c. 529 plan
    d. Diversification

6. _____ is the risk that the value of an investment will decrease due to moves in market factors. The five standard _____ factors are:

- Equity risk, the risk that stock prices will change.
- Interest rate risk, the risk that interest rates will change.
- Currency risk, the risk that foreign exchange rates will change.
- Commodity risk, the risk that commodity prices (e.g. grains, metals) will change.

As with other forms of risk, _____ may be measured in a number of ways. Traditionally, this is done using a Value at Risk methodology. Value at risk is well established as a risk management technique, but it contains a number of limiting assumptions that constrain its accuracy.

a. Tracking error
c. Market risk

b. Currency risk
d. Transaction risk

7. The _____ is a stock exchange based in New York City, New York. It is the largest stock exchange in the world by dollar value of its listed companies securities. As of October 2008, the combined capitalization of all domestic _____ listed companies was $10.1 trillion.

a. 529 plan
c. 4-4-5 Calendar

b. New York Stock Exchange
d. 7-Eleven

8. A _____, securities exchange or (in Europe) bourse is a corporation or mutual organization which provides 'trading' facilities for stock brokers and traders, to trade stocks and other securities. _____s also provide facilities for the issue and redemption of securities as well as other financial instruments and capital events including the payment of income and dividends. The securities traded on a _____ include: shares issued by companies, unit trusts and other pooled investment products and bonds.

a. Stock Exchange
c. 7-Eleven

b. 4-4-5 Calendar
d. 529 plan

9. In finance, _____ is that risk which is common to an entire market and not to any individual entity or component thereof. It should be distinguished from systemic risk which is the risk that the entire financial system will collapse as a result of some catastrophic event.

Risks can be reduced in four main ways: Avoidance, Reduction, Retention and Transfer.

a. Primary market
c. Capital surplus

b. Conglomerate merger
d. Systematic risk

10. In probability and statistics, the _____ of a collection of numbers is a measure of the dispersion of the numbers from their expected (mean) value. It can apply to a probability distribution, a random variable, a population or a data set. The _____ is usually denoted with the letter σ (lowercase sigma.)

a. Mean
c. Kurtosis

b. Sample size
d. Standard deviation

11.   In finance, a _____ is a debt security, in which the authorized issuer owes the holders a debt and, depending on the terms of the _____, is obliged to pay interest (the coupon) and/or to repay the principal at a later date, termed maturity.

Thus a _____ is a loan: the issuer is the borrower, the _____ holder is the lender, and the coupon is the interest. _____s provide the borrower with external funds to finance long-term investments, or, in the case of government _____s, to finance current expenditure.

a. Puttable bond   b. Convertible bond
c. Catastrophe bonds   d. Bond

12.   A _____ is a collective investment scheme that invests in bonds and other debt securities. _____s yield monthly dividends that include interest payments on the fund's underlying securities plus any capital appreciation in the prices of the portfolio's bonds. _____s tend to pay higher dividends than CDs and money market accounts, and they generally pay out dividends more frequently and regularly than individual bonds.

a. Private activity bond   b. Gilts
c. Premium bond   d. Bond fund

13.   In probability theory and statistics, _____ indicates the strength and direction of a linear relationship between two random variables. That is in contrast with the usage of the term in colloquial speech, which denotes any relationship, not necessarily linear. In general statistical usage, _____ or co-relation refers to the departure of two random variables from independence.

a. Variance   b. Probability distribution
c. Geometric mean   d. Correlation

14.   In probability theory and statistics, _____ is a measure of how much two variables change together (variance is a special case of the _____ when the two variables are identical.)

If two variables tend to vary together (that is, when one of them is above its expected value, then the other variable tends to be above its expected value too), then the _____ between the two variables will be positive. On the other hand, when one of them is above its expected value the other variable tends to be below its expected value, then the _____ between the two variables will be negative.

a. Frequency distribution   b. Covariance
c. Probability distribution   d. Stratified sampling

15.   In economics, a _____ is a general slowdown in economic activity in a country over a sustained period of time, or a business cycle contraction. During _____s, many macroeconomic indicators vary in a similar way. Production as measured by Gross Domestic Product (GDP), employment, investment spending, capacity utilization, household incomes and business profits all fall during _____s.

a. Behavioral finance   b. Recession
c. Mercantilism   d. Fixed exchange rate

16.   A _____ or equity fund is a fund that invests in Equities more commonly known as stocks. Such funds are typically held either in stock or cash, as opposed to Bonds, notes, or other securities. This may be a mutual fund or exchange-traded fund.

a. Closed-end fund

b. Mutual fund fees and expenses

c. Money market funds

d. Stock fund

17. The _____ is the market for securities, where companies and governments can raise longterm funds. The _____ includes the stock market and the bond market. Financial regulators, such as the U.S. Securities and Exchange Commission, oversee the _____s in their designated countries to ensure that investors are protected against fraud.

a. Forward market

b. Spot rate

c. Delta neutral

d. Capital market

18. _____ mature in one year or less. Like zero-coupon bonds, they do not pay interest prior to maturity; instead they are sold at a discount of the par value to create a positive yield to maturity. Many regard _____ as the least risky investment available to U.S. investors.

a. Treasury Inflation Protected Securities

b. Treasury bills

c. 4-4-5 Calendar

d. Treasury securities

19. In probability theory and statistics, the _____ of a random variable, probability distribution averaging the squared distance of its possible values from the expected value (mean.) Whereas the mean is a way to describe the location of a distribution, the _____ is a way to capture its scale or degree of being spread out. The unit of _____ is the square of the unit of the original variable.

a. Harmonic mean

b. Monte Carlo methods

c. Semivariance

d. Variance

20. In finance, _____, also known as return on investment is the ratio of money gained or lost on an investment relative to the amount of money invested. The amount of money gained or lost may be referred to as interest, profit/loss, gain/loss, or net income/loss. The money invested may be referred to as the asset, capital, principal, or the cost basis of the investment.

a. Doctrine of the Proper Law

b. Rate of return

c. Stock or scrip dividends

d. Composiition of Creditors

21. In statistics, _____ has two related meanings:

- the arithmetic _____
- the expected value of a random variable, which is also called the population _____.

It is sometimes stated that the '_____' is average. This is incorrect if '_____' is taken in the specific sense of 'arithmetic _____' as there are different types of averages: the _____, median, and mode. Other simple statistical analyses use measures of spread, such as range, interquartile range, or standard deviation. For a real-valued random variable X, the _____ is the expectation of X. Note that not every probability distribution has a defined _____; see the Cauchy distribution for an example.

a. Probability distribution

b. Sample size

c. Harmonic mean

d. Mean

22. The _____ is the relationship between the amount of return gained on an investment and the amount of risk undertaken in that investment. The more return sought, the more risk that must be undertaken.

There are various classes of possible investments, each with their own positions on the overall _____.

a. Blank endorsement   b. Fiscal sponsorship
c. Post earnings announcement drift   d. Risk-return spectrum

23.   A _____ is a situation that involves losing one quality or aspect of something in return for gaining another quality or aspect. It implies a decision to be made with full comprehension of both the upside and downside of a particular choice.

In economics the term is expressed as opportunity cost, referring the most preferred alternative given up.

a. Total revenue   b. Break-even point
c. Capital outflow   d. Trade-off

24.   The _____ is one of several stock market indices, created by nineteenth-century Wall Street Journal editor and Dow Jones ' Company co-founder Charles Dow. Dow compiled the index to gauge the performance of the industrial sector of the American stock market. It is the second-oldest U.S. market index, after the Dow Jones Transportation Average, which Dow also created.

a. 4-4-5 Calendar   b. 7-Eleven
c. 529 plan   d. Dow Jones Industrial Average

25.   The _____ is the weighted-average most likely outcome in gambling, probability theory, economics or finance.

In gambling and probability theory, there is usually a discrete set of possible outcomes. In this case, _____ is a measure of the relative balance of win or loss weighted by their chances of occurring.

a. ABN Amro   b. AAB
c. A Random Walk Down Wall Street   d. Expected return

26.   _____ proposes how rational investors will use diversification to optimize their portfolios, and how a risky asset should be priced. The basic concepts of the theory are Markowitz diversification, the efficient frontier, capital asset pricing model, the alpha and beta coefficients, the Capital Market Line and the Securities Market Line.

_____ models an asset's return as a random variable, and models a portfolio as a weighted combination of assets so that the return of a portfolio is the weighted combination of the assets' returns.

a. Payback period   b. Modern portfolio theory
c. Consumer basket   d. Market value

27.   _____ is a graph created by investors to measure the risk of risky and risk-free assets. The graph displays to the investors on the return they can make by taking on a certain level of risk. It is also known as a 'reward-to-variability ratio'.

a. Divestment   b. Portfolio investment
c. Dollar cost averaging   d. Capital allocation line

28.   In finance, the Acid-test or _____ or liquid ratio measures the ability of a company to use its near cash or quick assets to immediately extinguish or retire its current liabilities. Quick assets include those current assets that presumably can be quickly converted to cash at close to their book values.

Generally, the acid test ratio should be 1:1 or better, however this varies widely by industry.

a. Net assets

c. Financial ratio

b. P/E ratio

d. Quick ratio

29.   Modern portfolio theory (MPT) proposes how rational investors will use diversification to optimize their portfolios, and how a risky asset should be priced. The basic concepts of the theory are Markowitz diversification, the _____, capital asset pricing model, the alpha and beta coefficients, the Capital Market Line and the Securities Market Line.

MPT models an asset's return as a random variable, and models a portfolio as a weighted combination of assets so that the return of a portfolio is the weighted combination of the assets' returns.

a. A Random Walk Down Wall Street

c. Efficient frontier

b. ABN Amro

d. AAB

30.   Behavioral economics and _____ are closely related fields that have evolved to be a separate branch of economic and financial analysis which applies scientific research on human and social, cognitive and emotional factors to better understand economic decisions by, say, consumers, borrowers, investors, and how they affect market prices, returns and the allocation of resources.

The field is primarily concerned with the bounds of rationality (selfishness, self-control) of economic agents. Behavioral models typically integrate insights from psychology with neo-classical economic theory.

a. Recession

c. Medium of exchange

b. Market structure

d. Behavioral finance

31.   _____ are organizations which pool large sums of money and invest those sums in companies. They include banks, insurance companies, retirement or pension funds, hedge funds and mutual funds. Their role in the economy is to act as highly specialized investors on behalf of others.

a. A Random Walk Down Wall Street

c. ABN Amro

b. AAB

d. Institutional investors

32.   A _____ is a payment made by a corporation to its shareholder members. When a corporation earns a profit or surplus, that money can be put to two uses: it can either be re-invested in the business (called retained earnings), or it can be paid to the shareholders as a _____. Many corporations retain a portion of their earnings and pay the remainder as a _____.

a. Dividend

c. Dividend puzzle

b. Special dividend

d. Dividend yield

33.   The _____ on a company stock is the company's annual dividend payments divided by its market cap, or the dividend per share divided by the price per share. It is often expressed as a percentage.

Dividend payments on preferred shares are stipulated by the prospectus.

a. Dividend reinvestment plan   b. Dividend imputation

c. Special dividend   d. Dividend yield

34.   In finance, the term _____ describes the amount in cash that returns to the owners of a security. Normally it does not include the price variations, at the difference of the total return. _____ applies to various stated rates of return on stocks (common and preferred, and convertible), fixed income instruments (bonds, notes, bills, strips, zero coupon), and some other investment type insurance products (e.g. annuities.)

a. Macaulay duration   b. Yield

c. 4-4-5 Calendar   d. Yield to maturity

35.   In business and finance, a _____ (also referred to as equity _____) of stock means a _____ of ownership in a corporation (company.) In the plural, stocks is often used as a synonym for _____s especially in the United States, but it is less commonly used that way outside of North America.

In the United Kingdom, South Africa, and Australia, stock can also refer to completely different financial instruments such as government bonds or, less commonly, to all kinds of marketable securities.

a. Margin   b. Bucket shop

c. Procter ' Gamble   d. Share

36.   _____ is a risk-adjusted measure of the so-called active return on an investment. It is the return in excess of the compensation for the risk borne, and thus commonly used to assess active managers' performances. Often, the return of a benchmark is subtracted in order to consider relative performance, which yields Jensen's _____.

a. Alpha   b. Option

c. Amortization   d. Annuity

37.   The _____ is an asset pricing model commonly used in the finance industry to measure risk and return of a stock. Mathematically the SIM is expressed as:

where:

rit >− rf is the excess return on the stock

ai is the company's alpha

Bi is the company's beta

rmt >− rf is the excess return on the market index

Eit is the residual return

The accuracy of the model is enhanced by the stock return's influence by market (beta) and firm-specific risk factors (alpha), unexpected returns (residual) and the relation to the performance of a market index (such as the All Ordinaries.) Security analysts often use the SIM for such functions as computing stock betas, evaluating stock selection skills, and conducting event studies.

a. Political risk

c. Capital asset

b. Country risk

d. Single-index model

38. A _____ is a fungible, negotiable instrument representing financial value. They are broadly categorized into debt securities (such as banknotes, bonds and debentures), and equity securities; e.g., common stocks. The company or other entity issuing the _____ is called the issuer.

a. Tracking stock

c. Book entry

b. Securities lending

d. Security

39. In statistics, _____ refers to techniques for the modeling and analysis of numerical data consisting of values of a dependent variable and of one or more independent variables The dependent variable in the regression equation is modeled as a function of the independent variables, corresponding parameters, and an error term. The error term is treated as a random variable.

a. Regression analysis

c. 4-4-5 Calendar

b. 529 plan

d. 7-Eleven

40. A scatter plot is a type of display using Cartesian coordinates to display values for two variables for a set of data. The data is displayed as a collection of points, each having the value of one variable determining the position on the horizontal axis and the value of the other variable determining the position on the vertical axis. A scatter plot is also called a scatter chart, _____ and scatter graph.

a. 529 plan

c. 4-4-5 Calendar

b. 7-Eleven

d. Scatter diagram

41. In economics and finance, _____ is the practice of taking advantage of a price differential between two or more markets: striking a combination of matching deals that capitalize upon the imbalance, the profit being the difference between the market prices. When used by academics, an _____ is a transaction that involves no negative cash flow at any probabilistic or temporal state and a positive cash flow in at least one state; in simple terms, a risk-free profit.

a. Arbitrage

c. Efficient-market hypothesis

b. Issuer

d. Initial margin

42. _____ , in finance, is a general theory of asset pricing, that has become influential in the pricing of stocks.

_____ holds that the expected return of a financial asset can be modeled as a linear function of various macro-economic factors or theoretical market indices, where sensitivity to changes in each factor is represented by a factor-specific beta coefficient. The model-derived rate of return will then be used to price the asset correctly - the asset price should equal the expected end of period price discounted at the rate implied by model.

a. Arbitrage pricing theory

b. A Random Walk Down Wall Street

c. AAB

d. ABN Amro

43.   A _____ is a portfolio consisting of a weighted sum of every asset in the market, with weights in the proportions that they exist in the market (with the necessary assumption that these assets are infinitely divisible.)

Neha Tyagi's critique (1977) states that this is only a theoretical concept, as to create a _____ for investment purposes in practice would necessarily include every single possible available asset, including real estate, precious metals, stamp collections, jewelry, and anything with any worth, as the theoretical market being referred to would be the world market. As a result, proxies for the market are used in practice by investors.

a. Delta neutral

b. Market price

c. Central Securities Depository

d. Market Portfolio

44.   A '_____' is a 'Charge' that is paid to obtain the right to delay a payment. Essentially, the payer purchases the right to make a given payment in the future instead of in the Present. The '_____', or 'Charge' that must be paid to delay the payment, is simply the difference between what the payment amount would be if it were paid in the present and what the payment amount would be paid if it were paid in the future.

a. Value at risk

b. Discount

c. Risk aversion

d. Risk modeling

1. In economics and finance, _____ is the practice of taking advantage of a price differential between two or more markets: striking a combination of matching deals that capitalize upon the imbalance, the profit being the difference between the market prices. When used by academics, an _____ is a transaction that involves no negative cash flow at any probabilistic or temporal state and a positive cash flow in at least one state; in simple terms, a risk-free profit.

   a. Arbitrage
   b. Efficient-market hypothesis
   c. Initial margin
   d. Issuer

2. _____ , in finance, is a general theory of asset pricing, that has become influential in the pricing of stocks.

   _____ holds that the expected return of a financial asset can be modeled as a linear function of various macro-economic factors or theoretical market indices, where sensitivity to changes in each factor is represented by a factor-specific beta coefficient. The model-derived rate of return will then be used to price the asset correctly - the asset price should equal the expected end of period price discounted at the rate implied by model.

   a. Arbitrage pricing theory
   b. A Random Walk Down Wall Street
   c. ABN Amro
   d. AAB

3. In finance, the _____ is used to determine a theoretically appropriate required rate of return of an asset, if that asset is to be added to an already well-diversified portfolio, given that asset's non-diversifiable risk. The model takes into account the asset's sensitivity to non-diversifiable risk (also known as systemic risk or market risk), often represented by the quantity beta (β) in the financial industry, as well as the expected return of the market and the expected return of a theoretical risk-free asset.

   The model was introduced by Jack Treynor (1961, 1962), William Sharpe (1964), John Lintner (1965a,b) and Jan Mossin (1966) independently, building on the earlier work of Harry Markowitz on diversification and modern portfolio theory.

   a. Hull-White model
   b. Capital asset pricing model
   c. Random walk hypothesis
   d. Cox-Ingersoll-Ross model

4. The term _____ has three unrelated technical definitions, and is also used in a variety of non-technical ways.

- In financial economics, it refers to any asset used to make money, as opposed to assets used for personal enjoyment or consumption. This is an important distinction because two people can disagree sharply about the value of personal assets, one person might think a sports car is more valuable than a pickup truck, another person might have the opposite taste. But if an asset is held for the purpose of making money, taste has nothing to do with it, only differences of opinion about how much money the asset will produce. With the further assumption that people agree on the probability distribution of future cash flows, it is possible to have an objective _____ pricing model. Even without the assumption of agreement, it is possible to set rational limits on _____ value.
- In governmental accounting, it is defined as any asset used in operations with an initial useful life extending beyond one reporting period. Generally, government managers have a 'stewardship' duty to maintain _____s under their control. See International Public Sector Accounting Standards for details.
- In US tax accounting, it is defined as any property other than a list of exceptions. The main exceptions are anything held for sale, and any real estate or depreciable property used in business. Almost everything you own and use for personal purposes, pleasure or investment is a _____. If something is a _____ for tax purposes, gains or losses on sale or disposition are capital gains or capital losses. For individuals, however, capital losses on property held for personal use are generally not deductible. See the IRS publication Tax Facts about Capital Gains and Losses for details.

A well-known financial accounting textbook advises that the term be avoided except in tax accounting because it is used in so many different senses, not all of them well-defined. For example it is often used as a synonym for fixed assets or for investments in securities.

A common non-technical usage occurs when people ask that employees or the environment or something else be treated as a _____.

a. Solvency	b. Capital asset
c. Settlement date	d. Political risk

5. The _____ is the market for securities, where companies and governments can raise longterm funds. The _____ includes the stock market and the bond market. Financial regulators, such as the U.S. Securities and Exchange Commission, oversee the _____s in their designated countries to ensure that investors are protected against fraud.

a. Forward market	b. Delta neutral
c. Spot rate	d. Capital market

6. The _____ is the weighted-average most likely outcome in gambling, probability theory, economics or finance.

In gambling and probability theory, there is usually a discrete set of possible outcomes. In this case, _____ is a measure of the relative balance of win or loss weighted by their chances of occurring.

a. AAB	b. ABN Amro
c. A Random Walk Down Wall Street	d. Expected return

7. _____, is when a company issues common stock or shares to the public for the first time. They are often issued by smaller, younger companies seeking capital to expand, but can also be done by large privately-owned companies looking to become publicly traded.

In an _____ the issuer may obtain the assistance of an underwriting firm, which helps it determine what type of security to issue (common or preferred), best offering price and time to bring it to market.

a. Asian Financial Crisis

c. Initial public offering

b. Interest

d. Insolvency

8. In business and accounting, _____s are everything of value that is owned by a person or company. The balance sheet of a firm records the monetary value of the _____s owned by the firm. The two major _____ classes are tangible _____s and intangible _____s.

a. EBITDA

c. Accounts payable

b. Income

d. Asset

9. In finance, _____ is the process of estimating the potential market value of a financial asset or liability. they can be done on assets (for example, investments in marketable securities such as stocks, options, business enterprises, or intangible assets such as patents and trademarks) or on liabilities (e.g., Bonds issued by a company.) _____s are required in many contexts including investment analysis, capital budgeting, merger and acquisition transactions, financial reporting, taxable events to determine the proper tax liability, and in litigation.

a. Share

c. Margin

b. Procter ' Gamble

d. Valuation

10. In finance, _____ is the risk involved in using models to value financial securities. Rebonato considers alternative definitions including:

1) After observing a set of prices for the underlying and hedging instruments, different but identically calibrated models might produce different prices for the same exotic product. 2) Losses will be incurred because of an 'incorrect' hedging strategy suggested by a model.

a. Price-to-book ratio

c. Takeover

b. Duty of loyalty

d. Model Risk

11. Behavioral economics and _____ are closely related fields that have evolved to be a separate branch of economic and financial analysis which applies scientific research on human and social, cognitive and emotional factors to better understand economic decisions by, say, consumers, borrowers, investors, and how they affect market prices, returns and the allocation of resources.

The field is primarily concerned with the bounds of rationality (selfishness, self-control) of economic agents. Behavioral models typically integrate insights from psychology with neo-classical economic theory.

a. Recession

c. Medium of exchange

b. Market structure

d. Behavioral finance

12. The _____, in terms of finance and investing, describes how the expected return of a stock or portfolio is correlated to the return of the financial market as a whole.

An asset with a beta of 0 means that its price is not at all correlated with the market; that asset is independent. A positive beta means that the asset generally follows the market.

a. LIBOR market model   b. Perpetuity
c. Current yield   d. Beta coefficient

13. _____ proposes how rational investors will use diversification to optimize their portfolios, and how a risky asset should be priced. The basic concepts of the theory are Markowitz diversification, the efficient frontier, capital asset pricing model, the alpha and beta coefficients, the Capital Market Line and the Securities Market Line.

_____ models an asset's return as a random variable, and models a portfolio as a weighted combination of assets so that the return of a portfolio is the weighted combination of the assets' returns.

a. Market value   b. Modern portfolio theory
c. Consumer basket   d. Payback period

14. Modern portfolio theory (MPT) proposes how rational investors will use diversification to optimize their portfolios, and how a risky asset should be priced. The basic concepts of the theory are Markowitz diversification, the _____, capital asset pricing model, the alpha and beta coefficients, the Capital Market Line and the Securities Market Line.

MPT models an asset's return as a random variable, and models a portfolio as a weighted combination of assets so that the return of a portfolio is the weighted combination of the assets' returns.

a. AAB   b. ABN Amro
c. A Random Walk Down Wall Street   d. Efficient frontier

15. _____ are organizations which pool large sums of money and invest those sums in companies. They include banks, insurance companies, retirement or pension funds, hedge funds and mutual funds. Their role in the economy is to act as highly specialized investors on behalf of others.
a. AAB   b. A Random Walk Down Wall Street
c. Institutional investors   d. ABN Amro

16. A _____ is a portfolio consisting of a weighted sum of every asset in the market, with weights in the proportions that they exist in the market (with the necessary assumption that these assets are infinitely divisible.)

Neha Tyagi's critique (1977) states that this is only a theoretical concept, as to create a _____ for investment purposes in practice would necessarily include every single possible available asset, including real estate, precious metals, stamp collections, jewelry, and anything with any worth, as the theoretical market being referred to would be the world market. As a result, proxies for the market are used in practice by investors.

a. Market portfolio   b. Market price
c. Central Securities Depository   d. Delta neutral

17.

In finance, the _____ can be the expected rate of return above the risk-free interest rate. When measuring risk, a common sense approach is to compare the risk-free return on T-bills and the very risky return on other investments. The difference between these two returns can be interpreted as a measure of the excess return on the average risky asset. This excess return is known as the _____.

a. Risk aversion
c. Risk premium

b. Risk adjusted return on capital
d. Risk modeling

18. In finance, a _____ is a debt security, in which the authorized issuer owes the holders a debt and, depending on the terms of the _____, is obliged to pay interest (the coupon) and/or to repay the principal at a later date, termed maturity.

Thus a _____ is a loan: the issuer is the borrower, the _____ holder is the lender, and the coupon is the interest. _____s provide the borrower with external funds to finance long-term investments, or, in the case of government _____s, to finance current expenditure.

a. Catastrophe bonds
c. Puttable bond

b. Bond
d. Convertible bond

19. _____ is a graph created by investors to measure the risk of risky and risk-free assets. The graph displays to the investors on the return they can make by taking on a certain level of risk. It is also known as a 'reward-to-variability ratio'.

a. Capital allocation line
c. Dollar cost averaging

b. Divestment
d. Portfolio investment

20. _____ is the risk that the value of an investment will decrease due to moves in market factors. The five standard _____ factors are:

- Equity risk, the risk that stock prices will change.
- Interest rate risk, the risk that interest rates will change.
- Currency risk, the risk that foreign exchange rates will change.
- Commodity risk, the risk that commodity prices (e.g. grains, metals) will change.

As with other forms of risk, _____ may be measured in a number of ways. Traditionally, this is done using a Value at Risk methodology. Value at risk is well established as a risk management technique, but it contains a number of limiting assumptions that constrain its accuracy.

a. Currency risk
c. Market risk

b. Transaction risk
d. Tracking error

21. A _____ is a professionally managed type of collective investment scheme that pools money from many investors and invests it in stocks, bonds, short-term money market instruments, and/or other securities. The _____ will have a fund manager that trades the pooled money on a regular basis. Currently, the worldwide value of all _____s totals more than $26 trillion.

Since 1940, there have been three basic types of investment companies in the United States: open-end funds, also known in the US as _____s; unit investment trusts (UITs); and closed-end funds.

a. Mutual fund   b. Trust company
c. Net asset value   d. Financial intermediary

22.   _____ is a concept in economics, finance, and psychology related to the behaviour of consumers and investors under uncertainty. _____ is the reluctance of a person to accept a bargain with an uncertain payoff rather than another bargain with a more certain, but possibly lower, expected payoff.

The inverse of a person's _____ is sometimes called their risk tolerance

a. Risk premium   b. Risk adjusted return on capital
c. Discount factor   d. Risk aversion

23.   _____ is a risk-adjusted measure of the so-called active return on an investment. It is the return in excess of the compensation for the risk borne, and thus commonly used to assess active managers' performances. Often, the return of a benchmark is subtracted in order to consider relative performance, which yields Jensen's _____.
a. Alpha   b. Option
c. Annuity   d. Amortization

24.   In finance, _____, also known as return on investment is the ratio of money gained or lost on an investment relative to the amount of money invested. The amount of money gained or lost may be referred to as interest, profit/loss, gain/loss, or net income/loss. The money invested may be referred to as the asset, capital, principal, or the cost basis of the investment.
a. Composiition of Creditors   b. Stock or scrip dividends
c. Rate of return   d. Doctrine of the Proper Law

25.   A _____ is a fungible, negotiable instrument representing financial value. They are broadly categorized into debt securities (such as banknotes, bonds and debentures), and equity securities; e.g., common stocks. The company or other entity issuing the _____ is called the issuer.
a. Book entry   b. Security
c. Tracking stock   d. Securities lending

26.   In finance, _____ is that risk which is common to an entire market and not to any individual entity or component thereof. It should be distinguished from systemic risk which is the risk that the entire financial system will collapse as a result of some catastrophic event.

Risks can be reduced in four main ways: Avoidance, Reduction, Retention and Transfer.

a. Capital surplus   b. Primary market
c. Conglomerate merger   d. Systematic risk

27.   In Modern Portfolio Theory, the _____ is the graphical representation of the Capital Asset Pricing Model. It displays the expected rate of return for an overall market as a function of systematic (non-diversifiable) risk (beta.)

The Y-Intercept (beta=0) of the _____ is equal to the risk-free interest rate.

a. Security market line

b. Certificate in Investment Performance Measurement

c. Rebalancing

d. Divestment

28.   _____ is the planning process used to determine whether a firm's long term investments such as new machinery, replacement machinery, new plants, new products, and research development projects are worth pursuing. It is budget for major capital, or investment, expenditures.

Many formal methods are used in _____, including the techniques such as

- Net present value
- Profitability index
- Internal rate of return
- Modified Internal Rate of Return
- Equivalent annuity

These methods use the incremental cash flows from each potential investment, or project. Techniques based on accounting earnings and accounting rules are sometimes used - though economists consider this to be improper - such as the accounting rate of return, and 'return on investment.' Simplified and hybrid methods are used as well, such as payback period and discounted payback period.

a. Shareholder value

b. Financial distress

c. Preferred stock

d. Capital budgeting

29.   The _____ is the rate of return that must be met for a company to undertake a particular project. The _____ is usually determined by evaluating existing opportunities in operations expansion, rate of return for investments, and other factors deemed relevant by management. A risk premium can also be attached to the _____ if management feels that specific opportunities inherently contain more risk than others that could be pursued with the same resources.

a. Capital structure

b. Corporate finance

c. Gross profit

d. Hurdle rate

30.   The _____ is a capital budgeting metric used by firms to decide whether they should make investments. It is an indicator of the efficiency or quality of an investment, as opposed to net present value (NPV), which indicates value or magnitude.

The IRR is the annualized effective compounded return rate which can be earned on the invested capital, i.e., the yield on the investment.

a. A Random Walk Down Wall Street

b. Internal rate of return

c. ABN Amro

d. AAB

31.   In economics, _____ is a measure of the relative satisfaction from or desirability of consumption of various goods and services. Given this measure, one may speak meaningfully of increasing or decreasing _____, and thereby explain economic behavior in terms of attempts to increase one's _____. For illustrative purposes, changes in _____ are sometimes expressed in units called utils.

    a. AAB   b. Utility

    c. A Random Walk Down Wall Street   d. Utility function

32.   In statistics, _____ refers to techniques for the modeling and analysis of numerical data consisting of values of a dependent variable and of one or more independent variables The dependent variable in the regression equation is modeled as a function of the independent variables, corresponding parameters, and an error term. The error term is treated as a random variable.

    a. Regression analysis   b. 529 plan

    c. 7-Eleven   d. 4-4-5 Calendar

33.   In statistics, _____ or explained randomness measures the proportion to which a mathematical model accounts for the variation (= apparent randomness) of a given data set. Often, variation is quantified as variance; then, the more specific term explained variance can be used.

The complementary part of the total variation/randomness/variance is called unexplained or residual.

    a. ABN Amro   b. A Random Walk Down Wall Street

    c. AAB   d. Explained variation

34.   In probability and statistics, the _____ of a collection of numbers is a measure of the dispersion of the numbers from their expected (mean) value. It can apply to a probability distribution, a random variable, a population or a data set. The _____ is usually denoted with the letter σ (lowercase sigma.)

    a. Standard deviation   b. Sample size

    c. Mean   d. Kurtosis

35.   The _____ is an asset pricing model commonly used in the finance industry to measure risk and return of a stock. Mathematically the SIM is expressed as:

where:

        rit >− rf is the excess return on the stock
        ai is the company's alpha
        Bi is the company's beta
        rmt >− rf is the excess return on the market index
        Eit is the residual return

The accuracy of the model is enhanced by the stock return's influence by market (beta) and firm-specific risk factors (alpha), unexpected returns (residual) and the relation to the performance of a market index (such as the All Ordinaries.) Security analysts often use the SIM for such functions as computing stock betas, evaluating stock selection skills, and conducting event studies.

a. Country risk

b. Political risk

c. Capital asset

d. Single-index model

36.   In statistics, the _____, R^2 is used in the context of statistical models whose main purpose is the prediction of future outcomes on the basis of other related information. It is the proportion of variability in a data set that is accounted for by the statistical model. It provides a measure of how well future outcomes are likely to be predicted by the model.

a. 7-Eleven

b. Coefficient of determination

c. 4-4-5 Calendar

d. 529 plan

37.   In statistics, _____ is a collection of statistical models, and their associated procedures, in which the observed variance is partitioned into components due to different explanatory variables. The initial techniques of the _____ were developed by the statistician and geneticist R. A. Fisher in the 1920s and 1930s, and is sometimes known as Fisher's ANOVA or Fisher's _____, due to the use of Fisher's F-distribution as part of the test of statistical significance.

There are three conceptual classes of such models:

1.   Fixed-effects models assumes that the data came from normal populations which may differ only in their means. (Model 1)
2.   Random effects models assume that the data describe a hierarchy of different populations whose differences are constrained by the hierarchy. (Model 2)
3.   Mixed-effect models describe situations where both fixed and random effects are present. (Model 3)

a. Analysis of variance

b. AAB

c. A Random Walk Down Wall Street

d. ABN Amro

38.   In probability theory and statistics, the _____ of a random variable, probability distribution averaging the squared distance of its possible values from the expected value (mean.) Whereas the mean is a way to describe the location of a distribution, the _____ is a way to capture its scale or degree of being spread out. The unit of _____ is the square of the unit of the original variable.

a. Variance

b. Monte Carlo methods

c. Semivariance

d. Harmonic mean

39.   In business, a _____ is the purchase of one company (the target) by another (the acquirer or bidder). In the UK the term refers to the acquisition of a public company whose shares are listed on a stock exchange, in contrast to the acquisition of a private company.

Before a bidder makes an offer for another company, it usually first informs that company's board of directors.

a. Takeover   b. 529 plan
c. Stock swap   d. 4-4-5 Calendar

40. _____ most frequently refers to the standard deviation of the continuously compounded returns of a financial instrument with a specific time horizon. It is often used to quantify the risk of the instrument over that time period. _____ is typically expressed in annualized terms, and it may either be an absolute number ($5) or a fraction of the mean (5%).
   a. Currency swap   b. Seasoned equity offering
   c. Portfolio insurance   d. Volatility

41. In econometrics, an _____ model considers the variance of the current error term to be a function of the variances of the previous time period's error terms. _____ relates the error variance to the square of a previous period's error. It is employed commonly in modeling financial time series that exhibit time-varying volatility clustering, i.e. periods of swings followed by periods of relative calm.
   a. AAB   b. ABN Amro
   c. A Random Walk Down Wall Street   d. Autoregressive conditional heteroscedasticity

42. _____ is one of the authors of the Black-Scholes equation. In 1997 he was awarded the Nobel Memorial Prize in Economic Sciences for 'a new method to determine the value of derivatives'. The model provides the fundamental conceptual framework for valuing options, such as calls or puts, and is referred to as the Black-Scholes model, which has become the standard in financial markets globally.
   a. Adolph Coors   b. Robert James Shiller
   c. Myron Samuel Scholes   d. Andrew Tobias

43. _____ is a measure of the ability of a debtor to pay their debts as and when they fall due. It is usually expressed as a ratio or a percentage of current liabilities.

For a corporation with a published balance sheet there are various ratios used to calculate a measure of liquidity.

   a. Invested capital   b. Operating profit margin
   c. Accounting liquidity   d. Operating leverage

44. _____ arises from situations in which a party interested in trading an asset cannot do it because nobody in the market wants to trade that asset. _____ becomes particularly important to parties who are about to hold or currently hold an asset, since it affects their ability to trade.

Manifestation of _____ is very different from a drop of price to zero.

   a. Credit risk   b. Currency risk
   c. Tracking error   d. Liquidity Risk

45. _____ is the balance of the amounts of cash being received and paid by a business during a defined period of time, sometimes tied to a specific project. Measurement of _____ can be used

- to evaluate the state or performance of a business or project.
- to determine problems with liquidity. Being profitable does not necessarily mean being liquid. A company can fail because of a shortage of cash, even while profitable.
- to generate project rate of returns. The time of _____s into and out of projects are used as inputs to financial models such as internal rate of return, and net present value.
- to examine income or growth of a business when it is believed that accrual accounting concepts do not represent economic realities. Alternately, _____ can be used to 'validate' the net income generated by accrual accounting.

_____ as a generic term may be used differently depending on context, and certain _____ definitions may be adapted by analysts and users for their own uses. Common terms include operating _____ and free _____.

_____s can be classified into:

1. Operational _____s: Cash received or expended as a result of the company's core business activities.
2. Investment _____s: Cash received or expended through capital expenditure, investments or acquisitions.
3. Financing _____s: Cash received or expended as a result of financial activities, such as interests and dividends.

All three together - the net _____ - are necessary to reconcile the beginning cash balance to the ending cash balance. Loan draw downs or equity injections, that is just shifting of capital but no expenditure as such, are not considered in the net _____.

a. Cash flow
c. Corporate finance

b. Shareholder value
d. Real option

46. The _____ is a term coined by economists Rajnish Mehra and Edward C. Prescott. It is based on the observation that in order to reconcile the much higher return on equity stock compared to government bonds in the United States, individuals must have implausibly high risk aversion according to standard economics models. Similar situations prevail in many other industrialized countries.

a. A Random Walk Down Wall Street
c. Equity premium puzzle

b. ABN Amro
d. AAB

47. _____ is a fee paid on borrowed assets. It is the price paid for the use of borrowed money , or, money earned by deposited funds . Assets that are sometimes lent with _____ include money, shares, consumer goods through hire purchase, major assets such as aircraft, and even entire factories in finance lease arrangements.

a. Insolvency
c. A Random Walk Down Wall Street

b. AAB
d. Interest

48. An _____ is the price a borrower pays for the use of money they do not own, and the return a lender receives for deferring the use of funds, by lending it to the borrower. _____s are normally expressed as a percentage rate over the period of one year.

_____s targets are also a vital tool of monetary policy and are used to control variables like investment, inflation, and unemployment.

a. AAB

b. A Random Walk Down Wall Street

c. ABN Amro

d. Interest rate

49.   A _____, securities exchange or (in Europe) bourse is a corporation or mutual organization which provides 'trading' facilities for stock brokers and traders, to trade stocks and other securities. _____s also provide facilities for the issue and redemption of securities as well as other financial instruments and capital events including the payment of income and dividends. The securities traded on a _____ include: shares issued by companies, unit trusts and other pooled investment products and bonds.

a. 529 plan

b. 4-4-5 Calendar

c. 7-Eleven

d. Stock exchange

50.   In business and finance, a _____ (also referred to as equity _____) of stock means a _____ of ownership in a corporation (company.) In the plural, stocks is often used as a synonym for _____s especially in the United States, but it is less commonly used that way outside of North America.

In the United Kingdom, South Africa, and Australia, stock can also refer to completely different financial instruments such as government bonds or, less commonly, to all kinds of marketable securities.

a. Procter ' Gamble

b. Margin

c. Bucket shop

d. Share

51.   The _____ is one of several stock market indices, created by nineteenth-century Wall Street Journal editor and Dow Jones ' Company co-founder Charles Dow. Dow compiled the index to gauge the performance of the industrial sector of the American stock market. It is the second-oldest U.S. market index, after the Dow Jones Transportation Average, which Dow also created.

a. 529 plan

b. 4-4-5 Calendar

c. 7-Eleven

d. Dow Jones Industrial Average

52.   _____ is a branch of economics that deals with the performance, structure, and behavior of a national or regional economy as a whole. Along with microeconomics, _____ is one of the two most general fields in economics. Macroeconomists study aggregated indicators such as GDP, unemployment rates, and price indices to understand how the whole economy functions.

a. Macroeconomics

b. Recession

c. Human capital

d. Behavioral finance

53.   The _____ is a financial ratio used to compare a company's book value to its current market price. Book value is an accounting term denoting the portion of the company held by the shareholders; in other words, the company's total tangible assets less its total liabilities. The calculation can be performed in two ways, but the result should be the same each way. In the first way, the company's market capitalization can be divided by the company's total book value from its balance sheet. The second way, using per-share values, is to divide the company's current share price by the book value per share (i.e. its book value divided by the number of outstanding shares).

a. Stop order
c. Stock repurchase

b. Whisper numbers
d. Price-to-book ratio

54. The _____ is used by business and government to classify and measure economic activity in Canada, Mexico and the United States. It has largely replaced the older Standard Industrial Classification (SIC) system; however, certain government departments and agencies, such as the U.S. Securities and Exchange Commission (SEC), still use the SIC codes.

The _____ numbering system is a six-digit code.

a. 529 plan
c. 4-4-5 Calendar

b. 7-Eleven
d. NAICS

55. In finance, the Acid-test or _____ or liquid ratio measures the ability of a company to use its near cash or quick assets to immediately extinguish or retire its current liabilities. Quick assets include those current assets that presumably can be quickly converted to cash at close to their book values.

Generally, the acid test ratio should be 1:1 or better, however this varies widely by industry.

a. P/E ratio
c. Quick ratio

b. Financial ratio
d. Net assets

56. In finance, _____ occurs when a debtor has not met its legal obligations according to the debt contract, e.g. it has not made a scheduled payment, or has violated a loan covenant (condition) of the debt contract. _____ may occur if the debtor is either unwilling or unable to pay their debt. This can occur with all debt obligations including bonds, mortgages, loans, and promissory notes.

a. Vendor finance
c. Credit crunch

b. Default
d. Debt validation

57. In finance, the term _____ describes the amount in cash that returns to the owners of a security. Normally it does not include the price variations, at the difference of the total return. _____ applies to various stated rates of return on stocks (common and preferred, and convertible), fixed income instruments (bonds, notes, bills, strips, zero coupon), and some other investment type insurance products (e.g. annuities.)

a. Macaulay duration
c. Yield to maturity

b. Yield
d. 4-4-5 Calendar

58. The _____ or redemption yield is the yield promised to the bondholder on the assumption that the bond or other fixed-interest security such as gilts will be held to maturity, that all coupon and principal payments will be made and coupon payments are reinvested at the bond's promised yield at the same rate as invested. It is a measure of the return of the bond. This technique in theory allows investors to calculate the fair value of different financial instruments.

a. Yield
c. Yield to maturity

b. Macaulay duration
d. 4-4-5 Calendar

59. _____ is a life of security. It may also refer to the final payment date of a loan or other financial instrument, at which point all remaining interest and principal is due to be paid.

1, 3, 6 months _____ band can be calculated by using 30-day per month periods.

a. Replacement cost   b. False billing
c. Primary market   d. Maturity

60. A _____ is a variable associated with an increased risk of disease or infection. They are correlational and not necessarily causal, because correlation does not imply causation. For example, being young cannot be said to cause measles, but young people are more at risk as they are less likely to have developed immunity during a previous epidemic.

a. 4-4-5 Calendar   b. 7-Eleven
c. Risk factor   d. 529 plan

61. _____ is the difference between price and the costs of bringing to market whatever it is that is accounted as an enterprise (whether by harvest, extraction, manufacture, or purchase) in terms of the component costs of delivered goods and/or services and any operating or other expenses.

A key difficulty in measuring profit is in defining costs. Pure economic monetary profits can be zero or negative even in competitive equilibrium when accounted monetized costs exceed monetized price.

a. Accounting profit   b. AAB
c. Economic profit   d. A Random Walk Down Wall Street

62. The institution most often referenced by the word '_____' is a public or publicly traded _____, the shares of which are traded on a public stock exchange (e.g., the New York Stock Exchange or Nasdaq in the United States) where shares of stock of _____s are bought and sold by and to the general public. Most of the largest businesses in the world are publicly traded _____s. However, the majority of _____s are said to be closely held, privately held or close _____s, meaning that no ready market exists for the trading of shares.

a. Depository Trust Company   b. Corporation
c. Federal Home Loan Mortgage Corporation   d. Protect

1.   The term _____ or economic cycle refers to the fluctuations of economic activity (business fluctuations) around a long-term growth trend. The cycle involves shifts over time between periods of relatively rapid growth of output (recovery and prosperity), and periods of relative stagnation or decline (contraction or recession.) These fluctuations are often measured using the real gross domestic product.

a. Deflation   b. Business cycle
c. Fixed exchange rate   d. Behavioral finance

2.   The _____ is one of several stock market indices, created by nineteenth-century Wall Street Journal editor and Dow Jones ' Company co-founder Charles Dow. Dow compiled the index to gauge the performance of the industrial sector of the American stock market. It is the second-oldest U.S. market index, after the Dow Jones Transportation Average, which Dow also created.

a. 7-Eleven   b. 529 plan
c. Dow Jones Industrial Average   d. 4-4-5 Calendar

3.   A _____, is a mathematical formalization of a trajectory that consists of taking successive random steps. The results of _____ analysis have been applied to computer science, physics, ecology, economics and a number of other fields as a fundamental model for random processes in time. For example, the path traced by a molecule as it travels in a liquid or a gas, the search path of a foraging animal, the price of a fluctuating stock and the financial status of a gambler can all be modeled as _____s.

a. 7-Eleven   b. 529 plan
c. 4-4-5 Calendar   d. Random walk

4.   A _____ is a private or public market for the trading of company stock and derivatives of company stock at an agreed price; these are securities listed on a stock exchange as well as those only traded privately.

The size of the world _____ is estimated at about $36.6 trillion US at the beginning of October 2008 . The world derivatives market has been estimated at about $480 trillion face or nominal value, 12 times the size of the entire world economy.

a. Adolph Coors   b. Anton Gelonkin
c. Andrew Tobias   d. Stock market

5.   A _____ is the price of a single share of a no. of saleable stocks of the company. Once the stock is purchased, the owner becomes a shareholder of the company that issued the share.

a. Trading curb   b. Share price
c. Whisper numbers   d. Stock split

6.   _____ refers to a portfolio management strategy where the manager makes specific investments with the goal of outperforming an investment benchmark index. Investors or mutual funds that do not aspire to create a return in excess of a benchmark index will often invest in an index fund that replicates as closely as possible the investment weighting and returns of that index; this is called passive management. _____ is the opposite of passive management, because in passive management the manager does not seek to outperform the benchmark index.

a. A Random Walk Down Wall Street   b. ABN Amro
c. AAB   d. Active management

7. In finance, _____ is the process of estimating the potential market value of a financial asset or liability. they can be done on assets (for example, investments in marketable securities such as stocks, options, business enterprises, or intangible assets such as patents and trademarks) or on liabilities (e.g., Bonds issued by a company.) _____s are required in many contexts including investment analysis, capital budgeting, merger and acquisition transactions, financial reporting, taxable events to determine the proper tax liability, and in litigation.

    a. Margin   b. Procter ' Gamble

    c. Share   d. Valuation

8. A _____, securities exchange or (in Europe) bourse is a corporation or mutual organization which provides 'trading' facilities for stock brokers and traders, to trade stocks and other securities. _____s also provide facilities for the issue and redemption of securities as well as other financial instruments and capital events including the payment of income and dividends. The securities traded on a _____ include: shares issued by companies, unit trusts and other pooled investment products and bonds.

    a. 529 plan   b. 7-Eleven

    c. Stock exchange   d. 4-4-5 Calendar

9. In business, a _____ is the purchase of one company (the target) by another (the acquirer or bidder). In the UK the term refers to the acquisition of a public company whose shares are listed on a stock exchange, in contrast to the acquisition of a private company.

Before a bidder makes an offer for another company, it usually first informs that company's board of directors.

    a. Stock swap   b. 529 plan

    c. 4-4-5 Calendar   d. Takeover

10. In economics, a _____ is a mechanism that allows people to easily buy and sell (trade) financial securities (such as stocks and bonds), commodities (such as precious metals or agricultural goods), and other fungible items of value at low transaction costs and at prices that reflect the efficient-market hypothesis.

_____s have evolved significantly over several hundred years and are undergoing constant innovation to improve liquidity.

Both general markets (where many commodities are traded) and specialized markets (where only one commodity is traded) exist.

    a. Financial market   b. Delta hedging

    c. Cost of carry   d. Secondary market

11. The term _____ is used to describe a nation's social, or business activity in the process of rapid industrialization. _____ are generally less-wealthy than the developed world, and are wealthier (or the wealthiest of) the developing world. According to The Economist many people find the term dated, but a new term has yet to gain much traction.

    a. A Random Walk Down Wall Street   b. Emerging markets

    c. ABN Amro   d. AAB

12. _____ is the trading of a corporation's stock or other securities (e.g. bonds or stock options) by individuals with potential access to non-public information about the company. In most countries, trading by corporate insiders such as officers, key employees, directors, and large shareholders may be legal, if this trading is done in a way that does not take advantage of non-public information. However, the term is frequently used to refer to a practice in which an insider or a related party trades based on material non-public information obtained during the performance of the insider's duties at the corporation, or otherwise in breach of a fiduciary duty or other relationship of trust and confidence or where the non-public information was misappropriated from the company.

a. Equity investment   b. Intellidex

c. Open outcry   d. Insider trading

13. A _____ is a fungible, negotiable instrument representing financial value. They are broadly categorized into debt securities (such as banknotes, bonds and debentures), and equity securities; e.g., common stocks. The company or other entity issuing the _____ is called the issuer.

a. Securities lending   b. Security

c. Book entry   d. Tracking stock

14. The _____ of 1934 is a law governing the secondary trading of securities (stocks, bonds, and debentures) in the United States of America. The Act, 48 Stat. 881 (enacted June 6, 1934), codified at 15 U.S.C. Â§ 78a et seq., was a sweeping piece of legislation. The Act and related statutes form the basis of regulation of the financial markets and their participants in the United States.

a. 529 plan   b. 7-Eleven

c. 4-4-5 Calendar   d. Securities Exchange Act

15. _____ of a business involves analyzing its financial statements and health, its management and competitive advantages, and its competitors and markets. The term is used to distinguish such analysis from other types of investment analysis, such as quantitative analysis and technical analysis.

_____ is performed on historical and present data, but with the goal of making financial forecasts.

a. Stock valuation   b. Growth stocks

c. 4-4-5 Calendar   d. Fundamental analysis

16. _____ is a security analysis discipline for forecasting the future direction of prices through the study of past market data, primarily price and volume. In its purest form, _____ considers only the actual price and volume behavior of the market or instrument. Technical analysts may employ models and trading rules based on price and volume transformations, such as the relative strength index, moving averages, regressions, inter-market and intra-market price correlations, cycles or, classically, through recognition of chart patterns.

a. Point and figure   b. Support and resistance

c. Dow theory   d. Technical analysis

17. An _____ or index tracker is a collective investment scheme (usually a mutual fund or exchange-traded fund) that aims to replicate the movements of an index of a specific financial market regardless of market conditions.

Tracking can be achieved by trying to hold all of the securities in the index, in the same proportions as the index. Other methods include statistically sampling the market and holding 'representative' securities.

a. Index fund   b. AAB

c. Investment company   d. A Random Walk Down Wall Street

18. _____ is a financial strategy in which a fund manager makes as few portfolio decisions as possible, in order to minimize transaction costs, including the incidence of capital gains tax. One popular method is to mimic the performance of an externally specified index--called 'index funds'. The ethos of an index fund is aptly summed up in the injunction to an index fund manager: 'Don't just do something, sit there!'

_____ is most common on the equity market, where index funds track a stock market index, but it is becoming more common in other investment types, including bonds, commodities and hedge funds.

a. Savings and loan association   b. Trust company

c. Net asset value   d. Passive management

19. In business and accounting, _____s are everything of value that is owned by a person or company. The balance sheet of a firm records the monetary value of the _____s owned by the firm. The two major _____ classes are tangible _____s and intangible _____s.

a. Accounts payable   b. EBITDA

c. Income   d. Asset

20. _____ is a term used to refer to how an investor distributes his or her investments among various classes of investment vehicles (e.g., stocks and bonds.)

A large part of financial planning is finding an _____ that is appropriate for a given person in terms of their appetite for and ability to shoulder risk. This can depend on various factors; see investor profile.

a. Investment performance   b. Investing online

c. Alternative investment   d. Asset allocation

21. Behavioral economics and _____ are closely related fields that have evolved to be a separate branch of economic and financial analysis which applies scientific research on human and social, cognitive and emotional factors to better understand economic decisions by, say, consumers, borrowers, investors, and how they affect market prices, returns and the allocation of resources.

The field is primarily concerned with the bounds of rationality (selfishness, self-control) of economic agents. Behavioral models typically integrate insights from psychology with neo-classical economic theory.

a. Medium of exchange   b. Recession

c. Market structure   d. Behavioral finance

22. _____ are organizations which pool large sums of money and invest those sums in companies. They include banks, insurance companies, retirement or pension funds, hedge funds and mutual funds. Their role in the economy is to act as highly specialized investors on behalf of others.

a. A Random Walk Down Wall Street   b. AAB

c. Institutional investors   d. ABN Amro

23. In finance, a _____ is a debt security, in which the authorized issuer owes the holders a debt and, depending on the terms of the _____, is obliged to pay interest (the coupon) and/or to repay the principal at a later date, termed maturity.

Thus a _____ is a loan: the issuer is the borrower, the _____ holder is the lender, and the coupon is the interest. _____s provide the borrower with external funds to finance long-term investments, or, in the case of government _____s, to finance current expenditure.

  a. Puttable bond
  c. Catastrophe bonds

  b. Bond
  d. Convertible bond

24. _____ are made by investors and investment managers.

Investors commonly perform investment analysis by making use of fundamental analysis, technical analysis and gut feel.

_____ are often supported by decision tools.

  a. Investment decisions
  c. Asset allocation

  b. Investing online
  d. Investment performance

25. A _____ is a portfolio consisting of a weighted sum of every asset in the market, with weights in the proportions that they exist in the market (with the necessary assumption that these assets are infinitely divisible.)

Neha Tyagi's critique (1977) states that this is only a theoretical concept, as to create a _____ for investment purposes in practice would necessarily include every single possible available asset, including real estate, precious metals, stamp collections, jewelry, and anything with any worth, as the theoretical market being referred to would be the world market. As a result, proxies for the market are used in practice by investors.

  a. Central Securities Depository
  c. Market price

  b. Delta neutral
  d. Market Portfolio

26. _____ is used to assign the available resources in an economic way. It is part of resource management.

In strategic planning, a _____ decision is a plan for using available resources, for example human resources, especially in the near term, to achieve goals for the future.

  a. 7-Eleven
  c. 4-4-5 Calendar

  b. Resource allocation
  d. 529 plan

27. _____ is a distortion of evidence or data that arises from the way that the data are collected. It is sometimes referred to as the selection effect. The term _____ most often refers to the distortion of a statistical analysis, due to the method of collecting samples.

a. 529 plan   b. 7-Eleven
c. 4-4-5 Calendar   d. Selection bias

28. _____ is the strategy of making buy or sell decisions of financial assets (often stocks) by attempting to predict future market price movements. The prediction may be based on an outlook of market or economic conditions resulting from technical or fundamental analysis. This is an investment strategy based on the outlook for an aggregate market, rather than for a particular financial asset.
   a. Late trading   b. Portable alpha
   c. Divestment   d. Market timing

29. _____ are the inflation-indexed bonds issued by the U.S. Treasury. The principal is adjusted to the Consumer Price Index, the commonly used measure of inflation. The coupon rate is constant, but generates a different amount of interest when multiplied by the inflation-adjusted principal, thus protecting the holder against inflation. _____ are currently offered in 5-year, 10-year and 20-year maturities.
   a. Treasury Inflation-Protected Securities   b. Treasury securities
   c. 4-4-5 Calendar   d. Treasury Inflation Protected Securities

30. The _____ is a financial ratio used to compare a company's book value to its current market price. Book value is an accounting term denoting the portion of the company held by the shareholders; in other words, the company's total tangible assets less its total liabilities. The calculation can be performed in two ways, but the result should be the same each way. In the first way, the company's market capitalization can be divided by the company's total book value from its balance sheet. The second way, using per-share values, is to divide the company's current share price by the book value per share (i.e. its book value divided by the number of outstanding shares).
   a. Whisper numbers   b. Stock repurchase
   c. Stop order   d. Price-to-book ratio

31. In probability theory and statistics, _____ indicates the strength and direction of a linear relationship between two random variables. That is in contrast with the usage of the term in colloquial speech, which denotes any relationship, not necessarily linear. In general statistical usage, _____ or co-relation refers to the departure of two random variables from independence.
   a. Probability distribution   b. Variance
   c. Geometric mean   d. Correlation

32. In finance, a _____ is one who attempts to profit by investing in a manner that differs from the conventional wisdom, when the consensus opinion appears to be wrong.

A _____ believes that certain crowd behavior among investors can lead to exploitable mispricings in securities markets. For example, widespread pessimism about a stock can drive a price so low that it overstates the company's risks, and understates its prospects for returning to profitability.

   a. Direct access trading   b. Secured debt
   c. Contrarian   d. Day trading

33. _____ is the quotient of earnings per share divided by the share price. It is the reciprocal of the P/E ratio--the E/P or the EPS.

The _____ is quoted as a percentage, allowing an easy comparison to going bond rates.

a. Earnings yield   b. Assets turnover
c. Asset turnover   d. Average accounting return

34.

In finance, the _____ can be the expected rate of return above the risk-free interest rate. When measuring risk, a common sense approach is to compare the risk-free return on T-bills and the very risky return on other investments. The difference between these two returns can be interpreted as a measure of the excess return on the average risky asset. This excess return is known as the _____.

a. Risk adjusted return on capital   b. Risk aversion
c. Risk modeling   d. Risk premium

35.   In finance, the term _____ describes the amount in cash that returns to the owners of a security. Normally it does not include the price variations, at the difference of the total return. _____ applies to various stated rates of return on stocks (common and preferred, and convertible), fixed income instruments (bonds, notes, bills, strips, zero coupon), and some other investment type insurance products (e.g. annuities.)
a. 4-4-5 Calendar   b. Macaulay duration
c. Yield to maturity   d. Yield

36.   The _____ is the market for securities, where companies and governments can raise longterm funds. The _____ includes the stock market and the bond market. Financial regulators, such as the U.S. Securities and Exchange Commission, oversee the _____s in their designated countries to ensure that investors are protected against fraud.
a. Delta neutral   b. Capital market
c. Forward market   d. Spot rate

37.   The _____ of a stock is a measure of the price paid for a share relative to the annual income or profit earned by the firm per share. It is a financial ratio used for valuation: a higher _____ means that investors are paying more for each unit of income, so the stock is more expensive compared to one with lower _____.

The _____ has units of years, which can be interpreted as 'number of years of earnings to pay back purchase price'.

a. Quick ratio   b. P/E ratio
c. Sustainable growth rate   d. Return of capital

38.   The _____ is the tendency of the stock market to rise between December 31 and the end of the first week in January. There are many theories for why this happens, the main one being that it occurs because many investors choose to sell some of their stock right before the end of the year in order to claim a capital loss for tax purposes. Once the tax calendar rolls over to a new year on January 1st these same investors quickly reinvest their money in the market, causing stock prices to rise.

a. Death spiral financing

b. Sector rotation

c. Revaluation

d. January effect

39.   The institution most often referenced by the word '_____' is a public or publicly traded _____, the shares of which are traded on a public stock exchange (e.g., the New York Stock Exchange or Nasdaq in the United States) where shares of stock of _____s are bought and sold by and to the general public. Most of the largest businesses in the world are publicly traded _____s. However, the majority of _____s are said to be closely held, privately held or close _____s, meaning that no ready market exists for the trading of shares.

a. Depository Trust Company

b. Corporation

c. Federal Home Loan Mortgage Corporation

d. Protect

40.   _____ is a measure of the ability of a debtor to pay their debts as and when they fall due. It is usually expressed as a ratio or a percentage of current liabilities.

For a corporation with a published balance sheet there are various ratios used to calculate a measure of liquidity.

a. Accounting liquidity

b. Operating leverage

c. Operating profit margin

d. Invested capital

41.   In finance, the Acid-test or _____ or liquid ratio measures the ability of a company to use its near cash or quick assets to immediately extinguish or retire its current liabilities. Quick assets include those current assets that presumably can be quickly converted to cash at close to their book values.

Generally, the acid test ratio should be 1:1 or better, however this varies widely by industry.

a. Quick ratio

b. P/E ratio

c. Financial ratio

d. Net assets

42.   In accounting, _____ or *Carrying value* is the value of an asset according to its balance sheet account balance. For assets, the value is based on the original cost of the asset less any depreciation, amortization or impairment costs made against the asset. A company's _____ is its total assets minus intangible assets and liabilities.

a. Book value

b. Current liabilities

c. Retained earnings

d. Pro forma

43.   In finance, an _____ is the difference between the expected return of a security and the actual return. _____s are sometimes triggered by 'events.' Events can include mergers, dividend announcements, company earning announcements, interest rate increases, lawsuits, etc. all which can contribute to an _____.

a. Abnormal return

b. ABN Amro

c. A Random Walk Down Wall Street

d. AAB

44.   In economics and finance, _____ is the practice of taking advantage of a price differential between two or more markets: striking a combination of matching deals that capitalize upon the imbalance, the profit being the difference between the market prices. When used by academics, an _____ is a transaction that involves no negative cash flow at any probabilistic or temporal state and a positive cash flow in at least one state; in simple terms, a risk-free profit.

a. Initial margin   b. Arbitrage
c. Efficient-market hypothesis   d. Issuer

45.   _____ , in finance, is a general theory of asset pricing, that has become influential in the pricing of stocks.

_____ holds that the expected return of a financial asset can be modeled as a linear function of various macro-economic factors or theoretical market indices, where sensitivity to changes in each factor is represented by a factor-specific beta coefficient. The model-derived rate of return will then be used to price the asset correctly - the asset price should equal the expected end of period price discounted at the rate implied by model.

a. A Random Walk Down Wall Street   b. AAB
c. ABN Amro   d. Arbitrage pricing theory

46.   An _____ represents the ownership in the shares of a foreign company trading on US financial markets. The stock of many non-US companies trades on US exchanges through the use of _____s. _____s enable US investors to buy shares in foreign companies without undertaking cross-border transactions.

a. A Random Walk Down Wall Street   b. ABN Amro
c. American Depository Receipt   d. AAB

47.   _____ is an Israeli-American psychologist and Nobel laureate, notable for his work on behavioral finance and hedonic psychology.

With Amos Tversky and others, he established a cognitive basis for common human errors using heuristics and biases and developed Prospect theory. He was awarded the 2002 Nobel Prize in Economics for his work in Prospect theory.

a. Myron Samuel Scholes   b. Adolph Coors
c. Andrew Tobias   d. Daniel Kahneman

48.   _____ is a theory which assumes that restrictions placed upon funds, that would ordinarily be used by rational traders to arbitrage away pricing inefficiencies, leave prices in a non-equilibrium state for protracted periods of time.

The efficient market hypothesis assumes that whenever mispricing of a publicly-traded stock occurs as a result of an over-reaction to news, or some similar event, an opportuntity for low-risk profit is created for rational traders. The low-risk profit opportunity exists through the tool of arbitrage, which, briefly, is buying and selling differently priced items of the same value, and pocketing the difference.

a. Delta hedging   b. Forward market
c. Limits to Arbitrage   d. Market anomaly

49. _____ most frequently refers to the standard deviation of the continuously compounded returns of a financial instrument with a specific time horizon. It is often used to quantify the risk of the instrument over that time period. _____ is typically expressed in annualized terms, and it may either be an absolute number ($5) or a fraction of the mean (5%).

a. Portfolio insurance
b. Seasoned equity offering
c. Currency swap
d. Volatility

50. The _____ of a statistical sample is the number of observations that constitute it. It is typically denoted n, a positive integer (natural number.)

Typically, all else being equal, a larger _____ leads to increased precision in estimates of various properties of the population.

a. Sample size
b. Harmonic mean
c. Correlation
d. Frequency distribution

51. The _____ Options Exchange is a futures exchange based in London. _____ is now part of NYSE Euronext following its takeover by Euronext in January 2002 and Euronext's merger with New York Stock Exchange in April 2007.

The _____ started life on September 30, 1982, to take advantage of the removal of currency controls in the UK in 1979.

a. 529 plan
b. 4-4-5 Calendar
c. 7-Eleven
d. LIFFE

52. In economics, business, and accounting, a _____ is the value of money that has been used up to produce something, and hence is not available for use anymore. In business, the _____ may be one of acquisition, in which case the amount of money expended to acquire it is counted as _____. In this case, money is the input that is gone in order to acquire the thing.

a. Fixed costs
b. Marginal cost
c. Sliding scale fees
d. Cost

53. A concept first named by Richard Thaler (1980), _____ attempts to describe the process whereby people code, categorize and evaluate economic outcomes. _____ theorists argue that people group their assets into a number of non-fungible mental accounts.

One detailed application of _____, the behavioral life cycle hypothesis (Shefrin ' Thaler, 1988), posits that people mentally frame assets as belonging to either current income, current wealth or future income and this has implications for their behavior as the accounts are largely non-fungible and marginal propensity to consume out of each account is different.

a. Mental accounting
b. Quantitative behavioral finance
c. Disposition effect
d. Psychological level

54. In business, investment, and accounting, the principle or convention of _____ has at least two meanings.

In investment and finance, it is a strategy which aims at long-term capital appreciation with low risk. It can be characterized as moderate or cautious and is the opposite of aggressive behavior.

a. Conservatism
c. Debt-snowball method

b. Duration gap
d. Barcampbank

55. _____ is a risk-adjusted measure of the so-called active return on an investment. It is the return in excess of the compensation for the risk borne, and thus commonly used to assess active managers' performances. Often, the return of a benchmark is subtracted in order to consider relative performance, which yields Jensen's _____.

a. Amortization
c. Option

b. Annuity
d. Alpha

56. A _____ is a professionally managed type of collective investment scheme that pools money from many investors and invests it in stocks, bonds, short-term money market instruments, and/or other securities. The _____ will have a fund manager that trades the pooled money on a regular basis. Currently, the worldwide value of all _____s totals more than $26 trillion.

Since 1940, there have been three basic types of investment companies in the United States: open-end funds, also known in the US as _____s; unit investment trusts (UITs); and closed-end funds.

a. Net asset value
c. Financial intermediary

b. Trust company
d. Mutual fund

57. In finance, the _____ is used to determine a theoretically appropriate required rate of return of an asset, if that asset is to be added to an already well-diversified portfolio, given that asset's non-diversifiable risk. The model takes into account the asset's sensitivity to non-diversifiable risk (also known as systemic risk or market risk), often represented by the quantity beta (β) in the financial industry, as well as the expected return of the market and the expected return of a theoretical risk-free asset.

The model was introduced by Jack Treynor (1961, 1962), William Sharpe (1964), John Lintner (1965a,b) and Jan Mossin (1966) independently, building on the earlier work of Harry Markowitz on diversification and modern portfolio theory.

a. Hull-White model
c. Cox-Ingersoll-Ross model

b. Random walk hypothesis
d. Capital asset pricing model

58. The _____ is a financial market where participants buy and sell debt securities, usually in the form of bonds. As of 2006, the size of the international _____ is an estimated $45 trillion, of which the size of the outstanding U.S. _____ debt was $25.2 trillion.

Nearly all of the $923 billion average daily trading volume in the U.S. _____ takes place between broker-dealers and large institutions in a decentralized, over-the-counter market.

a. Bond market

b. 4-4-5 Calendar

c. Fixed income

d. 529 plan

1.   In finance, a _____ is a debt security, in which the authorized issuer owes the holders a debt and, depending on the terms of the _____, is obliged to pay interest (the coupon) and/or to repay the principal at a later date, termed maturity.

Thus a _____ is a loan: the issuer is the borrower, the _____ holder is the lender, and the coupon is the interest. _____s provide the borrower with external funds to finance long-term investments, or, in the case of government _____s, to finance current expenditure.

a. Convertible bond   b. Catastrophe bonds
c. Bond   d. Puttable bond

2.   _____ are dollar-denominated bonds, issued mostly by Latin American countries in the 1980s, named after U.S. Treasury Secretary Nicholas Brady.

_____ were created in March 1989 in order to convert bonds issued by mostly Latin American countries into a variety or 'menu' of new bonds after many of those countries defaulted on their debt in the 1980's. At that time, the market for sovereign debt was small and illiquid, and the standardization of emerging-market debt facilitated risk-spreading and trading.

a. Municipal bond   b. Coupon rate
c. Nominal yield   d. Brady bonds

3.   The coupon or _____ of a bond is the amount of interest paid per year expressed as a percentage of the face value of the bond.

For example if you hold $10,000 nominal of a bond described as a 4.5% loan stock, you will receive $450 in interest each year (probably in two installments of $225 each.)

Not all bonds have coupons.

a. Revenue bonds   b. Zero-coupon bond
c. Puttable bond   d. Coupon rate

4.   _____ is that which is owed; usually referencing assets owed, but the term can cover other obligations. In the case of assets, _____ is a means of using future purchasing power in the present before a summation has been earned. Some companies and corporations use _____ as a part of their overall corporate finance strategy.
a. Cross-collateralization   b. Credit cycle
c. Partial Payment   d. Debt

5.   _____ refers to any type of investment that yields a regular (or fixed) return.

For example, if you lend money to a borrower and the borrower has to pay interest once a month, you have been issued a fixed-income security. When a company does this, it is often called a bond or corporate bank debt (although preferred stock is also sometimes considered to be _____).

a. 529 plan	b. 4-4-5 Calendar
c. Bond market	d. Fixed income

6. A _____ is a fungible, negotiable instrument representing financial value. They are broadly categorized into debt securities (such as banknotes, bonds and debentures), and equity securities; e.g., common stocks. The company or other entity issuing the _____ is called the issuer.

a. Tracking stock	b. Book entry
c. Securities lending	d. Security

7. In finance, _____ is the interest that has accumulated since the principal investment, or since the previous interest payment if there has been one already. For a financial instrument such as a bond, interest is calculated and paid in set intervals.

The primary formula for calculating the interest accrued in a given period is:

$$I_A = T \times P \times R$$

where I_A is the _____, T is the fraction of the year, P is the principal, and R is the annualized interest rate.

a. ABN Amro	b. Accrued interest
c. A Random Walk Down Wall Street	d. AAB

8. _____ offer, asking price is a price a seller of a good is willing to accept for that particular good.

In bid and ask, the term _____ is used in contrast to the term bid price. The difference between the _____ and the bid price is called the spread.

a. Interest rate parity	b. A Random Walk Down Wall Street
c. AAB	d. Ask price

9. A _____ is the highest price that a buyer (i.e., bidder) is willing to pay for a good. It is usually referred to simply as the 'bid.'

In bid and ask, the _____ stands in contrast to the ask price or 'offer', and the difference between the two is called the bid/ask spread.

An unsolicited bid or offer is when a person or company receives a bid even though they are not looking to sell.

a. Political risk	b. Bid price
c. Settlement date	d. Mid price

10. _____ (also trust indenture or deed of trust) is a legal document issued to lenders and describes key terms such as the interest rate, maturity date, convertibility, pledge, promises, representations, covenants, and other terms of the bond offering. When the Offering Memorandum is prepared in advance of marketing a Bond, the indenture will typically be summarised in the 'Description of Notes' section.

a. McFadden Act

b. Fair Labor Standards Act

c. Court of Audit of Belgium

d. Bond indenture

11. _____s are deposits denominated in United States dollars at banks outside the United States, and thus are not under the jurisdiction of the Federal Reserve. Consequently, such deposits are subject to much less regulation than similar deposits within the United States, allowing for higher margins. There is nothing 'European' about _____ deposits; a US dollar-denominated deposit in Tokyo or Caracas would likewise be deemed _____ deposits.

a. A Random Walk Down Wall Street

b. AAB

c. ABN Amro

d. Eurodollar

12. _____ is a fee paid on borrowed assets. It is the price paid for the use of borrowed money , or, money earned by deposited funds . Assets that are sometimes lent with _____ include money, shares, consumer goods through hire purchase, major assets such as aircraft, and even entire factories in finance lease arrangements.

a. AAB

b. Interest

c. A Random Walk Down Wall Street

d. Insolvency

13. An _____ or bill is a commercial document issued by a seller to the buyer, indicating the products, quantities, and agreed prices for products or services the seller has provided the buyer. An _____ indicates the buyer must pay the seller, according to the payment terms.

In the rental industry, an _____ must include a specific reference to the duration of the time being billed, so rather than quantity, price and discount the invoicing amount is based on quantity, price, discount and duration.

a. ABN Amro

b. A Random Walk Down Wall Street

c. AAB

d. Invoice

14. _____, in finance and accounting, means stated value or face value. From this comes the expressions at par (at the _____), over par (over _____) and under par (under _____.)

The term '_____' has several meanings depending on context and geography.

a. Sinking fund

b. FIDC

c. Global Squeeze

d. Par value

15. _____ are government bonds issued by the United States Department of the Treasury through the Bureau of the Public Debt. They are the debt financing instruments of the U.S. Federal government, and they are often referred to simply as Treasuries or Treasurys. There are four types of marketable _____: Treasury bills, Treasury notes, Treasury bonds, and Treasury Inflation Protected Securities (TIPS.)

a. 4-4-5 Calendar

b. Treasury Inflation-Protected Securities

c. Treasury Inflation Protected Securities

d. Treasury securities

16.   A _____ is a bond bought at a price lower than its face value, with the face value repaid at the time of maturity. It does not make periodic interest payments, or have so-called 'coupons,' hence the term _____. Investors earn return from the compounded interest all paid at maturity plus the difference between the discounted price of the bond and its par value.
  a. Clean price   b. Bond fund
  c. Corporate bond   d. Zero-coupon bond

17.   An _____ represents the ownership in the shares of a foreign company trading on US financial markets. The stock of many non-US companies trades on US exchanges through the use of _____s. _____s enable US investors to buy shares in foreign companies without undertaking cross-border transactions.
  a. American Depository Receipt   b. ABN Amro
  c. A Random Walk Down Wall Street   d. AAB

18.   A _____ is a document that indicates that the bearer of the document has title to property, such as shares or bonds. They differ from normal registered instruments, in that no records are kept of who owns the underlying property, or of the transactions involving transfer of ownership. Whoever physically holds the bearer bond papers owns the property.
  a. Marketable   b. Bearer instrument
  c. Book entry   d. Securities lending

19.   A _____ is different from normal stock in that it is unregistered - no records are kept of the owner, or the transactions involving ownership. Whoever physically holds the _____ papers owns the stock or corporation. This is useful for investors and corporate officers who wish to retain anonymity.
  a. Revenue bonds   b. Gilts
  c. Bearer bond   d. Clean price

20.   The _____ is a financial market where participants buy and sell debt securities, usually in the form of bonds. As of 2006, the size of the international _____ is an estimated $45 trillion, of which the size of the outstanding U.S. _____ debt was $25.2 trillion.

Nearly all of the $923 billion average daily trading volume in the U.S. _____ takes place between broker-dealers and large institutions in a decentralized, over-the-counter market.

  a. Fixed income   b. 4-4-5 Calendar
  c. 529 plan   d. Bond market

21.   _____ is a type of bond that allows the issuer of the bond to retain the privilege of redeeming the bond at some point before the bond reaches the date of maturity. In other words, on the call dates, the issuer has the right, but not the obligation, to buy back the bonds from the bond holders at the call price. Technically speaking, the bonds are not really bought and held by the issuer but cancelled immediately.
  a. Bond fund   b. Coupon rate
  c. Gilts   d. Callable bond

22.   A _____ is a bond issued by a corporation. The term is usually applied to longer-term debt instruments, generally with a maturity date falling at least a year after their issue date. (The term 'commercial paper' is sometimes used for instruments with a shorter maturity.)

a. Brady bonds   b. Corporate bond
c. Government bond   d. Serial bond

23. _____ is the provision of resources (such as granting a loan) by one party to another party where that second party does not reimburse the first party immediately, thereby generating a debt, and instead arranges either to repay or return those resources (or material(s) of equal value) at a later date. The first party is called a creditor, also known as a lender, while the second party is called a debtor, also known as a borrower.

Movements of financial capital are normally dependent on either _____ or equity transfers.

a. Warrant   b. Comparable
c. Clearing house   d. Credit

24. _____ is the risk of loss due to a debtor's non-payment of a loan or other line of credit (either the principal or interest (coupon) or both)

Most lenders employ their own models (credit scorecards) to rank potential and existing customers according to risk, and then apply appropriate strategies. With products such as unsecured personal loans or mortgages, lenders charge a higher price for higher risk customers and vice versa. With revolving products such as credit cards and overdrafts, risk is controlled through careful setting of credit limits.

a. Market risk   b. Liquidity risk
c. Credit risk   d. Transaction risk

25. _____, in accrual accounting, is any account where the asset or liability is not realized until a future date, e.g. annuities, charges, taxes, income, etc. The _____ item may be carried, dependent on type of deferral, as either an asset or liability.See also: accrual

_____ is also used in the university admissions process. It is the action by which a school rejects a student for early admission but still opts to review that student in the general admissions pool.

a. Current asset   b. Revenue
c. Net profit   d. Deferred

26. The _____ is a stock exchange based in New York City, New York. It is the largest stock exchange in the world by dollar value of its listed companies securities. As of October 2008, the combined capitalization of all domestic _____ listed companies was $10.1 trillion.
a. 529 plan   b. 4-4-5 Calendar
c. 7-Eleven   d. New York Stock Exchange

27. _____ occurs when an entity that has issued callable bonds calls those debt securities from the debt holders with the express purpose of reissuing new debt at a lower coupon rate. In essence, the issue of new, lower-interest debt allows the company to prematurely refund the older, higher-interest debt.

On the contrary, NonRefundable Bonds may be callable but they cannot be re-issued with a lower coupon rate.

a. No-arbitrage bounds	b. Market neutral
c. Refunding	d. Systematic risk

28.   A _____, securities exchange or (in Europe) bourse is a corporation or mutual organization which provides 'trading' facilities for stock brokers and traders, to trade stocks and other securities. _____s also provide facilities for the issue and redemption of securities as well as other financial instruments and capital events including the payment of income and dividends. The securities traded on a _____ include: shares issued by companies, unit trusts and other pooled investment products and bonds.

a. 529 plan	b. 4-4-5 Calendar
c. Stock Exchange	d. 7-Eleven

29.   In financial accounting, _____s are precautions for which the amount or probability of occurrence are not known. Typical examples are _____s for warranty costs and _____ for taxes the term reserve is used instead of term _____; such a use, however, is inconsistent with the terminology suggested by International Accounting Standards Board.

a. Momentum Accounting and Triple-Entry Bookkeeping	b. Money measurement concept
c. Provision	d. Petty cash

30.   In finance, a _____ is a type of bond that can be converted into shares of stock in the issuing company, usually at some pre-announced ratio. It is a hybrid security with debt- and equity-like features. Although it typically has a low coupon rate, the holder is compensated with the ability to convert the bond to common stock, usually at a substantial discount to the stock's market value.

a. Gilts	b. Corporate bond
c. Bond fund	d. Convertible bond

31.   A _____ is a payment made by a corporation to its shareholder members. When a corporation earns a profit or surplus, that money can be put to two uses: it can either be re-invested in the business (called retained earnings), or it can be paid to the shareholders as a _____. Many corporations retain a portion of their earnings and pay the remainder as a _____.

a. Special dividend	b. Dividend yield
c. Dividend puzzle	d. Dividend

32.   _____ is typically a higher ranking stock than voting shares, and its terms are negotiated between the corporation and the investor.

_____ usually carry no voting rights, but may carry superior priority over common stock in the payment of dividends and upon liquidation. _____ may carry a dividend that is paid out prior to any dividends to common stock holders.

a. Follow-on offering	b. Trade-off theory
c. Second lien loan	d. Preferred stock

33.   _____ is a combination of straight bond and embedded put option. The holder of the _____ has the right, but not the obligation, to demand early repayment of the principal. The put option is usually exercisable on specified dates.

a. Brady bonds   b. Callable bond
c. Convertible bond   d. Puttable bond

34.   In finance, the Acid-test or _____ or liquid ratio measures the ability of a company to use its near cash or quick
assets to immediately extinguish or retire its current liabilities. Quick assets include those current assets that presumably can be
quickly converted to cash at close to their book values.

Generally, the acid test ratio should be 1:1 or better, however this varies widely by industry.

a. P/E ratio   b. Financial ratio
c. Net assets   d. Quick ratio

35.   _____ are those dividends paid out in form of additional stock shares of the issuing corporation or other corporation
They are usually issued in proportion to shares owned (for example for every 100 shares of stock owned, 5% stock dividend will
yield 5 extra shares). If this payment involves the issue of new shares, this is very similar to a stock split in that it increases the
total number of shares while lowering the price of each share and does not change the market capitalization or the total value of
the shares held
a. Database auditing   b. Time-based currency
c. Stock or scrip dividends   d. The Hong Kong Securities Institute

36.   A _____ is an international bond that is denominated in a currency not native to the country where it is issued. It can
be categorised according to the currency in which it is issued. London is one of the centers of the _____ market, but
_____s may be traded throughout the world - for example in Singapore or Tokyo.
a. Eurobond   b. Interest rate option
c. Education production function   d. Economic entity

37.   A _____ is an annuity in which the periodic payments begin on a fixed date and continue indefinitely. It is sometimes
referred to as a perpetual annuity. Fixed coupon payments on permanently invested (irredeemable) sums of money are prime
examples of these. Scholarships paid perpetually from an endowment fit the definition of _____.
a. LIBOR market model   b. Stochastic volatility
c. Current yield   d. Perpetuity

38.   _____ are asset-backed securities of current and future revenues of the first 25 albums (287 songs) of David
Bowie's collection recorded before 1990. Issued by David Bowie in 1997, they were bought for $55 million by the Prudential
Insurance Company. The 287 included songs also acted as collateral to insure the bond.
a. Clean price   b. Corporate bond
c. Revenue bonds   d. Bowie bonds

39.   _____ are risk-linked securities that transfer a specified set of risks from a sponsor to investors. They are often
structured as floating rate corporate bonds whose principal is forgiven if specified trigger conditions are met. They are typically
used by insurers as an alternative to traditional catastrophe reinsurance.

a. Clean price   b. Brady bonds
c. Catastrophe bonds   d. Callable bond

40.   In economics, _____ is a rise in the general level of prices of goods and services in an economy over a period of time. The term '_____' once referred to increases in the money supply (monetary _____); however, economic debates about the relationship between money supply and price levels have led to its primary use today in describing price _____. _____ can also be described as a decline in the real value of money--a loss of purchasing power in the medium of exchange which is also the monetary unit of account.
   a. ABN Amro   b. AAB
   c. A Random Walk Down Wall Street   d. Inflation

41.   An _____ is a type of bond or other type of debt instrument used in finance whose coupon rate has an inverse relationship to short-term interest rates (or its reference rate.) With an _____, as interest rates rise the coupon rate falls. The basic structure is the same as an ordinary floating rate note except for the direction in which the coupon rate is adjusted.
   a. ABN Amro   b. A Random Walk Down Wall Street
   c. AAB   d. Inverse floater

42.   Treasury securities are government bonds issued by the United States Department of the Treasury through the Bureau of the Public Debt. They are the debt financing instruments of the U.S. Federal government, and they are often referred to simply as Treasuries or Treasurys. There are four types of marketable treasury securities: Treasury bills, Treasury notes, Treasury bonds, and _____ (_____.)
   a. Treasury Inflation Protected Securities   b. 4-4-5 Calendar
   c. Treasury Inflation-Protected Securities   d. Treasury securities

43.   _____ are bonds that have a variable coupon, equal to a money market reference rate, like LIBOR or federal funds rate, plus a spread. The spread is a rate that remains constant. Almost all _____ have quarterly coupons, i.e. they pay out interest every three months, though counter examples do exist.
   a. CVECAs   b. Loan participation
   c. Gordon growth model   d. Floating rate notes

44.   An _____ can be defined as a contract which provides an income stream in return for an initial payment.

An immediate _____ is an _____ for which the time between the contract date and the date of the first payment is not longer than the time interval between payments. A common use for an immediate _____ is to provide a pension to a retired person or persons.

   a. Amortization   b. AT'T Inc.
   c. Intrinsic value   d. Annuity

45.   _____ is the value on a given date of a future payment or series of future payments, discounted to reflect the time value of money and other factors such as investment risk. _____ calculations are widely used in business and economics to provide a means to compare cash flows at different times on a meaningful 'like to like' basis.

The most commonly applied model of the time value of money is compound interest.

a. Negative gearing

b. Present value

c. Present value of benefits

d. Net present value

46. In finance, _____, also known as return on investment is the ratio of money gained or lost on an investment relative to the amount of money invested. The amount of money gained or lost may be referred to as interest, profit/loss, gain/loss, or net income/loss. The money invested may be referred to as the asset, capital, principal, or the cost basis of the investment.

a. Composiition of Creditors

b. Rate of return

c. Doctrine of the Proper Law

d. Stock or scrip dividends

47. The _____ is the financial market where previously issued securities and financial instruments such as stock, bonds, options, and futures are bought and sold. The term '_____' is also used refer to the market for any used goods or assets, or an alternative use for an existing product or asset where the customer base is the second market

With primary issuances of securities or financial instruments, or the primary market, investors purchase these securities directly from issuers such as corporations issuing shares in an IPO or private placement, or directly from the federal government in the case of treasuries.

a. Performance attribution

b. Delta neutral

c. Financial market

d. Secondary market

48. In finance, the term _____ describes the amount in cash that returns to the owners of a security. Normally it does not include the price variations, at the difference of the total return. _____ applies to various stated rates of return on stocks (common and preferred, and convertible), fixed income instruments (bonds, notes, bills, strips, zero coupon), and some other investment type insurance products (e.g. annuities.)

a. Yield to maturity

b. Yield

c. 4-4-5 Calendar

d. Macaulay duration

49. _____ is a securities industry term describing the date on which a trade (bonds, equities, foreign exchange, commodities etc) settles. That is, the actual day on which transfer of cash or assets is completed.

It is not necessarily the same as value date (when the settlement amount is calculated.)

a. Single-index model

b. Mid price

c. Political risk

d. Settlement date

50. The _____ for an investment is a calculated annual yield for an investment, which may not pay out yearly. This allows investments which payout with different frequencies to be compared.

a. 529 plan

b. 4-4-5 Calendar

c. 7-Eleven

d. Bond equivalent yield

51. The _____ is a capital budgeting metric used by firms to decide whether they should make investments. It is an indicator of the efficiency or quality of an investment, as opposed to net present value (NPV), which indicates value or magnitude.

The IRR is the annualized effective compounded return rate which can be earned on the invested capital, i.e., the yield on the investment.

a. A Random Walk Down Wall Street

b. ABN Amro

c. Internal rate of return

d. AAB

52.   The _____ or redemption yield is the yield promised to the bondholder on the assumption that the bond or other fixed-interest security such as gilts will be held to maturity, that all coupon and principal payments will be made and coupon payments are reinvested at the bond's promised yield at the same rate as invested. It is a measure of the return of the bond. This technique in theory allows investors to calculate the fair value of different financial instruments.

a. Yield

b. 4-4-5 Calendar

c. Macaulay duration

d. Yield to maturity

53.   _____ is a life of security. It may also refer to the final payment date of a loan or other financial instrument, at which point all remaining interest and principal is due to be paid.

1, 3, 6 months _____ band can be calculated by using 30-day per month periods.

a. False billing

b. Replacement cost

c. Primary market

d. Maturity

54.   The _____, interest yield, income yield, flat yield or running yield is a financial term used in reference to bonds and other fixed-interest securities such as gilts. It is the ratio of the annual interest payment and the bond's current price.

The _____ only therefore refers to the yield of the bond at the current moment. It does not reflect the total return over the life of the bond. In particular, it takes no account of reinvestment risk (the uncertainty about the rate at which future cashflows can be reinvested) or the fact that bonds usually mature at par value, which can be an important component of a bond's return.

a. Modified Internal Rate of Return

b. Perpetuity

c. Stochastic volatility

d. Current yield

55.   A '_____' is a 'Charge' that is paid to obtain the right to delay a payment. Essentially, the payer purchases the right to make a given payment in the future instead of in the Present. The '_____', or 'Charge' that must be paid to delay the payment, is simply the difference between what the payment amount would be if it were paid in the present and what the payment amount would be paid if it were paid in the future.

a. Discount

b. Risk modeling

c. Value at risk

d. Risk aversion

56.   A _____ is a bond bought at a price lower than its face value, with the face value repaid at the time of maturity. It does not make periodic interest payments, or so-called 'coupons,' hence the term zero-coupon bond. Investors earn return from the compounded interest all paid at maturity plus the difference between the discounted price of the bond and its par value.

a. Bowie bonds
c. Municipal bond

b. Callable bond
d. Zero coupon bond

57.   A _____ is a generic term for any bond selling for more than 100% of par value, i.e., at a price greater than 100.00, which typically occurs for high coupon bonds in a falling interest rate climate.

a. Revenue bonds
c. Municipal bond

b. Nominal yield
d. Premium bond

58.   An _____ is the price a borrower pays for the use of money they do not own, and the return a lender receives for deferring the use of funds, by lending it to the borrower. _____s are normally expressed as a percentage rate over the period of one year.

_____s targets are also a vital tool of monetary policy and are used to control variables like investment, inflation, and unemployment.

a. ABN Amro
c. A Random Walk Down Wall Street

b. AAB
d. Interest rate

59.   In economic models, the _____ time frame assumes no fixed factors of production. Firms can enter or leave the marketplace, and the cost (and availability) of land, labor, raw materials, and capital goods can be assumed to vary. In contrast, in the short-run time frame, certain factors are assumed to be fixed, because there is not sufficient time for them to change.

a. 529 plan
c. Long-run

b. Short-run
d. 4-4-5 Calendar

60.   In business, _____ is income that a company receives from its normal business activities, usually from the sale of goods and services to customers. Some companies also receive _____ from interest, dividends or royalties paid to them by other companies. _____ may refer to business income in general, or it may refer to the amount, in a monetary unit, received during a period of time, as in 'Last year, Company X had _____ of $32 million.'

In many countries, including the UK, _____ is referred to as turnover.

a. Bottom line
c. Revenue

b. Matching principle
d. Furniture, Fixtures and Equipment

61.   In economics, the concept of the _____ refers to the decision-making time frame of a firm in which at least one factor of production is fixed. Costs which are fixed in the _____ have no impact on a firms decisions. For example a firm can raise output by increasing the amount of labour through overtime.

a. 529 plan
c. 4-4-5 Calendar

b. Long-run
d. Short-run

62.   _____ mature in one year or less. Like zero-coupon bonds, they do not pay interest prior to maturity; instead they are sold at a discount of the par value to create a positive yield to maturity. Many regard _____ as the least risky investment available to U.S. investors.

a. Treasury Inflation Protected Securities   b. 4-4-5 Calendar
c. Treasury securities   d. Treasury bills

63.   The institution most often referenced by the word '_____' is a public or publicly traded _____, the shares of
which are traded on a public stock exchange (e.g., the New York Stock Exchange or Nasdaq in the United States) where shares
of stock of _____s are bought and sold by and to the general public. Most of the largest businesses in the world are
publicly traded _____s. However, the majority of _____s are said to be closely held, privately held or close
_____s, meaning that no ready market exists for the trading of shares.
   a. Protect   b. Depository Trust Company
   c. Federal Home Loan Mortgage Corporation   d. Corporation

64.   In finance, _____ occurs when a debtor has not met its legal obligations according to the debt contract, e.g. it has
not made a scheduled payment, or has violated a loan covenant (condition) of the debt contract. _____ may occur if the
debtor is either unwilling or unable to pay their debt. This can occur with all debt obligations including bonds, mortgages, loans,
and promissory notes.
   a. Vendor finance   b. Debt validation
   c. Credit crunch   d. Default

65.   The value of speculative bonds is affected to a higher degree than investment grade bonds by the possibility of default.
For example, in a recession interest rates may drop, and the drop in interest rates tends to increase the value of investment
grade bonds; however, a recession tends to increase the possibility of default in speculative-grade bonds.

The original speculative grade bonds were bonds that once had been investment grade at time of issue, but where the credit
rating of the issuer had slipped and the possibility of default increased significantly. These bonds are called '_____'.

   a. Seed round   b. Return on capital employed
   c. Fallen angels   d. Sharpe ratio

66.   In finance, a _____ (non-investment grade bond, speculative grade bond or junk bond) is a bond that is rated below
investment grade at the time of purchase. These bonds have a higher risk of default or other adverse credit events, but typically
pay higher yields than better quality bonds in order to make them attractive to investors.
   a. Sharpe ratio   b. High yield bond
   c. Volatility   d. Private equity

67.   A bond is considered _____ if its credit rating is BBB- or higher by Standard and Poor's or Baa3 or higher by
Moody's or BBB(low) or higher by DBRS. Generally they are bonds that are judged by the rating agency as likely enough to
meet payment obligations that banks are allowed to invest in them.

Ratings play a critical role in determining how much companies and other entities that issue debt, including sovereign
governments, have to pay to access credit markets, i.e., the amount of interest they pay on their issued debt.

   a. ABN Amro   b. AAB
   c. A Random Walk Down Wall Street   d. Investment grade

68.   The _____ is a financial ratio that measures whether or not a firm has enough resources to pay its debts over the next 12 months. It compares a firm's current assets to its current liabilities. It is expressed as follows:

$$\text{Current ratio} = \frac{\text{Current Assets}}{\text{Current Liabilities}}$$

For example, if WXY Company's current assets are $50,000,000 and its current liabilities are $40,000,000, then its _____ would be $50,000,000 divided by $40,000,000, which equals 1.25.

a. PEG ratio   b. Current ratio
c. Debt service coverage ratio   d. Sustainable growth rate

69.   In finance, _____ (or gearing) is borrowing money to supplement existing funds for investment in such a way that the potential positive or negative outcome is magnified and/or enhanced. It generally refers to using borrowed funds, or debt, so as to attempt to increase the returns to equity. Deleveraging is the action of reducing borrowings.

a. Financial endowment   b. Pension fund
c. Limited partnership   d. Leverage

70.   A _____ occurs when a financial sponsor acquires a controlling interest in a company's equity and where a significant percentage of the purchase price is financed through leverage (borrowing.) The assets of the acquired company are used as collateral for the borrowed capital, sometimes with assets of the acquiring company. The bonds or other paper issued for _____s are commonly considered not to be investment grade because of the significant risks involved.

a. Limited partnership   b. Leveraged buyout
c. Leverage   d. Pension fund

71.   _____ is a measure of the ability of a debtor to pay their debts as and when they fall due. It is usually expressed as a ratio or a percentage of current liabilities.

For a corporation with a published balance sheet there are various ratios used to calculate a measure of liquidity.

a. Accounting liquidity   b. Invested capital
c. Operating profit margin   d. Operating leverage

72.   The _____ percentage shows how profitable a company's assets are in generating revenue.

_____ can be computed as:

$$\text{ROA} = \frac{\text{Net Income}}{\text{Total Assets}}$$

This number tells you 'what the company can do with what it's got', i.e. how many dollars of earnings they derive from each dollar of assets they control. It's a useful number for comparing competing companies in the same industry.

a. P/E ratio   b. Return on sales
c. Receivables turnover ratio   d. Return on assets

73.   In business and accounting, _____s are everything of value that is owned by a person or company. The balance sheet of a firm records the monetary value of the _____s owned by the firm. The two major _____ classes are tangible _____s and intangible _____s.
a. EBITDA   b. Asset
c. Accounts payable   d. Income

74.   In lending agreements, _____ is a borrower's pledge of specific property to a lender, to secure repayment of a loan. The _____ serves as protection for a lender against a borrower's risk of default - that is, a borrower failing to pay the principal and interest under the terms of a loan obligation. If a borrower does default on a loan (due to insolvency or other event), that borrower forfeits (gives up) the property pledged as _____ *ollateral* - and the lender then becomes the owner of the _____.
a. Refinancing risk   b. Nominal value
c. Collateral   d. Future-oriented

75.   An _____ (or business indicator) is a statistic about the economy. _____s allow analysis of economic performance and predictions of future performance.

_____s include various indices, earnings reports, and economic summaries, such as unemployment, housing starts, Consumer Price Index (a measure for inflation), industrial production, bankruptcies, Gross Domestic Product, broadband internet penetration, retail sales, stock market prices, and money supply changes.

a. Economic indicator   b. A Random Walk Down Wall Street
c. ABN Amro   d. AAB

76.   In business, a _____ is the purchase of one company (the target) by another (the acquirer or bidder). In the UK the term refers to the acquisition of a public company whose shares are listed on a stock exchange, in contrast to the acquisition of a private company.

Before a bidder makes an offer for another company, it usually first informs that company's board of directors.

a. 4-4-5 Calendar   b. 529 plan
c. Stock swap   d. Takeover

77.   _____ or interest coverage ratio is a measure of a company's ability to honor its debt payments. It may be calculated as either EBIT or EBITDA divided by the total interest payable.

$$\text{Times-Interest-Earned} = \frac{\text{EBIT or EBITDA}}{\text{Interest Charges}}$$

- Financial ratio
- Financial leverage
- EBIT
- EBITDA
- Debt service coverage ratio

Interest Charges = Traditionally 'charges' refers to interest expense found on the income statement.

_____ or Interest Coverage is a great tool when measuring a company's ability to meet its debt obligations.

a. Return of capital

b. Cash conversion cycle

c. Net assets

d. Times interest earned

78. In finance, a _____ or accounting ratio is a ratio of two selected numerical values taken from an enterprise's financial statements. There are many standard ratios used to try to evaluate the overall financial condition of a corporation or other organization. They may be used by managers within a firm, by current and potential shareholders (owners) of a firm, and by a firm's creditors. Security analysts use these to compare the strengths and weaknesses in various companies.

a. Sustainable growth rate

b. Price/cash flow ratio

c. Return on capital employed

d. Financial ratio

79. _____s are financial bonds that mature in installments over a period of time. In effect, a $100,000, 5-year _____ would mature in a $20,000 annuity over a 5-year interval. Bond issues consisting of a series of blocks of securities maturing in sequence, the coupon rate can be different.

a. Callable bond

b. Bond fund

c. Serial bond

d. Brady bonds

80. In finance, _____ is debt which ranks after other debts should a company fall into receivership or be closed.

Such debt is referred to as subordinate, because the debt providers have subordinate status in relationship to the normal debt. A typical example for this would be when a promoter of a company invests money in the form of debt, rather than in the form of stock.

a. Credit rating

b. Participation loan

c. Cross-collateralization

d. Subordinated debt

81. In accounting, _____ or *Carrying value* is the value of an asset according to its balance sheet account balance. For assets, the value is based on the original cost of the asset less any depreciation, amortization or impairment costs made against the asset. A company's _____ is its total assets minus intangible assets and liabilities.

a. Current liabilities

b. Retained earnings

c. Pro forma

d. Book value

82.   An _____ is a contract written by a seller that conveys to the buyer the right -- but not the obligation -- to buy (in the case of a call _____) or to sell (in the case of a put _____) a particular asset, such as a piece of property such as, among others, a futures contract. In return for granting the _____, the seller collects a payment (the premium) from the buyer.

For example, buying a call _____ provides the right to buy a specified quantity of a security at a set strike price at some time on or before expiration, while buying a put _____ provides the right to sell.

a. Amortization   b. AT'T Mobility LLC
c. Annuity   d. Option

83.   A _____ is a fund established by a government agency or business for the purpose of reducing debt.

The _____ was first used in Great Britain in the 18th century to reduce national debt. While used by Robert Walpole in 1716 and effectively in the 1720s and early 1730s, it originated in the commercial tax syndicates of the Italian peninsula of the 14th century to retire redeemable public debt of those cities.

a. Security interest   b. Debtor
c. Sinking fund   d. Modern portfolio theory

84.   A _____, in its most general sense, is a solemn promise to engage in or refrain from a specified action.

More specifically, a _____, in contrast to a contract, is a one-way agreement whereby the _____er is the only party bound by the promise. A _____ may have conditions and prerequisites that qualify the undertaking, including the actions of second or third parties, but there is no inherent agreement by such other parties to fulfill those requirements.

a. Partnership   b. Clayton Antitrust Act
c. Federal Trade Commission Act   d. Covenant

85.   A _____ is defined as a certificate of agreement of loans which is given under the company's stamp and carries an undertaking that the _____ holder will get a fixed return (fixed on the basis of interest rates) and the principal amount whenever the _____ matures.

In finance, a _____ is a long-term debt instrument used by governments and large companies to obtain funds. It is defined as 'a debt secured only by the debtor's earning power, not by a lien on any specific asset.' It is similar to a bond except the securitization conditions are different.

a. Collection agency   b. Partial Payment
c. Debenture   d. Collateral Management

86.   In finance, the yield curve is the relation between the interest rate (or cost of borrowing) and the time to maturity of the debt for a given borrower in a given currency. For example, the current U.S. dollar interest rates paid on U.S. Treasury securities for various maturities are closely watched by many traders, and are commonly plotted on a graph such as the one on the right which is informally called 'the yield curve.' More formal mathematical descriptions of this relation are often called the _____.

The yield of a debt instrument is the annualized percentage increase in the value of the investment.

a. 7-Eleven   b. Term structure of interest rates
c. 4-4-5 Calendar   d. 529 plan

87.   In finance, the _____ is the relation between the interest rate (or cost of borrowing) and the time to maturity of the debt for a given borrower in a given currency. For example, the current U.S. dollar interest rates paid on U.S. Treasury securities for various maturities are closely watched by many traders, and are commonly plotted on a graph such as the one on the right which is informally called 'the _____.' More formal mathematical descriptions of this relation are often called the term structure of interest rates.

The yield of a debt instrument is the annualized percentage increase in the value of the investment.

a. 4-4-5 Calendar   b. 529 plan
c. 7-Eleven   d. Yield curve

88.   _____ is the risk that the value of an investment will decrease due to moves in market factors. The five standard _____ factors are:

- Equity risk, the risk that stock prices will change.
- Interest rate risk, the risk that interest rates will change.
- Currency risk, the risk that foreign exchange rates will change.
- Commodity risk, the risk that commodity prices (e.g. grains, metals) will change.

As with other forms of risk, _____ may be measured in a number of ways. Traditionally, this is done using a Value at Risk methodology. Value at risk is well established as a risk management technique, but it contains a number of limiting assumptions that constrain its accuracy.

a. Transaction risk   b. Tracking error
c. Currency risk   d. Market risk

89.   The terms _____ , nominal _____, and effective _____ describe the interest rate for a whole year (annualized), rather than just a monthly fee/rate, as applied on a loan, mortgage, credit card, etc. Those terms have formal, legal definitions in some countries or legal jurisdictions, but in general:

- The nominal _____ is the simple-interest rate (for a year.)
- The effective _____ is the fee+compound interest rate (calculated across a year.)

The nominal _____ is calculated as: the rate, for a payment period, multiplied by the number of payment periods in a year. However, the exact legal definition of 'effective _____' can vary greatly in each jurisdiction, depending on the type of fees included, such as participation fees, loan origination fees, monthly service charges, or late fees. The effective _____ has been called the 'mathematically-true' interest rate for each year. The computation for the effective _____, as the fee+compound interest rate, can also vary depending on whether the up-front fees, such as origination or participation fees, are added to the entire amount, or treated as a short-term loan due in the first payment.

a. A Random Walk Down Wall Street   b. Annual percentage rate
c. ABN Amro   d. AAB

90.   The _____ or forward rate is the agreed upon price of an asset in a forward contract. Using the rational pricing assumption, we can express the _____ in terms of the spot price and any dividends etc., so that there is no possibility for arbitrage.

The _____ is given by:

$$\boxed{\times}\,,$$

where

F is the _____ to be paid at time T
e^x is the exponential function
r is the risk-free interest rate
q is the cost-of-carry
S_0 is the spot price of the asset (i.e. what it would sell for at time 0)
D_i is a dividend which is guaranteed to be paid at time t_i where $0 < t_i < T$.

The two questions here are what price the short position (the seller of the asset) should offer to maximize his gain, and what price the long position (the buyer of the asset) should accept to maximize his gain?

At the very least we know that both do not want to lose any money in the deal.

a. Biweekly Mortgage   b. Financial Gerontology
c. Security interest   d. Forward price

91.   _____ refers to government attempts to influence the direction of the economy through changes in government taxes, or through some spending (fiscal allowances.)

_____ can be contrasted with the other main type of economic policy, monetary policy, which attempts to stabilize the economy by controlling interest rates and the supply of money. The two main instruments of _____ are government spending and taxation.

a. Qualified residence interest

b. Tax incidence

c. Tax exemption

d. Fiscal policy

92. _____ is a branch of economics that deals with the performance, structure, and behavior of a national or regional economy as a whole. Along with microeconomics, _____ is one of the two most general fields in economics. Macroeconomists study aggregated indicators such as GDP, unemployment rates, and price indices to understand how the whole economy functions.

a. Recession

b. Macroeconomics

c. Human capital

d. Behavioral finance

93. _____ is the risk (variability in value) borne by an interest-bearing asset, such as a loan or a bond, due to variability of interest rates. In general, as rates rise, the price of a fixed rate bond will fall, and vice versa. _____ is commonly measured by the bond's duration.

a. Interest rate risk

b. A Random Walk Down Wall Street

c. International Fisher effect

d. Official bank rate

94. John Maynard Keynes developed the _____ of Interest in the General Theory of Employment Interest and Money. The primary consideration of the _____ is the demand for money as an asset, as a means for holding wealth. Interest rates, he argues, cannot be a reward for savings as such because, if a person hoards his savings in cash, keeping it under his mattress say, he will receive no interest, although he has nevertheless, refrained from consuming all his current income.

a. 529 plan

b. Liquidity preference

c. 4-4-5 Calendar

d. 7-Eleven

95. _____ is a term used to explain a difference between two types of financial securities (e.g. stocks), that have all the same qualities except liquidity. For example:

_____ is a segment of a three-part theory that works to explain the behavior of yield curves for interest rates. The upwards-curving component of the interest yield can be explained by the _____.

a. 7-Eleven

b. 4-4-5 Calendar

c. 529 plan

d. Liquidity premium

1. _____ refers to a portfolio management strategy where the manager makes specific investments with the goal of outperforming an investment benchmark index. Investors or mutual funds that do not aspire to create a return in excess of a benchmark index will often invest in an index fund that replicates as closely as possible the investment weighting and returns of that index; this is called passive management. _____ is the opposite of passive management, because in passive management the manager does not seek to outperform the benchmark index.

   a. A Random Walk Down Wall Street   b. ABN Amro

   c. Active management   d. AAB

2. In finance, a _____ is a debt security, in which the authorized issuer owes the holders a debt and, depending on the terms of the _____, is obliged to pay interest (the coupon) and/or to repay the principal at a later date, termed maturity.

Thus a _____ is a loan: the issuer is the borrower, the _____ holder is the lender, and the coupon is the interest. _____s provide the borrower with external funds to finance long-term investments, or, in the case of government _____s, to finance current expenditure.

   a. Bond   b. Catastrophe bonds

   c. Convertible bond   d. Puttable bond

3. _____ is a fee paid on borrowed assets. It is the price paid for the use of borrowed money , or, money earned by deposited funds . Assets that are sometimes lent with _____ include money, shares, consumer goods through hire purchase, major assets such as aircraft, and even entire factories in finance lease arrangements.

   a. Insolvency   b. AAB

   c. Interest   d. A Random Walk Down Wall Street

4. An _____ is the price a borrower pays for the use of money they do not own, and the return a lender receives for deferring the use of funds, by lending it to the borrower. _____s are normally expressed as a percentage rate over the period of one year.

_____s targets are also a vital tool of monetary policy and are used to control variables like investment, inflation, and unemployment.

   a. ABN Amro   b. A Random Walk Down Wall Street

   c. AAB   d. Interest rate

5. _____ is the risk (variability in value) borne by an interest-bearing asset, such as a loan or a bond, due to variability of interest rates. In general, as rates rise, the price of a fixed rate bond will fall, and vice versa. _____ is commonly measured by the bond's duration.

   a. A Random Walk Down Wall Street   b. Official bank rate

   c. Interest rate risk   d. International Fisher effect

6. In finance, the term _____ describes the amount in cash that returns to the owners of a security. Normally it does not include the price variations, at the difference of the total return. _____ applies to various stated rates of return on stocks (common and preferred, and convertible), fixed income instruments (bonds, notes, bills, strips, zero coupon), and some other investment type insurance products (e.g. annuities.)

a. 4-4-5 Calendar

b. Yield to maturity

c. Macaulay duration

d. Yield

7. The _____ or redemption yield is the yield promised to the bondholder on the assumption that the bond or other fixed-interest security such as gilts will be held to maturity, that all coupon and principal payments will be made and coupon payments are reinvested at the bond's promised yield at the same rate as invested. It is a measure of the return of the bond. This technique in theory allows investors to calculate the fair value of different financial instruments.

a. 4-4-5 Calendar

b. Yield

c. Yield to maturity

d. Macaulay duration

8. In business and accounting, _____s are everything of value that is owned by a person or company. The balance sheet of a firm records the monetary value of the _____s owned by the firm. The two major _____ classes are tangible _____s and intangible _____s.

a. Accounts payable

b. Income

c. EBITDA

d. Asset

9. _____ is a term used to refer to how an investor distributes his or her investments among various classes of investment vehicles (e.g., stocks and bonds.)

A large part of financial planning is finding an _____ that is appropriate for a given person in terms of their appetite for and ability to shoulder risk. This can depend on various factors; see investor profile.

a. Investment performance

b. Alternative investment

c. Investing online

d. Asset allocation

10. _____ is a life of security. It may also refer to the final payment date of a loan or other financial instrument, at which point all remaining interest and principal is due to be paid.

1, 3, 6 months _____ band can be calculated by using 30-day per month periods.

a. False billing

b. Primary market

c. Replacement cost

d. Maturity

11. The coupon or _____ of a bond is the amount of interest paid per year expressed as a percentage of the face value of the bond.

For example if you hold $10,000 nominal of a bond described as a 4.5% loan stock, you will receive $450 in interest each year (probably in two installments of $225 each.)

Not all bonds have coupons.

a. Zero-coupon bond

b. Coupon rate

c. Puttable bond

d. Revenue bonds

12. In economic models, the _____ time frame assumes no fixed factors of production. Firms can enter or leave the marketplace, and the cost (and availability) of land, labor, raw materials, and capital goods can be assumed to vary. In contrast, in the short-run time frame, certain factors are assumed to be fixed, because there is not sufficient time for them to change.
   a. 4-4-5 Calendar
   b. 529 plan
   c. Short-run
   d. Long-run

13. In economics, the concept of the _____ refers to the decision-making time frame of a firm in which at least one factor of production is fixed. Costs which are fixed in the _____ have no impact on a firms decisions. For example a firm can raise output by increasing the amount of labour through overtime.
   a. 4-4-5 Calendar
   b. Long-run
   c. 529 plan
   d. Short-run

14. A _____ is a bond bought at a price lower than its face value, with the face value repaid at the time of maturity. It does not make periodic interest payments, or have so-called 'coupons,' hence the term _____. Investors earn return from the compounded interest all paid at maturity plus the difference between the discounted price of the bond and its par value.
   a. Clean price
   b. Zero-coupon bond
   c. Corporate bond
   d. Bond fund

15. In finance, the _____ of a financial asset measures the sensitivity of the asset's price to interest rate movements, expressed as a number of years. The reason for expressing this sensitivity in years is that the time that will elapse until a cash flow is received allows more interest to accumulate. Therefore the price of an asset with long term cashflows has more interest rate sensitivity than an asset with cashflows in the near future.
   a. 4-4-5 Calendar
   b. Yield to maturity
   c. Macaulay duration
   d. Duration

16. An _____ (or business indicator) is a statistic about the economy. _____s allow analysis of economic performance and predictions of future performance.

_____s include various indices, earnings reports, and economic summaries, such as unemployment, housing starts, Consumer Price Index (a measure for inflation), industrial production, bankruptcies, Gross Domestic Product, broadband internet penetration, retail sales, stock market prices, and money supply changes.

   a. A Random Walk Down Wall Street
   b. AAB
   c. ABN Amro
   d. Economic indicator

17. _____ is the balance of the amounts of cash being received and paid by a business during a defined period of time, sometimes tied to a specific project. Measurement of _____ can be used

- to evaluate the state or performance of a business or project.
- to determine problems with liquidity. Being profitable does not necessarily mean being liquid. A company can fail because of a shortage of cash, even while profitable.
- to generate project rate of returns. The time of _____s into and out of projects are used as inputs to financial models such as internal rate of return, and net present value.
- to examine income or growth of a business when it is believed that accrual accounting concepts do not represent economic realities. Alternately, _____ can be used to 'validate' the net income generated by accrual accounting.

_____ as a generic term may be used differently depending on context, and certain _____ definitions may be adapted by analysts and users for their own uses. Common terms include operating _____ and free _____.

_____s can be classified into:

1. Operational _____s: Cash received or expended as a result of the company's core business activities.
2. Investment _____s: Cash received or expended through capital expenditure, investments or acquisitions.
3. Financing _____s: Cash received or expended as a result of financial activities, such as interests and dividends.

All three together - the net _____ - are necessary to reconcile the beginning cash balance to the ending cash balance. Loan draw downs or equity injections, that is just shifting of capital but no expenditure as such, are not considered in the net _____.

a. Cash flow
c. Shareholder value

b. Corporate finance
d. Real option

18. _____ or financing is to provide capital (funds), which means money for a project, a person, a business or any other private or public institutions.

Those funds can be allocated for either short term or long term purposes. The health fund is a new way of _____ private healthcare centers.

a. Product life cycle
c. Proxy fight

b. Synthetic CDO
d. Funding

19. _____ proposes how rational investors will use diversification to optimize their portfolios, and how a risky asset should be priced. The basic concepts of the theory are Markowitz diversification, the efficient frontier, capital asset pricing model, the alpha and beta coefficients, the Capital Market Line and the Securities Market Line.

_____ models an asset's return as a random variable, and models a portfolio as a weighted combination of assets so that the return of a portfolio is the weighted combination of the assets' returns.

a. Payback period   b. Consumer basket
c. Modern portfolio theory   d. Market value

20. A _____ is a pool of assets forming an independent legal entity that are bought with the contributions to a pension plan for the exclusive purpose of financing pension plan benefits.

_____s are important shareholders of listed and private companies. They are especially important to the stock market where large institutional investors like the Ontario Teachers' Pension Plan dominate.

a. Pension fund   b. Leverage
c. Leveraged buyout   d. Limited liability company

21. A _____ is an annuity in which the periodic payments begin on a fixed date and continue indefinitely. It is sometimes referred to as a perpetual annuity. Fixed coupon payments on permanently invested (irredeemable) sums of money are prime examples of these. Scholarships paid perpetually from an endowment fit the definition of _____.
a. Current yield   b. LIBOR market model
c. Stochastic volatility   d. Perpetuity

22. The _____ is the over-the-counter financial market in contracts for future delivery, so called forward contracts. Forward contracts are personalized between parties. The _____ is a general term used to describe the informal market by which these contracts are entered into.
a. Forward market   b. Limits to arbitrage
c. Delta hedging   d. Spot rate

23. _____ is a financial strategy in which a fund manager makes as few portfolio decisions as possible, in order to minimize transaction costs, including the incidence of capital gains tax. One popular method is to mimic the performance of an externally specified index--called 'index funds'. The ethos of an index fund is aptly summed up in the injunction to an index fund manager: 'Don't just do something, sit there!'

_____ is most common on the equity market, where index funds track a stock market index, but it is becoming more common in other investment types, including bonds, commodities and hedge funds.

a. Trust company   b. Passive management
c. Savings and loan association   d. Net asset value

24. In finance, _____, also known as return on investment is the ratio of money gained or lost on an investment relative to the amount of money invested. The amount of money gained or lost may be referred to as interest, profit/loss, gain/loss, or net income/loss. The money invested may be referred to as the asset, capital, principal, or the cost basis of the investment.
a. Doctrine of the Proper Law   b. Composiition of Creditors
c. Stock or scrip dividends   d. Rate of return

25. A _____, securities exchange or (in Europe) bourse is a corporation or mutual organization which provides 'trading' facilities for stock brokers and traders, to trade stocks and other securities. _____s also provide facilities for the issue and redemption of securities as well as other financial instruments and capital events including the payment of income and dividends. The securities traded on a _____ include: shares issued by companies, unit trusts and other pooled investment products and bonds.

a. 7-Eleven
b. 529 plan
c. Stock exchange
d. 4-4-5 Calendar

26. In finance, an _____ occurs when the financial terms of the assets and liabilities do not correspond. For example, a bank that chose to borrow entirely in U.S. dollars and lend in Russian rubles would have a significant (currency) mismatch: if the value of the ruble were to fall dramatically, the bank would lose money. In extreme cases, such movements in the value of the assets and liabilities could lead to bankruptcy, liquidity problems and wealth transfer.

a. Intelligent investor
b. ASCOT
c. Inflation derivatives
d. Asset-liability mismatch

27. _____ is one of the main genres of financial risk. The term describes the risk that a particular investment might be canceled or stopped somehow, that one may have to find a new place to invest that money with the risk being there might not be a similarly attractive investment available. This primarily occurs if bonds (which are portions of loans to entities) are paid back earlier then expected.

a. Debt cash flow
b. Reinvestment risk
c. Standard of deferred payment
d. Biweekly Mortgage

28. _____ measures the nominal future sum of money that a given sum of money is 'worth' at a specified time in the future assuming a certain interest rate rate of return; it is the present value multiplied by the accumulation function.

The value does not include corrections for inflation or other factors that affect the true value of money in the future. This is used in time value of money calculations.

a. Future-oriented
b. Discounted cash flow
c. Present value of costs
d. Future value

29. _____ is the value on a given date of a future payment or series of future payments, discounted to reflect the time value of money and other factors such as investment risk. _____ calculations are widely used in business and economics to provide a means to compare cash flows at different times on a meaningful 'like to like' basis.

The most commonly applied model of the time value of money is compound interest.

a. Present value
b. Negative gearing
c. Net present value
d. Present value of benefits

30. _____ is the action of bringing a portfolio of investments that has deviated away from one's target asset allocation back into line. Under-weighted securities can be purchased with newly saved money; alternatively, over-weighted securities can be sold to purchase under-weighted securities.

The investments in a portfolio will perform according to the market.

a. Security market line   b. Divestment
c. Market timing   d. Rebalancing

31. _____ are dollar-denominated bonds, issued mostly by Latin American countries in the 1980s, named after U.S. Treasury Secretary Nicholas Brady.

_____ were created in March 1989 in order to convert bonds issued by mostly Latin American countries into a variety or 'menu' of new bonds after many of those countries defaulted on their debt in the 1980's. At that time, the market for sovereign debt was small and illiquid, and the standardization of emerging-market debt facilitated risk-spreading and trading.

a. Coupon rate   b. Brady bonds
c. Nominal yield   d. Municipal bond

32. Behavioral economics and _____ are closely related fields that have evolved to be a separate branch of economic and financial analysis which applies scientific research on human and social, cognitive and emotional factors to better understand economic decisions by, say, consumers, borrowers, investors, and how they affect market prices, returns and the allocation of resources.

The field is primarily concerned with the bounds of rationality (selfishness, self-control) of economic agents. Behavioral models typically integrate insights from psychology with neo-classical economic theory.

a. Medium of exchange   b. Behavioral finance
c. Market structure   d. Recession

33. _____ are organizations which pool large sums of money and invest those sums in companies. They include banks, insurance companies, retirement or pension funds, hedge funds and mutual funds. Their role in the economy is to act as highly specialized investors on behalf of others.

a. A Random Walk Down Wall Street   b. AAB
c. Institutional investors   d. ABN Amro

34. In finance, an _____ is the difference between the expected return of a security and the actual return. _____s are sometimes triggered by 'events.' Events can include mergers, dividend announcements, company earning announcements, interest rate increases, lawsuits, etc. all which can contribute to an _____.

a. ABN Amro   b. AAB
c. Abnormal return   d. A Random Walk Down Wall Street

35. An _____ is an exchange of tangible assets for intangible assets or vice versa. Since it is a swap of assets, the procedure takes place on the active side of the balance sheet and has no impact on the latter in regards to volume. As an example, a company may sell equity and receive the value in cash thus increasing liquidity.

a. Asset swap   b. A Random Walk Down Wall Street
c. ABN Amro   d. AAB

36. _____ refers to any type of investment that yields a regular (or fixed) return.

For example, if you lend money to a borrower and the borrower has to pay interest once a month, you have been issued a fixed-income security. When a company does this, it is often called a bond or corporate bank debt (although preferred stock is also sometimes considered to be _____).

a. Bond market   b. 4-4-5 Calendar

c. Fixed income   d. 529 plan

37.   The _____ is the market for securities, where companies and governments can raise longterm funds. The _____ includes the stock market and the bond market. Financial regulators, such as the U.S. Securities and Exchange Commission, oversee the _____s in their designated countries to ensure that investors are protected against fraud.

a. Delta neutral   b. Spot rate

c. Forward market   d. Capital market

38.   _____ is the difference between price and the costs of bringing to market whatever it is that is accounted as an enterprise (whether by harvest, extraction, manufacture, or purchase) in terms of the component costs of delivered goods and/or services and any operating or other expenses.

A key difficulty in measuring profit is in defining costs. Pure economic monetary profits can be zero or negative even in competitive equilibrium when accounted monetized costs exceed monetized price.

a. A Random Walk Down Wall Street   b. Economic profit

c. AAB   d. Accounting profit

39.   In finance, a _____ is a derivative in which two counterparties agree to exchange one stream of cash flows against another stream. These streams are called the legs of the _____.

The cash flows are calculated over a notional principal amount, which is usually not exchanged between counterparties.

a. Volatility swap   b. Volatility arbitrage

c. Local volatility   d. Swap

40.   The _____ is a financial market where participants buy and sell debt securities, usually in the form of bonds. As of 2006, the size of the international _____ is an estimated $45 trillion, of which the size of the outstanding U.S. _____ debt was $25.2 trillion.

Nearly all of the $923 billion average daily trading volume in the U.S. _____ takes place between broker-dealers and large institutions in a decentralized, over-the-counter market.

a. Fixed income   b. 529 plan

c. 4-4-5 Calendar   d. Bond market

41. The institution most often referenced by the word '_____' is a public or publicly traded _____, the shares of which are traded on a public stock exchange (e.g., the New York Stock Exchange or Nasdaq in the United States) where shares of stock of _____s are bought and sold by and to the general public. Most of the largest businesses in the world are publicly traded _____s. However, the majority of _____s are said to be closely held, privately held or close _____s, meaning that no ready market exists for the trading of shares.

a. Depository Trust Company   b. Corporation

c. Federal Home Loan Mortgage Corporation   d. Protect

1.   The institution most often referenced by the word '_____' is a public or publicly traded _____, the shares of which are traded on a public stock exchange (e.g., the New York Stock Exchange or Nasdaq in the United States) where shares of stock of _____s are bought and sold by and to the general public. Most of the largest businesses in the world are publicly traded _____s. However, the majority of _____s are said to be closely held, privately held or close _____s, meaning that no ready market exists for the trading of shares.

  a. Federal Home Loan Mortgage Corporation   b. Protect

  c. Corporation   d. Depository Trust Company

2.   _____ of a business involves analyzing its financial statements and health, its management and competitive advantages, and its competitors and markets. The term is used to distinguish such analysis from other types of investment analysis, such as quantitative analysis and technical analysis.

_____ is performed on historical and present data, but with the goal of making financial forecasts.

  a. Stock valuation   b. 4-4-5 Calendar

  c. Growth stocks   d. Fundamental analysis

3.   _____ is the branch of economics that studies the dynamics of exchange rates, foreign investment, and how these affect international trade. It also studies international projects, international investments and capital flows, and trade deficits. It includes the study of futures, options and currency swaps.

  a. AAB   b. ABN Amro

  c. A Random Walk Down Wall Street   d. International finance

4.   In finance, _____ (or gearing) is borrowing money to supplement existing funds for investment in such a way that the potential positive or negative outcome is magnified and/or enhanced. It generally refers to using borrowed funds, or debt, so as to attempt to increase the returns to equity. Deleveraging is the action of reducing borrowings.

  a. Financial endowment   b. Pension fund

  c. Leverage   d. Limited partnership

5.   A _____ is a tax designation for a corporation investing in real estate that reduces or eliminates corporate income taxes. In return, _____s are required to distribute 95% of their income, which may be taxable in the hands of the investors. The _____ structure was designed to provide a similar structure for investment in real estate as mutual funds provide for investment in stocks.

  a. REIT   b. Liquidation value

  c. Real Estate Investment Trust   d. Real estate investing

6.   In accounting, _____ or *Carrying value* is the value of an asset according to its balance sheet account balance. For assets, the value is based on the original cost of the asset less any depreciation, amortization or impairment costs made against the asset. A company's _____ is its total assets minus intangible assets and liabilities.

  a. Book value   b. Retained earnings

  c. Pro forma   d. Current liabilities

7.   A _____ is a private or public market for the trading of company stock and derivatives of company stock at an agreed price; these are securities listed on a stock exchange as well as those only traded privately.

The size of the world _____ is estimated at about $36.6 trillion US at the beginning of October 2008 . The world derivatives market has been estimated at about $480 trillion face or nominal value, 12 times the size of the entire world economy.

a. Adolph Coors	b. Andrew Tobias
c. Anton Gelonkin	d. Stock market

8.   In finance, the _____ between two currencies specifies how much one currency is worth in terms of the other. For example an _____ of 102 Japanese yen to the United States dollar means that JPY 102 is worth the same as USD 1. The foreign exchange market is one of the largest markets in the world.

a. AAB	b. A Random Walk Down Wall Street
c. Exchange rate	d. ABN Amro

9.   _____ is a type of risk faced by investors, corporations, and governments. It is a risk that can be understood and managed with proper aforethought and investment.

Broadly, _____ refers to the complications businesses and governments may face as a result of what are commonly referred to as political decisions--or 'any political change that alters the expected outcome and value of a given economic action by changing the probability of achieving business objectives.' .

a. Mid price	b. Capital asset
c. Political risk	d. Single-index model

10.   _____ refers to a business or organization attempting to acquire goods or services to accomplish the goals of the enterprise. Though there are several organizations that attempt to set standards in the _____ process, processes can vary greatly between organizations. Typically the word '_____' is not used interchangeably with the word 'procurement', since procurement typically includes Expediting, Supplier Quality, and Traffic and Logistics (T'L) in addition to _____.

a. 4-4-5 Calendar	b. Purchasing
c. 7-Eleven	d. 529 plan

11.   _____ is the value of goods/services compared to the amount paid with a currency. Currency can be either a commodity money, like gold or silver, or fiat currency like US dollars which are the world reserve currency. As Adam Smith noted, having money gives one the ability to 'command' others' labor, so _____ to some extent is power over other people, to the extent that they are willing to trade their labor or goods for money or currency.

a. 529 plan	b. 4-4-5 Calendar
c. 7-Eleven	d. Purchasing power

12.   An _____ (or business indicator) is a statistic about the economy. _____s allow analysis of economic performance and predictions of future performance.

_____s include various indices, earnings reports, and economic summaries, such as unemployment, housing starts, Consumer Price Index (a measure for inflation), industrial production, bankruptcies, Gross Domestic Product, broadband internet penetration, retail sales, stock market prices, and money supply changes.

a. ABN Amro

b. AAB

c. A Random Walk Down Wall Street

d. Economic indicator

13. _____ is a mathematical science pertaining to the collection, analysis, interpretation or explanation, and presentation of data. It also provides tools for prediction and forecasting based on data. It is applicable to a wide variety of academic disciplines, from the natural and social sciences to the humanities, government and business.

a. Sample size

b. Covariance

c. Mean

d. Statistics

14. _____ most frequently refers to the standard deviation of the continuously compounded returns of a financial instrument with a specific time horizon. It is often used to quantify the risk of the instrument over that time period. _____ is typically expressed in annualized terms, and it may either be an absolute number ($5) or a fraction of the mean (5%).

a. Currency swap

b. Volatility

c. Portfolio insurance

d. Seasoned equity offering

15. The _____ is one of several stock market indices, created by nineteenth-century Wall Street Journal editor and Dow Jones ' Company co-founder Charles Dow. Dow compiled the index to gauge the performance of the industrial sector of the American stock market. It is the second-oldest U.S. market index, after the Dow Jones Transportation Average, which Dow also created.

a. 7-Eleven

b. 4-4-5 Calendar

c. 529 plan

d. Dow Jones Industrial Average

16. _____ are the earnings returned on the initial investment amount.

In the US, the Financial Accounting Standards Board (FASB) requires companies' income statements to report _____ for each of the major categories of the income statement: continuing operations, discontinued operations, extraordinary items, and net income.

The _____ formula does not include preferred dividends for categories outside of continued operations and net income.

a. Inventory turnover

b. Earnings per share

c. Average accounting return

d. Assets turnover

17. The _____ is one of the measures of national income and input for a given country's economy. _____ is defined as the total cost of all finished goods and services produced within the country in a stipulated period of time (usually a 365-day year.) It is sometimes regarded as the sum of profits added at every level of production (the intermediate stages) of all final goods and services produced within a country in a stipulated timeframe, and it is rarely given a monetary value.

a. Macroeconomics

b. Recession

c. Behavioral finance

d. Gross domestic product

18. _____ is a branch of economics that deals with the performance, structure, and behavior of a national or regional economy as a whole. Along with microeconomics, _____ is one of the two most general fields in economics. Macroeconomists study aggregated indicators such as GDP, unemployment rates, and price indices to understand how the whole economy functions.

a. Human capital
c. Macroeconomics

b. Behavioral finance
d. Recession

19. In business and finance, a _____ (also referred to as equity _____) of stock means a _____ of ownership in a corporation (company.) In the plural, stocks is often used as a synonym for _____s especially in the United States, but it is less commonly used that way outside of North America.

In the United Kingdom, South Africa, and Australia, stock can also refer to completely different financial instruments such as government bonds or, less commonly, to all kinds of marketable securities.

a. Share
c. Margin

b. Procter ' Gamble
d. Bucket shop

20. _____ is a concept in economics which refers to the extent to which an enterprise or a nation actually uses its installed productive capacity. Thus, it refers to the relationship between actual output that 'is' produced with the installed equipment and the potential output which 'could' be produced with it, if capacity was fully used.

If market demand grows, _____ will rise.

a. 529 plan
c. 4-4-5 Calendar

b. Capacity utilization
d. Long-run

21. In economics, _____ is a rise in the general level of prices of goods and services in an economy over a period of time. The term '_____' once referred to increases in the money supply (monetary _____); however, economic debates about the relationship between money supply and price levels have led to its primary use today in describing price _____. _____ can also be described as a decline in the real value of money--a loss of purchasing power in the medium of exchange which is also the monetary unit of account.

a. A Random Walk Down Wall Street
c. ABN Amro

b. AAB
d. Inflation

22. Unemployment occurs when a person is available to work and currently seeking work, but the person is without work. The prevalence of unemployment is usually measured using the _____, which is defined as the percentage of those in the labor force who are unemployed. The _____ is also used in economic studies and economic indexes such as the United States' Conference Board's Index of Leading Indicators as a measure of the state of the macroeconomics.

a. ABN Amro
c. AAB

b. A Random Walk Down Wall Street
d. Unemployment rate

23. In finance, a _____ is a debt security, in which the authorized issuer owes the holders a debt and, depending on the terms of the _____, is obliged to pay interest (the coupon) and/or to repay the principal at a later date, termed maturity.

Thus a _____ is a loan: the issuer is the borrower, the _____ holder is the lender, and the coupon is the interest. _____s provide the borrower with external funds to finance long-term investments, or, in the case of government _____s, to finance current expenditure.

a. Bond

b. Catastrophe bonds

c. Puttable bond

d. Convertible bond

24. _____ is the amount by which a government, private company, or individual's spending exceeds income over a particular period of time, the opposite of budget surplus.

When the expenditures of a government to individuals and corporations) are greater than its tax revenues, it creates a deficit in the government budget; such a deficit is known as _____. This causes the government to borrow capital from the 'world market', increasing further debt, debt service and interest rates

a. 4-4-5 Calendar

b. 529 plan

c. 7-Eleven

d. Deficit spending

25. _____ is a fee paid on borrowed assets. It is the price paid for the use of borrowed money , or, money earned by deposited funds . Assets that are sometimes lent with _____ include money, shares, consumer goods through hire purchase, major assets such as aircraft, and even entire factories in finance lease arrangements.

a. AAB

b. Interest

c. Insolvency

d. A Random Walk Down Wall Street

26. An _____ is the price a borrower pays for the use of money they do not own, and the return a lender receives for deferring the use of funds, by lending it to the borrower. _____s are normally expressed as a percentage rate over the period of one year.

_____s targets are also a vital tool of monetary policy and are used to control variables like investment, inflation, and unemployment.

a. Interest rate

b. AAB

c. A Random Walk Down Wall Street

d. ABN Amro

27. The terms _____ , nominal _____, and effective _____ describe the interest rate for a whole year (annualized), rather than just a monthly fee/rate, as applied on a loan, mortgage, credit card, etc. Those terms have formal, legal definitions in some countries or legal jurisdictions, but in general:

- The nominal _____ is the simple-interest rate (for a year.)
- The effective _____ is the fee+compound interest rate (calculated across a year.)

The nominal _____ is calculated as: the rate, for a payment period, multiplied by the number of payment periods in a year. However, the exact legal definition of 'effective _____' can vary greatly in each jurisdiction, depending on the type of fees included, such as participation fees, loan origination fees, monthly service charges, or late fees. The effective _____ has been called the 'mathematically-true' interest rate for each year. The computation for the effective _____, as the fee+compound interest rate, can also vary depending on whether the up-front fees, such as origination or participation fees, are added to the entire amount, or treated as a short-term loan due in the first payment.

a. AAB

b. A Random Walk Down Wall Street

c. ABN Amro

d. Annual percentage rate

28. A _____ is a situation that involves losing one quality or aspect of something in return for gaining another quality or aspect. It implies a decision to be made with full comprehension of both the upside and downside of a particular choice.

In economics the term is expressed as opportunity cost, referring the most preferred alternative given up.

a. Total revenue

b. Break-even point

c. Capital outflow

d. Trade-off

29. _____ refers to government attempts to influence the direction of the economy through changes in government taxes, or through some spending (fiscal allowances.)

_____ can be contrasted with the other main type of economic policy, monetary policy, which attempts to stabilize the economy by controlling interest rates and the supply of money. The two main instruments of _____ are government spending and taxation.

a. Tax exemption

b. Tax incidence

c. Fiscal policy

d. Qualified residence interest

30. _____ is the process by which the government, or monetary authority of a country controls (i) the supply of money central bank (ii) availability of money, and (iii) cost of money or rate of interest, in order to attain a set of objectives oriented towards the growth and stability of the economy. Monetary theory provides insight into how to craft optimal _____.

_____ is referred to as either being an expansionary policy where an expansionary policy increases the total supply of money in the economy, and a contractionary policy decreases the total money supply.

a. Federal Open Market Committee

b. Natural resources consumption tax

c. Tax exemption

d. Monetary policy

31. In finance and economics _____ refers to the rate of interest before adjustment for inflation (in contrast with the real interest rate); or, for interest balls stated' without adjustment for the full effect of compounding (also referred to as the nominal annual rate.) An interest rate is called nominal if the frequency of compounding (e.g. a month) is not identical to the basic time unit (normally a year.)

The real interest rate includes compensation for the lender's lost value due to inflation, whereas the _____ excludes inflation.

a. SIBOR

b. Nominal interest rate

c. Cash accumulation equation

d. Shanghai Interbank Offered Rate

32. The '_____' is approximately the nominal interest rate minus the inflation rate Since the inflation rate over the course of a loan is not known initially, volatility in inflation represents a risk to both the lender and the borrower.

In economics and finance, an individual who lends money for repayment at a later point in time expects to be compensated for the time value of money, or not having the use of that money while it is lent.

a. 529 plan

b. Real interest rate

c. 4-4-5 Calendar

d. 7-Eleven

33. _____ is an economic model based on price, utility and quantity in a market. It predicts that in a competitive market, price will function to equalize the quantity demanded by consumers, and the quantity supplied by producers, resulting in an economic equilibrium of price and quantity. Similarly, an increase in the number of workers tends to result in lower wages and vice-versa.

a. Loan participation

b. Rural credit cooperatives

c. Supply and demand

d. Price channel

34. In financial accounting, a _____ or statement of financial position is a summary of a person's or organization's balances. Assets, liabilities and ownership equity are listed as of a specific date, such as the end of its financial year. A _____ is often described as a snapshot of a company's financial condition.

a. Balance sheet

b. Statement of retained earnings

c. Financial statements

d. Statement on Auditing Standards No. 70: Service Organizations

35. In economics, a _____ is a sudden event that increases or decreases demand for goods or services temporarily. A positive _____ increases demand and a negative _____ decreases demand. Prices of goods and services are affected in both cases.

a. Deregulation

b. Value added

c. Supply shock

d. Demand shock

36. A _____ is an event that suddenly changes the price of a commodity or service. It may be caused by a sudden increase or decrease in the supply of a particular good. This sudden change affects the equilibrium price.

a. Value added

b. Supply shock

c. Deregulation

d. Demand shock

37. _____ is a security analysis discipline for forecasting the future direction of prices through the study of past market data, primarily price and volume. In its purest form, _____ considers only the actual price and volume behavior of the market or instrument. Technical analysts may employ models and trading rules based on price and volume transformations, such as the relative strength index, moving averages, regressions, inter-market and intra-market price correlations, cycles or, classically, through recognition of chart patterns.

a. Dow theory

b. Point and figure

c. Support and resistance

d. Technical analysis

38. In finance, _____ is the process of estimating the potential market value of a financial asset or liability. they can be done on assets (for example, investments in marketable securities such as stocks, options, business enterprises, or intangible assets such as patents and trademarks) or on liabilities (e.g., Bonds issued by a company.) _____s are required in many contexts including investment analysis, capital budgeting, merger and acquisition transactions, financial reporting, taxable events to determine the proper tax liability, and in litigation.

a. Margin
c. Valuation

b. Share
d. Procter ' Gamble

39. In economics, _____ is the total amount of money available in an economy at a particular point in time. There are several ways to define 'money', but each includes currency in circulation and demand deposits.

_____ data are recorded and published.

a. 7-Eleven
c. Money supply

b. 4-4-5 Calendar
d. 529 plan

40. _____ are the means of implementing monetary policy by which a central bank controls its national money supply by buying and selling government securities, or other financial instruments. Monetary targets, such as interest rates or exchange rates, are used to guide this implementation.

Since most money is now in the form of electronic records, rather than paper records such as banknotes, _____ are conducted simply by electronically increasing or decreasing ('crediting' or 'debiting') the amount of money that a bank has, e.g., in its reserve account at the central bank, in exchange for a bank selling or buying a financial instrument.

a. Open market operations
c. A Random Walk Down Wall Street

b. AAB
d. ABN Amro

41. A '_____' is a 'Charge' that is paid to obtain the right to delay a payment. Essentially, the payer purchases the right to make a given payment in the future instead of in the Present. The '_____', or 'Charge' that must be paid to delay the payment, is simply the difference between what the payment amount would be if it were paid in the present and what the payment amount would be paid if it were paid in the future.

a. Discount
c. Risk modeling

b. Value at risk
d. Risk aversion

42. The _____ is an interest rate a central bank charges depository institutions that borrow reserves from it.

The term _____ has two meanings:

- the same as interest rate; the term 'discount' does not refer to the meaning of the word, but to the purpose of using the quantity, such as computations of present value, e.g. net present value / discounted cash flow

- the annual effective _____, which is the annual interest divided by the capital including that interest; this rate is lower than the interest rate; it corresponds to using the value after a year as the nominal value, and seeing the initial value as the nominal value minus a discount; it is used for Treasury Bills and similar financial instruments

The annual effective _____ is the annual interest divided by the capital including that interest, which is the interest rate divided by 100% plus the interest rate. It is the annual discount factor to be applied to the future cash flow, to find the discount, subtracted from a future value to find the value one year earlier.

For example, suppose there is a government bond that sells for $95 and pays $100 in a year's time.

a. Fisher equation   b. Black-Scholes
c. Stochastic volatility   d. Discount rate

43.   In the United States, _____ are overnight borrowings by banks to maintain their bank reserves at the Federal Reserve. Banks keep reserves at Federal Reserve Banks to meet their reserve requirements and to clear financial transactions. Transactions in the _____ market enable depository institutions with reserve balances in excess of reserve requirements to lend reserves to institutions with reserve deficiencies.
a. Federal funds rate   b. Federal funds
c. 4-4-5 Calendar   d. Regulation T

44.   In the United States, the _____ is the interest rate at which private depository institutions (mostly banks) lend balances (federal funds) at the Federal Reserve to other depository institutions, usually overnight. Changing the target rate is one form of open market operations that the Chairman of the Federal Reserve uses to regulate the supply of money in the U.S. economy.

U.S. banks and thrift institutions are obligated by law to maintain certain levels of reserves, either as reserves with the Fed or as vault cash.

a. 4-4-5 Calendar   b. Regulation T
c. Taylor rule   d. Federal funds rate

45.   _____ is the action of bringing a portfolio of investments that has deviated away from one's target asset allocation back into line. Under-weighted securities can be purchased with newly saved money; alternatively, over-weighted securities can be sold to purchase under-weighted securities.

The investments in a portfolio will perform according to the market.

a. Security market line   b. Divestment
c. Market timing   d. Rebalancing

46.   In financial accounting, the term _____ is most commonly used to describe any part of shareholders' equity, except for basic share capital. Sometimes, the term is used instead of the term provision; such a use, however, is inconsistent with the terminology suggested by International Accounting Standards Board. For more information about provisions, see provision (accounting.)
a. FIFO and LIFO accounting   b. Treasury stock
c. Closing entries   d. Reserve

47.   The _____ is a bank regulation that sets the minimum reserves each bank must hold to customer deposits and notes. These reserves are designed to satisfy withdrawal demands, and would normally be in the form of fiat currency stored in a bank vault (vault cash), or with a central bank.

The reserve ratio is sometimes used as a tool in the monetary policy, influencing the country's economy, borrowing, and interest rates.

a. Prime rate   b. Variable rate mortgage
c. Wall Street Journal prime rate   d. Reserve requirement

48.   The term _____ or economic cycle refers to the fluctuations of economic activity (business fluctuations) around a long-term growth trend. The cycle involves shifts over time between periods of relatively rapid growth of output (recovery and prosperity), and periods of relative stagnation or decline (contraction or recession.) These fluctuations are often measured using the real gross domestic product.
a. Behavioral finance   b. Fixed exchange rate
c. Deflation   d. Business cycle

49.   The _____ is the over-the-counter financial market in contracts for future delivery, so called forward contracts. Forward contracts are personalized between parties. The _____ is a general term used to describe the informal market by which these contracts are entered into.
a. Forward market   b. Limits to arbitrage
c. Delta hedging   d. Spot rate

50.   In business and accounting, _____s are everything of value that is owned by a person or company. The balance sheet of a firm records the monetary value of the _____s owned by the firm. The two major _____ classes are tangible _____s and intangible _____s.
a. Income   b. Asset
c. Accounts payable   d. EBITDA

51.   _____ is a term used to refer to how an investor distributes his or her investments among various classes of investment vehicles (e.g., stocks and bonds.)

A large part of financial planning is finding an _____ that is appropriate for a given person in terms of their appetite for and ability to shoulder risk. This can depend on various factors; see investor profile.

a. Investment performance   b. Alternative investment
c. Investing online   d. Asset allocation

52.   A _____ is the price of a single share of a no. of saleable stocks of the company. Once the stock is purchased, the owner becomes a shareholder of the company that issued the share.
a. Trading curb   b. Share price
c. Whisper numbers   d. Stock split

53.   A _____ is a method of measuring a section of the stock market. Many indices are cited by news or financial services firms and are used to benchmark the performance of portfolios such as mutual funds.
a. Program trading   b. Stop order
c. Trading curb   d. Stock market index

54.   In investments, _____ refers to the annual rate of growth of earnings. When the dividend payout ratio is the same, the dividend growth rate is equal to the _____ rate.

_____ rate is a key value that is needed when the DCF model, or the Gordon's model is used for stock valuation.

a. Annuity

b. Alternative asset

c. Earnings growth

d. Alternative display facility

55. The _____ is used by business and government to classify and measure economic activity in Canada, Mexico and the United States. It has largely replaced the older Standard Industrial Classification (SIC) system; however, certain government departments and agencies, such as the U.S. Securities and Exchange Commission (SEC), still use the SIC codes.

The _____ numbering system is a six-digit code.

a. 4-4-5 Calendar

b. 7-Eleven

c. 529 plan

d. NAICS

56. _____ are business expenses that are not dependent on the level of production or sales. They tend to be time-related, such as salaries or rents being paid per month. This is in contrast to Variable costs, which are volume-related (and are paid per quantity.)

a. Marginal cost

b. Sliding scale fees

c. Transaction cost

d. Fixed costs

57. The _____ is a measure of how revenue growth translates into growth in operating income. It is a measure of leverage, and of how risky (volatile) a company's operating income is.

There are various measures of _____, which can be interpreted analogously to financial leverage.

a. Average accounting return

b. Asset turnover

c. Invested capital

d. Operating leverage

58. _____ are expenses that change in proportion to the activity of a business. In other words, _____ are the sum of marginal costs. It can also be considered normal costs. Along with fixed costs, _____ make up the two components of total cost. Direct Costs, however, are costs that can be associated with a particular cost object.

a. Cost accounting

b. Transaction cost

c. Variable costs

d. Fixed costs

59. In economics, business, and accounting, a _____ is the value of money that has been used up to produce something, and hence is not available for use anymore. In business, the _____ may be one of acquisition, in which case the amount of money expended to acquire it is counted as _____. In this case, money is the input that is gone in order to acquire the thing.

a. Cost

b. Sliding scale fees

c. Fixed costs

d. Marginal cost

60. _____ is a term normally applied to stock market trading patterns. In this context, a sector is understood to mean a group of stocks representing companies in similar lines of business.

For example, an investor or trader may describe the current market movements as favoring basic material stocks over semiconductor stocks by calling the environment a _____ from semiconductors to basic materials.

a. Commercial finance   b. Refunding
c. Conglomerate merger   d. Sector rotation

61.   In business, a _____ is a product or a business unit that generates unusually high profit margins: so high that it is responsible for a large amount of a company's operating profit. This profit far exceeds the amount necessary to maintain the _____ business, and the excess is used by the business for other purposes.

A firm is said to be acting as a _____ when its earnings per share (EPS) is equal to its dividends per share (DPS), or in other words, when a firm pays out 100% of its free cash flow (FCF) to its shareholders as dividends at the end of each accounting term.

a. Performance measurement   b. Corporate Transparency
c. Management by exception   d. Cash cow

62.   _____ or amalgamation is the act of merging many things into one. In business, it often refers to the mergers or acquisitions of many smaller companies into much larger ones. The financial accounting term of _____ refers to the aggregated financial statements of a group company as consolidated account.
a. Cost of goods sold   b. Retained earnings
c. Write-off   d. Consolidation

63.   _____ is a life of security. It may also refer to the final payment date of a loan or other financial instrument, at which point all remaining interest and principal is due to be paid.

1, 3, 6 months _____ band can be calculated by using 30-day per month periods.

a. Primary market   b. Maturity
c. False billing   d. Replacement cost

64.   _____, in marketing, consists of a consumer's commitment to repurchase the brand and can be demonstrated by repeated buying of a product or service or other positive behaviors such as word of mouth advocacy. True _____ implies that the consumer is willing, at least on occasion, to put aside their own desires in the interest of the brand. _____ has been proclaimed by some to be the ultimate goal of marketing.
a. 529 plan   b. 7-Eleven
c. Brand loyalty   d. 4-4-5 Calendar

65.   A _____ is a set of exclusive rights granted by a state to an inventor or his assignee for a limited period of time in exchange for a disclosure of an invention.

The procedure for granting _____s, the requirements placed on the _____ee and the extent of the exclusive rights vary widely between countries according to national laws and international agreements. Typically, however, a _____ application must include one or more claims defining the invention which must be new, inventive, and useful or industrially applicable.

a. Foreclosure

b. National Securities Markets Improvement Act of 1996

c. Patent

d. Vesting

66. _____ is a type of calendar that is intended to inform financiers and traders about the scheduled major economic numbers (like CPI, PMI, Jobless Claims), government reports and speeches of the most influential persons of the financial world. _____s are usually issued on a hourly basis.

a. ABN Amro

b. A Random Walk Down Wall Street

c. Economic calendar

d. AAB

67. _____ is the strategy of making buy or sell decisions of financial assets (often stocks) by attempting to predict future market price movements. The prediction may be based on an outlook of market or economic conditions resulting from technical or fundamental analysis. This is an investment strategy based on the outlook for an aggregate market, rather than for a particular financial asset.

a. Portable alpha

b. Divestment

c. Market timing

d. Late trading

68. A _____, reserve bank, or monetary authority is the entity responsible for the monetary policy of a country or of a group of member states. It is a bank that can lend money to other banks in times of need. Its primary responsibility is to maintain the stability of the national currency and money supply, but more active duties include controlling subsidized-loan interest rates, and acting as a lender of last resort to the banking sector during times of financial crisis (private banks often being integral to the national financial system.)

a. Central bank

b. 7-Eleven

c. 4-4-5 Calendar

d. 529 plan

1. In finance, _____ is the process of estimating the potential market value of a financial asset or liability. they can be done on assets (for example, investments in marketable securities such as stocks, options, business enterprises, or intangible assets such as patents and trademarks) or on liabilities (e.g., Bonds issued by a company.) _____s are required in many contexts including investment analysis, capital budgeting, merger and acquisition transactions, financial reporting, taxable events to determine the proper tax liability, and in litigation.

   a. Valuation   b. Margin

   c. Share   d. Procter ' Gamble

2. The institution most often referenced by the word '_____' is a public or publicly traded _____, the shares of which are traded on a public stock exchange (e.g., the New York Stock Exchange or Nasdaq in the United States) where shares of stock of _____s are bought and sold by and to the general public. Most of the largest businesses in the world are publicly traded _____s. However, the majority of _____s are said to be closely held, privately held or close _____s, meaning that no ready market exists for the trading of shares.

   a. Federal Home Loan Mortgage Corporation   b. Depository Trust Company

   c. Protect   d. Corporation

3. _____ of a business involves analyzing its financial statements and health, its management and competitive advantages, and its competitors and markets. The term is used to distinguish such analysis from other types of investment analysis, such as quantitative analysis and technical analysis.

_____ is performed on historical and present data, but with the goal of making financial forecasts.

   a. 4-4-5 Calendar   b. Growth stocks

   c. Stock valuation   d. Fundamental analysis

4. _____ is a security analysis discipline for forecasting the future direction of prices through the study of past market data, primarily price and volume. In its purest form, _____ considers only the actual price and volume behavior of the market or instrument. Technical analysts may employ models and trading rules based on price and volume transformations, such as the relative strength index, moving averages, regressions, inter-market and intra-market price correlations, cycles or, classically, through recognition of chart patterns.

   a. Support and resistance   b. Dow theory

   c. Point and figure   d. Technical analysis

5. _____s is a real estate appraisal term referring to properties with characteristics that are similar to a subject property whose value is being sought. This can be accomplished either by a real estate agent who attempts to establish the value of a potential client's home or property through market analysis or, by a licensed or certified appraiser or surveyor using more defined methods, when performing a real estate appraisal.

Five factors are usually considered when determining _____s:

- Conditions of Sale -- Did the _____ recently transact under conditions (e.g. -- arms length, distress sale, estate settlement) which are consistent with the standard of value under which the appraisal is being performed?
- Financing Conditions -- Was the _____ transaction influenced by non-market or other favorable (or even unfavorable) financing terms? For example, if the _____ sold with a below-market interest rate provided by the seller, and if the standard of value (e.g. -- market value) assumes no such abnormal financing, then the appraiser may need to adjust the _____ price by an amount equal to the estimated impact of the favorable financing.
- Market Conditions -- This is often referred to as the time adjustment and accounts for changing prices over time.
- Locational Comparability -- Are the _____ and the subject property influenced by the same locational characteristics? For example, even two houses in the same neighborhood may have different views which cause one to be more valuable than the other.
- Physical Comparability -- This includes such factors as size, condition, quality, and age.

A real estate appraisal is like any other statistical sampling process. The _____s are the samples drawn and measured, and the outcome is an estimate of value -- called an 'opinion of value' in the terminology of real estate appraisal.

a. Bucket shop

b. Procter ' Gamble

c. Margin

d. Comparable

6. In accounting, _____ or *Carrying value* is the value of an asset according to its balance sheet account balance. For assets, the value is based on the original cost of the asset less any depreciation, amortization or impairment costs made against the asset. A company's _____ is its total assets minus intangible assets and liabilities.

a. Book value

b. Retained earnings

c. Current liabilities

d. Pro forma

7. _____ is an economic concept with commonplace familiarity. It is the price that a good or service is offered at, or will fetch, in the marketplace. It is of interest mainly in the study of microeconomics.

a. Central Securities Depository

b. Convertible arbitrage

c. Delta hedging

d. Market price

8. In financial accounting, a _____ or statement of financial position is a summary of a person's or organization's balances. Assets, liabilities and ownership equity are listed as of a specific date, such as the end of its financial year. A _____ is often described as a snapshot of a company's financial condition.

a. Balance sheet

b. Statement of retained earnings

c. Statement on Auditing Standards No. 70: Service Organizations

d. Financial statements

9.   The term _____ has three unrelated technical definitions, and is also used in a variety of non-technical ways.

- In financial economics, it refers to any asset used to make money, as opposed to assets used for personal enjoyment or consumption. This is an important distinction because two people can disagree sharply about the value of personal assets, one person might think a sports car is more valuable than a pickup truck, another person might have the opposite taste. But if an asset is held for the purpose of making money, taste has nothing to do with it, only differences of opinion about how much money the asset will produce. With the further assumption that people agree on the probability distribution of future cash flows, it is possible to have an objective _____ pricing model. Even without the assumption of agreement, it is possible to set rational limits on _____ value.
- In governmental accounting, it is defined as any asset used in operations with an initial useful life extending beyond one reporting period. Generally, government managers have a 'stewardship' duty to maintain _____s under their control. See International Public Sector Accounting Standards for details.
- In US tax accounting, it is defined as any property other than a list of exceptions. The main exceptions are anything held for sale, and any real estate or depreciable property used in business. Almost everything you own and use for personal purposes, pleasure or investment is a _____. If something is a _____ for tax purposes, gains or losses on sale or disposition are capital gains or capital losses. For individuals, however, capital losses on property held for personal use are generally not deductible. See the IRS publication Tax Facts about Capital Gains and Losses for details.

A well-known financial accounting textbook advises that the term be avoided except in tax accounting because it is used in so many different senses, not all of them well-defined. For example it is often used as a synonym for fixed assets or for investments in securities.

A common non-technical usage occurs when people ask that employees or the environment or something else be treated as a _____.

a. Capital asset	b. Political risk
c. Solvency	d. Settlement date

10.   A _____ is a profit that results from investments into a capital asset, such as stocks, bonds or real estate, which exceeds the purchase price. It is the difference between a higher selling price and a lower purchase price, resulting in a financial gain for the seller. Conversely, a capital loss arises if the proceeds from the sale of a capital asset are less than the purchase price.

a. Capital gains tax	b. Tax brackets
c. Payroll tax	d. Capital gain

11.   _____ is the difference between a lower selling price and a higher purchase price, resulting in a financial loss for the seller. Pursuant to IRS TAX TIP 2009-35 'If your _____ exceeds your capital gain, the excess can be deducted on your tax return, up to an annual limit of $3,000 ($1,500 if you are married filing separately.)' .

a. Capital loss	b. 529 plan
c. 7-Eleven	d. 4-4-5 Calendar

12.   A _____ is a payment made by a corporation to its shareholder members. When a corporation earns a profit or surplus, that money can be put to two uses: it can either be re-invested in the business (called retained earnings), or it can be paid to the shareholders as a _____. Many corporations retain a portion of their earnings and pay the remainder as a _____.

a. Special dividend

b. Dividend puzzle

c. Dividend

d. Dividend yield

13.   In finance, _____ refers to the value of a security which is intrinsic to or contained in the security itself. It is also frequently called fundamental value. It is ordinarily calculated by summing the future income generated by the asset, and discounting it to the present value.

a. Intrinsic value

b. Alpha

c. Accretion

d. Amortization

14.   In law, _____ refers to the process by which a company (or part of a company) is brought to an end, and the assets and property of the company redistributed. _____ can also be referred to as winding-up or dissolution, although dissolution technically refers to the last stage of _____. The process of _____ also arises when customs, an authority or agency in a country responsible for collecting and safeguarding customs duties, determines the final computation or ascertainment of the duties or drawback accruing on an entry.

a. Liquidation

b. 529 plan

c. Debt settlement

d. 4-4-5 Calendar

15.   _____ is the likely price of an asset when it is allowed insufficient time to sell on the open market, thereby reducing its exposure to potential buyers. _____ is typically lower than fair market value. Unlike cash or securities, certain illiquid assets, like real estate, often require a period of several months in order to obtain their fair market value in a sale, and will generally sell for a significantly lower price if a sale is forced to occur in a shorter time period.

a. Tenancy

b. Real estate investing

c. REIT

d. Liquidation value

16.   In finance, _____, also known as return on investment is the ratio of money gained or lost on an investment relative to the amount of money invested. The amount of money gained or lost may be referred to as interest, profit/loss, gain/loss, or net income/loss. The money invested may be referred to as the asset, capital, principal, or the cost basis of the investment.

a. Rate of return

b. Composiition of Creditors

c. Stock or scrip dividends

d. Doctrine of the Proper Law

17.   The term _____ or replacement value refers to the amount that an entity would have to pay, at the present time, to replace any one of its assets.

In the insurance industry, '_____' is a method of computing the value of an item insured. _____ is not market value, but is instead the cost to replace an item or structure at its pre-loss condition.

a. False billing

b. Replacement cost

c. January effect

d. Bonus share

18.   In business and accounting, _____s are everything of value that is owned by a person or company. The balance sheet of a firm records the monetary value of the _____s owned by the firm. The two major _____ classes are tangible _____s and intangible _____s.

a. Income

b. EBITDA

c. Asset

d. Accounts payable

19.   In economics, business, and accounting, a _____ is the value of money that has been used up to produce something, and hence is not available for use anymore. In business, the _____ may be one of acquisition, in which case the amount of money expended to acquire it is counted as _____. In this case, money is the input that is gone in order to acquire the thing.

a. Sliding scale fees   b. Marginal cost
c. Fixed costs   d. Cost

20.   A '_____' is a 'Charge' that is paid to obtain the right to delay a payment. Essentially, the payer purchases the right to make a given payment in the future instead of in the Present. The '_____', or 'Charge' that must be paid to delay the payment, is simply the difference between what the payment amount would be if it were paid in the present and what the payment amount would be paid if it were paid in the future.

a. Risk aversion   b. Risk modeling
c. Value at risk   d. Discount

21.   _____ is a measurement of corporate or economic size equal to the share price times the number of shares outstanding of a public company. As owning stock represents owning the company, including all its equity, capitalization could represent the public opinion of a company's net worth and is a determining factor in stock valuation. Likewise, the capitalization of stock markets or economic regions may be compared to other economic indicators.

a. Synthetic CDO   b. Just-in-time
c. Proxy fight   d. Market capitalization

22.   _____ is a measure of the ratio between the net operating income produced by an asset (usually real estate) and its capital cost (the original price paid to buy the asset) or alternatively its current market value. The rate is calculated in a simple fashion as follows:

- annual net operating income / cost (or value) = _____

For example, if a building is purchased for $1,000,000 sale price and it produces $100,000 in positive net operating income (the amount left over after fixed costs and variable costs are subtracted from gross lease income) during one year, then:

- $100,000 / $1,000,000 = 0.10 = 10%

The asset's _____ is ten percent.

_____s are an indirect measure of how fast an investment will pay for itself. In the example above, the purchased building will be fully capitalized (pay for itself) after ten years (100% divided by 10%.)

a. Conditional prepayment rate   b. Profitability index
c. Capitalization rate   d. Cash concentration

23.   _____ is a variant of the Discounted cash flow model, a method for valuing a stock or business. Often used to provide difficult-to-resolve valuation issues for litigation, tax planning, and business transactions that are currently off market.

It assumes that the company issues a dividend that has a current value of D that grows at a constant rate g. It also assumes that the required rate of return for the stock remains constant at k which is equal to the cost of equity for that company. It involves summing the infinite series which gives the value of price current P.

a. Stock or scrip dividends   b. Securitization
c. Special journals   d. Gordon growth model

24.   A _____ is an annuity in which the periodic payments begin on a fixed date and continue indefinitely. It is sometimes referred to as a perpetual annuity. Fixed coupon payments on permanently invested (irredeemable) sums of money are prime examples of these. Scholarships paid perpetually from an endowment fit the definition of _____.
a. LIBOR market model   b. Stochastic volatility
c. Current yield   d. Perpetuity

25.   _____ is typically a higher ranking stock than voting shares, and its terms are negotiated between the corporation and the investor.

_____ usually carry no voting rights, but may carry superior priority over common stock in the payment of dividends and upon liquidation. _____ may carry a dividend that is paid out prior to any dividends to common stock holders.

a. Preferred stock   b. Second lien loan
c. Follow-on offering   d. Trade-off theory

26.   In finance, the _____ approach describes a method of valuing a project, company, or asset using the concepts of the time value of money. All future cash flows are estimated and discounted to give their present values. The discount rate used is generally the appropriate cost of capital and may incorporate judgments of the uncertainty (riskiness) of the future cash flows.
a. Discounted cash flow   b. Present value of benefits
c. Net present value   d. Future-oriented

27.   In economics, _____ is a measure of the relative satisfaction from or desirability of consumption of various goods and services. Given this measure, one may speak meaningfully of increasing or decreasing _____, and thereby explain economic behavior in terms of attempts to increase one's _____. For illustrative purposes, changes in _____ are sometimes expressed in units called utils.
a. Utility   b. Utility function
c. AAB   d. A Random Walk Down Wall Street

28. _____ is the balance of the amounts of cash being received and paid by a business during a defined period of time, sometimes tied to a specific project. Measurement of _____ can be used

- to evaluate the state or performance of a business or project.
- to determine problems with liquidity. Being profitable does not necessarily mean being liquid. A company can fail because of a shortage of cash, even while profitable.
- to generate project rate of returns. The time of _____s into and out of projects are used as inputs to financial models such as internal rate of return, and net present value.
- to examine income or growth of a business when it is believed that accrual accounting concepts do not represent economic realities. Alternately, _____ can be used to 'validate' the net income generated by accrual accounting.

_____ as a generic term may be used differently depending on context, and certain _____ definitions may be adapted by analysts and users for their own uses. Common terms include operating _____ and free _____.

_____s can be classified into:

1. Operational _____s: Cash received or expended as a result of the company's core business activities.
2. Investment _____s: Cash received or expended through capital expenditure, investments or acquisitions.
3. Financing _____s: Cash received or expended as a result of financial activities, such as interests and dividends.

All three together - the net _____ - are necessary to reconcile the beginning cash balance to the ending cash balance. Loan draw downs or equity injections, that is just shifting of capital but no expenditure as such, are not considered in the net _____.

a. Shareholder value
c. Corporate finance

b. Real option
d. Cash flow

29. The _____ is one of several stock market indices, created by nineteenth-century Wall Street Journal editor and Dow Jones ' Company co-founder Charles Dow. Dow compiled the index to gauge the performance of the industrial sector of the American stock market. It is the second-oldest U.S. market index, after the Dow Jones Transportation Average, which Dow also created.

a. 4-4-5 Calendar
c. 7-Eleven

b. 529 plan
d. Dow Jones Industrial Average

30. A _____ is the price of a single share of a no. of saleable stocks of the company. Once the stock is purchased, the owner becomes a shareholder of the company that issued the share.

a. Share price
c. Stock split

b. Trading curb
d. Whisper numbers

31. _____ is the fraction of net income a firm pays to its stockholders in dividends:

The part of the earnings not paid to investors is left for investment to provide for future earnings growth. Investors seeking high current income and limited capital growth prefer companies with high _____. However investors seeking capital growth may prefer lower payout ratio because capital gains are taxed at a lower rate.

a. Dividend puzzle
c. Dividend payout ratio

b. Dividend imputation
d. Dividend yield

32. _____ measures the rate of return on the ownership interest (shareholders' equity) of the common stock owners. _____ is viewed as one of the most important financial ratios. It measures a firm's efficiency at generating profits from every dollar of shareholders' equity (also known as net assets or assets minus liabilities.)

a. Return of capital
c. Diluted Earnings Per Share

b. Return on sales
d. Return on equity

33. In finance, the Acid-test or _____ or liquid ratio measures the ability of a company to use its near cash or quick assets to immediately extinguish or retire its current liabilities. Quick assets include those current assets that presumably can be quickly converted to cash at close to their book values.

Generally, the acid test ratio should be 1:1 or better, however this varies widely by industry.

a. Financial ratio
c. P/E ratio

b. Net assets
d. Quick ratio

34. _____ indicates the percentage of a company's earnings that are not paid out in dividends but credited to retained earnings. It is the opposite of the dividend payout ratio, so that also called the retention rate.

_____ = 1 - Dividend Payout Ratio

a. Dow Jones Indexes
c. Fair market value

b. Bankassurer
d. Retention ratio

35. _____ is the value on a given date of a future payment or series of future payments, discounted to reflect the time value of money and other factors such as investment risk. _____ calculations are widely used in business and economics to provide a means to compare cash flows at different times on a meaningful 'like to like' basis.

The most commonly applied model of the time value of money is compound interest.

a. Negative gearing
c. Net present value

b. Present value of benefits
d. Present value

36. In finance, a _____ or accounting ratio is a ratio of two selected numerical values taken from an enterprise's financial statements. There are many standard ratios used to try to evaluate the overall financial condition of a corporation or other organization. They may be used by managers within a firm, by current and potential shareholders (owners) of a firm, and by a firm's creditors. Security analysts use these to compare the strengths and weaknesses in various companies.

a. Price/cash flow ratio
b. Sustainable growth rate
c. Return on capital employed
d. Financial ratio

37. In finance, _____ occurs when a debtor has not met its legal obligations according to the debt contract, e.g. it has not made a scheduled payment, or has violated a loan covenant (condition) of the debt contract. _____ may occur if the debtor is either unwilling or unable to pay their debt. This can occur with all debt obligations including bonds, mortgages, loans, and promissory notes.

a. Vendor finance
b. Credit crunch
c. Debt validation
d. Default

38. _____ is the risk of loss due to a debtor's non-payment of a loan or other line of credit (either the principal or interest (coupon) or both)

Most lenders employ their own models (credit scorecards) to rank potential and existing customers according to risk, and then apply appropriate strategies. With products such as unsecured personal loans or mortgages, lenders charge a higher price for higher risk customers and vice versa. With revolving products such as credit cards and overdrafts, risk is controlled through careful setting of credit limits.

a. Credit risk
b. Market risk
c. Transaction risk
d. Liquidity risk

39. A _____ rocket is a rocket that uses two or more stages, each of which contains its own engines and propellant. A tandem or serial stage is mounted on top of another stage; a parallel stage is attached alongside another stage. The result is effectively two or more rockets stacked on top of or attached next to each other.

a. 529 plan
b. 7-Eleven
c. Multistage
d. 4-4-5 Calendar

40. _____ is the study of how the variation (uncertainty) in the output of a mathematical model can be apportioned, qualitatively or quantitatively, to different sources of variation in the input of a model .

In more general terms uncertainty and sensitivity analyses investigate the robustness of a study when the study includes some form of mathematical modelling. While uncertainty analysis studies the overall uncertainty in the conclusions of the study, _____ tries to identify what source of uncertainty weights more on the study's conclusions.

a. Sensitivity analysis
b. Synthetic CDO
c. Proxy fight
d. Golden parachute

41. The _____ (Price/Earnings To Growth ratio) is a valuation metric for determining the relative trade-off between the price of a stock, the earnings generated per share (EPS), and the company's expected growth.

In general, the P/E ratio is higher for a company with a higher growth rate. Thus using just the P/E ratio would make high-growth companies overvalued relative to others.

a. Return on equity   b. Return on assets
c. Current ratio   d. PEG ratio

42.   A _____ is a type of auction where the auctioneer begins with a high asking price which is lowered until some participant is willing to accept the auctioneer's price, or a predetermined reserve price (the seller's minimum acceptable price) is reached. The winning participant pays the last announced price. This is also known as a 'clock auction' or an open-outcry descending-price auction.

a. Dutch auction   b. 529 plan
c. 4-4-5 Calendar   d. 7-Eleven

43.   The term _____ or economic cycle refers to the fluctuations of economic activity (business fluctuations) around a long-term growth trend. The cycle involves shifts over time between periods of relatively rapid growth of output (recovery and prosperity), and periods of relative stagnation or decline (contraction or recession.) These fluctuations are often measured using the real gross domestic product.

a. Fixed exchange rate   b. Deflation
c. Behavioral finance   d. Business cycle

44.   _____ and earnings management are euphemisms referring to accounting practices that may follow the letter of the rules of standard accounting practices, but certainly deviate from the spirit of those rules. They are characterized by excessive complication and the use of novel ways of characterizing income, assets, or liabilities and the intent to influence readers towards the interpretations desired by the authors. The terms 'innovative' or 'aggressive' are also sometimes used.

a. Creative accounting   b. Debit and credit
c. Non Performing Asset   d. Controlling account

45.   _____ is the standard framework of guidelines for financial accounting used in the United States of America. It includes the standards, conventions, and rules accountants follow in recording and summarizing transactions, and in the preparation of financial statements. _____ are now issued by the Financial Accounting Standards Board (FASB).

a. Net income   b. Depreciation
c. Revenue   d. Generally accepted accounting principles

46.   The term _____ is a term applied to practices that are perfunctory, or seek to satisfy the minimum requirements or to conform to a convention or doctrine. It has different meanings in different fields.

In accounting, _____ earnings are those earnings of companies in addition to actual earnings calculated under the Generally Accepted Accounting Principles (GAAP) in their quarterly and yearly financial reports.

a. Long-term liabilities   b. Deferred financing costs
c. Pro forma   d. Deferred income

47.   Accrual, in accounting, describes the accounting method known as _____, whereby revenues and expenses are recognized when they are accrued, i.e. accumulated (earned or incurred), regardless when the actual cash is received or paid out.

E.g. a company delivers a product to a customer who will pay for it 30 days later in the next fiscal year starting a week after the delivery. The company recognizes the proceeds as a revenue in its current income statement still for the fiscal year of the delivery, even though it will get paid in cash during the following accounting period.

a. A Random Walk Down Wall Street   b. Accrual basis
c. AAB   d. ABN Amro

48.   The _____ of a stock is a measure of the price paid for a share relative to the annual income or profit earned by the firm per share. It is a financial ratio used for valuation: a higher _____ means that investors are paying more for each unit of income, so the stock is more expensive compared to one with lower _____.

The _____ has units of years, which can be interpreted as 'number of years of earnings to pay back purchase price'.

a. P/E ratio   b. Sustainable growth rate
c. Return of capital   d. Quick ratio

49.   The _____ is a financial ratio used to compare a company's book value to its current market price. Book value is an accounting term denoting the portion of the company held by the shareholders; in other words, the company's total tangible assets less its total liabilities. The calculation can be performed in two ways, but the result should be the same each way. In the first way, the company's market capitalization can be divided by the company's total book value from its balance sheet. The second way, using per-share values, is to divide the company's current share price by the book value per share (i.e. its book value divided by the number of outstanding shares).

a. Whisper numbers   b. Price-to-book ratio
c. Stop order   d. Stock repurchase

50.   In corporate finance, _____ is a cash flow available for distribution among all the security holders of a company. They include equity holders, debt holders, preferred stock holders, convertible security holders, and so on.

Note that the first three lines above are calculated for you on the standard Statement of Cash Flows.

a. Safety stock   b. Forfaiting
c. Funding   d. Free cash flow

51.   The _____ is an interest rate a central bank charges depository institutions that borrow reserves from it.

The term _____ has two meanings:

- the same as interest rate; the term 'discount' does not refer to the meaning of the word, but to the purpose of using the quantity, such as computations of present value, e.g. net present value / discounted cash flow

- the annual effective _____, which is the annual interest divided by the capital including that interest; this rate is lower than the interest rate; it corresponds to using the value after a year as the nominal value, and seeing the initial value as the nominal value minus a discount; it is used for Treasury Bills and similar financial instruments

The annual effective _____ is the annual interest divided by the capital including that interest, which is the interest rate divided by 100% plus the interest rate. It is the annual discount factor to be applied to the future cash flow, to find the discount, subtracted from a future value to find the value one year earlier.

For example, suppose there is a government bond that sells for $95 and pays $100 in a year's time.

a. Fisher equation   b. Black-Scholes
c. Discount rate   d. Stochastic volatility

52.   In financial and business accounting, _____ is a measure of a firm's profitability that excludes interest and income tax expenses.

EBIT = Operating Revenue - Operating Expenses (OPEX) + Non-operating Income

Operating Income = Operating Revenue - Operating Expenses

Operating income is the difference between operating revenues and operating expenses, but it is also sometimes used as a synonym for EBIT and operating profit. This is true if the firm has no non-operating income.

a. Earnings before interest and taxes   b. ABN Amro
c. A Random Walk Down Wall Street   d. AAB

53.   In finance, the _____ (continuing value or horizon value) of a security is the present value at a future point in time of all future cash flows when we expect stable growth rate forever. It is most often used in multi-stage discounted cash flow analysis, and allows for the limitation of cash flow projections to a several-year period. Forecasting results beyond such a period is impractical and exposes such projections to a variety of risks limiting their validity, primarily the great uncertainty involved in predicting industry and macroeconomic conditions beyond a few years.
a. Refinancing risk   b. Negative gearing
c. Discounted cash flow   d. Terminal value

54.   The _____ is an expected return that the provider of capital plans to earn on their investment.

Capital (money) used for funding a business should earn returns for the capital providers who risk their capital. For an investment to be worthwhile, the expected return on capital must be greater than the _____.

a. 4-4-5 Calendar
c. Capital intensity

b. Weighted average cost of capital
d. Cost of capital

55. _____ is a fee paid on borrowed assets. It is the price paid for the use of borrowed money , or, money earned by deposited funds . Assets that are sometimes lent with _____ include money, shares, consumer goods through hire purchase, major assets such as aircraft, and even entire factories in finance lease arrangements.
   a. AAB
   c. Insolvency

   b. A Random Walk Down Wall Street
   d. Interest

56. _____ is that which is owed; usually referencing assets owed, but the term can cover other obligations. In the case of assets, _____ is a means of using future purchasing power in the present before a summation has been earned. Some companies and corporations use _____ as a part of their overall corporate finance strategy.
   a. Debt
   c. Credit cycle

   b. Partial Payment
   d. Cross-collateralization

57. _____ is the quotient of earnings per share divided by the share price. It is the reciprocal of the P/E ratio--the E/P or the EPS.

The _____ is quoted as a percentage, allowing an easy comparison to going bond rates.

   a. Average accounting return
   c. Asset turnover

   b. Earnings yield
   d. Assets turnover

58. In finance, the term _____ describes the amount in cash that returns to the owners of a security. Normally it does not include the price variations, at the difference of the total return. _____ applies to various stated rates of return on stocks (common and preferred, and convertible), fixed income instruments (bonds, notes, bills, strips, zero coupon), and some other investment type insurance products (e.g. annuities.)
   a. 4-4-5 Calendar
   c. Macaulay duration

   b. Yield
   d. Yield to maturity

59. In economics, _____ is a rise in the general level of prices of goods and services in an economy over a period of time. The term '_____' once referred to increases in the money supply (monetary _____); however, economic debates about the relationship between money supply and price levels have led to its primary use today in describing price _____. _____ can also be described as a decline in the real value of money--a loss of purchasing power in the medium of exchange which is also the monetary unit of account.
   a. A Random Walk Down Wall Street
   c. Inflation

   b. ABN Amro
   d. AAB

60. _____ are government bonds issued by the United States Department of the Treasury through the Bureau of the Public Debt. They are the debt financing instruments of the U.S. Federal government, and they are often referred to simply as Treasuries or Treasurys. There are four types of marketable _____: Treasury bills, Treasury notes, Treasury bonds, and Treasury Inflation Protected Securities (TIPS.)
   a. Treasury Inflation-Protected Securities
   c. 4-4-5 Calendar

   b. Treasury Inflation Protected Securities
   d. Treasury securities

61. In finance, a _____ is a debt security, in which the authorized issuer owes the holders a debt and, depending on the terms of the _____, is obliged to pay interest (the coupon) and/or to repay the principal at a later date, termed maturity.

Thus a _____ is a loan: the issuer is the borrower, the _____ holder is the lender, and the coupon is the interest. _____s provide the borrower with external funds to finance long-term investments, or, in the case of government _____s, to finance current expenditure.

a. Puttable bond
c. Catastrophe bonds

b. Bond
d. Convertible bond

62. A _____ is a private or public market for the trading of company stock and derivatives of company stock at an agreed price; these are securities listed on a stock exchange as well as those only traded privately.

The size of the world _____ is estimated at about $36.6 trillion US at the beginning of October 2008 . The world derivatives market has been estimated at about $480 trillion face or nominal value, 12 times the size of the entire world economy.

a. Stock market
c. Andrew Tobias

b. Adolph Coors
d. Anton Gelonkin

63. A _____, securities exchange or (in Europe) bourse is a corporation or mutual organization which provides 'trading' facilities for stock brokers and traders, to trade stocks and other securities. _____s also provide facilities for the issue and redemption of securities as well as other financial instruments and capital events including the payment of income and dividends. The securities traded on a _____ include: shares issued by companies, unit trusts and other pooled investment products and bonds.

a. 529 plan
c. 4-4-5 Calendar

b. 7-Eleven
d. Stock exchange

1. The institution most often referenced by the word '_____' is a public or publicly traded _____, the shares of which are traded on a public stock exchange (e.g., the New York Stock Exchange or Nasdaq in the United States) where shares of stock of _____s are bought and sold by and to the general public. Most of the largest businesses in the world are publicly traded _____s. However, the majority of _____s are said to be closely held, privately held or close _____s, meaning that no ready market exists for the trading of shares.

   a. Corporation
   c. Federal Home Loan Mortgage Corporation

   b. Depository Trust Company
   d. Protect

2. In financial and business accounting, _____ is a measure of a firm's profitability that excludes interest and income tax expenses.

EBIT = Operating Revenue - Operating Expenses (OPEX) + Non-operating Income

Operating Income = Operating Revenue - Operating Expenses

Operating income is the difference between operating revenues and operating expenses, but it is also sometimes used as a synonym for EBIT and operating profit. This is true if the firm has no non-operating income.

   a. AAB
   c. Earnings before interest and taxes

   b. A Random Walk Down Wall Street
   d. ABN Amro

3. _____ are formal records of a business' financial activities.

   _____ provide an overview of a business' financial condition in both short and long term. There are four basic _____:

   1. **Balance sheet**: also referred to as statement of financial position or condition, reports on a company's assets, liabilities, and net equity as of a given point in time.
   2. **Income statement**: also referred to as Profit and Loss statement (or a 'P'L'), reports on a company's income, expenses, and profits over a period of time.
   3. **Statement of retained earnings**: explains the changes in a company's retained earnings over the reporting period.
   4. **Statement of cash flows**: reports on a company's cash flow activities, particularly its operating, investing and financing activities.

   a. Notes to the Financial Statements
   c. Statement on Auditing Standards No. 70: Service Organizations

   b. Statement of retained earnings
   d. Financial statements

4. _____, refers to consumption opportunity gained by an entity within a specified time frame, which is generally expressed in monetary terms. However, for households and individuals, '_____ is the sum of all the wages, salaries, profits, interests payments, rents and other forms of earnings received... in a given period of time.' For firms, _____ generally refers to net-profit: what remains of revenue after expenses have been subtracted.

   a. Annual report
   c. Income

   b. Accrual
   d. OIBDA

5.   An _____ is a financial statement for companies that indicates how Revenue is transformed into net income The purpose of the _____ is to show managers and investors whether the company made or lost money during the period being reported.

The important thing to remember about an _____ is that it represents a period of time.

   a. ABN Amro   b. Income statement
   c. A Random Walk Down Wall Street   d. AAB

6.   _____ is a fee paid on borrowed assets. It is the price paid for the use of borrowed money , or, money earned by deposited funds . Assets that are sometimes lent with _____ include money, shares, consumer goods through hire purchase, major assets such as aircraft, and even entire factories in finance lease arrangements.

   a. Insolvency   b. AAB
   c. Interest   d. A Random Walk Down Wall Street

7.   _____ relates to the cost of borrowing money. It is the price that a lender charges a borrower for the use of the lender's money. _____ is different from OPEX and CAPEX, for it relates to the capital structure of a company.
   a. A Random Walk Down Wall Street   b. ABN Amro
   c. AAB   d. Interest expense

8.   An _____, operating expenditure, operational expense, operational expenditure or OPEX is an on-going cost for running a product, business, or system. Its counterpart, a capital expenditure (CAPEX), is the cost of developing or providing non-consumable parts for the product or system. For example, the purchase of a photocopier is the CAPEX, and the annual paper and toner cost is the OPEX.
   a. AAB   b. A Random Walk Down Wall Street
   c. ABN Amro   d. Operating expense

9.   _____ is the difference between operating revenues and operating expenses, but it is also sometimes used as a synonym for EBIT and operating profit. This is true if the firm has no non-_____.

A professional investor contemplating a change to the capital structure of a firm (e.g., through a leveraged buyout) first evaluates a firm's fundamental earnings potential (reflected by Earnings Before Interest, Taxes, Depreciation and Amortization EBITDA and EBIT), and then determines the optimal use of debt vs. equity.

   a. A Random Walk Down Wall Street   b. ABN Amro
   c. Operating income   d. AAB

10.   In business and accounting, _____s are everything of value that is owned by a person or company. The balance sheet of a firm records the monetary value of the _____s owned by the firm. The two major _____ classes are tangible _____s and intangible _____s.
   a. Accounts payable   b. Asset
   c. Income   d. EBITDA

11.   In financial accounting, a _____ or statement of financial position is a summary of a person's or organization's balances. Assets, liabilities and ownership equity are listed as of a specific date, such as the end of its financial year. A _____ is often described as a snapshot of a company's financial condition.

a. Financial statements

c. Balance sheet

b. Statement of retained earnings

d. Statement on Auditing Standards No. 70: Service Organizations

12. _____ is an accounting term used to reflect the portion of the book value of a business entity not directly attributable to its assets and liabilities; it normally arises only in case of an acquisition. It reflects the ability of the entity to make a higher profit than would be derived from selling the tangible assets. _____ is also known as an intangible asset.

a. Consolidation

c. Cost of goods sold

b. Goodwill

d. Net profit

13. In economic models, the _____ time frame assumes no fixed factors of production. Firms can enter or leave the marketplace, and the cost (and availability) of land, labor, raw materials, and capital goods can be assumed to vary. In contrast, in the short-run time frame, certain factors are assumed to be fixed, because there is not sufficient time for them to change.

a. 4-4-5 Calendar

c. 529 plan

b. Long-run

d. Short-run

14. In economics, the concept of the _____ refers to the decision-making time frame of a firm in which at least one factor of production is fixed. Costs which are fixed in the _____ have no impact on a firms decisions. For example a firm can raise output by increasing the amount of labour through overtime.

a. 529 plan

c. Long-run

b. 4-4-5 Calendar

d. Short-run

15. _____ is that which is owed; usually referencing assets owed, but the term can cover other obligations. In the case of assets, _____ is a means of using future purchasing power in the present before a summation has been earned. Some companies and corporations use _____ as a part of their overall corporate finance strategy.

a. Partial Payment

c. Debt

b. Cross-collateralization

d. Credit cycle

16. _____, in bookkeeping, refers to assets, liabilities, income, and expenses recorded on individual pages of the so called book of final entry or ledger. Changes in _____ value are made by chronologically posting debit (DR) and credit (CR) entries to its page. Examples of _____s are cash, _____s receivable, mortgages, loans, land and buildings, common stock, sales, services provided, wages, and payroll overhead.

a. Option

c. Accretion

b. Account

d. Alpha

17. _____ is a file or account that contains money that a person or company owes to suppliers, but hasn't paid yet (a form of debt.) When you receive an invoice you add it to the file, and then you remove it when you pay. Thus, the A/P is a form of credit that suppliers offer to their purchasers by allowing them to pay for a product or service after it has already been received.

a. Accrual

c. Accounts payable

b. Outstanding balance

d. Earnings before interest, taxes, depreciation and amortization

18. _____ is one of a series of accounting transactions dealing with the billing of customers who owe money to a person, company or organization for goods and services that have been provided to the customer. In most business entities this is typically done by generating an invoice and mailing or electronically delivering it to the customer, who in turn must pay it within an established timeframe called credit or payment terms.

An example of a common payment term is Net 30, meaning payment is due in the amount of the invoice 30 days from the date of invoice.

a. Income
c. Accounts receivable

b. Impaired asset
d. Accounting methods

19. Accrual, in accounting, describes the accounting method known as _____, whereby revenues and expenses are recognized when they are accrued, i.e. accumulated (earned or incurred), regardless when the actual cash is received or paid out.

E.g. a company delivers a product to a customer who will pay for it 30 days later in the next fiscal year starting a week after the delivery. The company recognizes the proceeds as a revenue in its current income statement still for the fiscal year of the delivery, even though it will get paid in cash during the following accounting period.

a. AAB
c. ABN Amro

b. A Random Walk Down Wall Street
d. Accrual basis

20. In financial accounting, a _____ or statement of cash flows is a financial statement that shows a company's flow of cash. The money coming into the business is called cash inflow, and money going out from the business is called cash outflow. The statement shows how changes in balance sheet and income accounts affect cash and cash equivalents, and breaks the analysis down to operating, investing, and financing activities.

a. 7-Eleven
c. 4-4-5 Calendar

b. 529 plan
d. Cash flow statement

21. _____ is the balance of the amounts of cash being received and paid by a business during a defined period of time, sometimes tied to a specific project. Measurement of _____ can be used

- to evaluate the state or performance of a business or project.
- to determine problems with liquidity. Being profitable does not necessarily mean being liquid. A company can fail because of a shortage of cash, even while profitable.
- to generate project rate of returns. The time of _____ s into and out of projects are used as inputs to financial models such as internal rate of return, and net present value.
- to examine income or growth of a business when it is believed that accrual accounting concepts do not represent economic realities. Alternately, _____ can be used to 'validate' the net income generated by accrual accounting.

_____ as a generic term may be used differently depending on context, and certain _____ definitions may be adapted by analysts and users for their own uses. Common terms include operating _____ and free _____.

_____s can be classified into:

1. Operational _____s: Cash received or expended as a result of the company's core business activities.
2. Investment _____s: Cash received or expended through capital expenditure, investments or acquisitions.
3. Financing _____s: Cash received or expended as a result of financial activities, such as interests and dividends.

All three together - the net _____ - are necessary to reconcile the beginning cash balance to the ending cash balance. Loan draw downs or equity injections, that is just shifting of capital but no expenditure as such, are not considered in the net _____.

a. Real option   b. Corporate finance
c. Shareholder value   d. Cash flow

22. _____ is a term used in accounting, economics and finance to spread the cost of an asset over the span of several years.

In simple words we can say that _____ is the reduction in the value of an asset due to usage, passage of time, wear and tear, technological outdating or obsolescence, depletion or other such factors.

In accounting, _____ is a term used to describe any method of attributing the historical or purchase cost of an asset across its useful life, roughly corresponding to normal wear and tear.

a. Matching principle   b. Depreciation
c. Deferred financing costs   d. Bottom line

23. _____ or financing is to provide capital (funds), which means money for a project, a person, a business or any other private or public institutions.

Those funds can be allocated for either short term or long term purposes. The health fund is a new way of _____ private healthcare centers.

a. Proxy fight   b. Synthetic CDO
c. Product life cycle   d. Funding

24. _____ is the standard framework of guidelines for financial accounting used in the United States of America. It includes the standards, conventions, and rules accountants follow in recording and summarizing transactions, and in the preparation of financial statements. _____ are now issued by the Financial Accounting Standards Board (FASB).
a. Depreciation   b. Revenue
c. Generally accepted accounting principles   d. Net income

25. _____ is equal to the income that a firm has after subtracting costs and expenses from the total revenue.
_____ can be distributed among holders of common stock as a dividend or held by the firm as retained earnings.
_____ is an accounting term; in some countries (such as the UK) profit is the usual term.

  a. Furniture, Fixtures and Equipment   b. Historical cost
  c. Write-off   d. Net income

26. _____ measures the rate of return on the ownership interest (shareholders' equity) of the common stock owners.
_____ is viewed as one of the most important financial ratios. It measures a firm's efficiency at generating profits from every dollar of shareholders' equity (also known as net assets or assets minus liabilities.)

  a. Return of capital   b. Return on sales
  c. Diluted Earnings Per Share   d. Return on equity

27. In finance, the Acid-test or _____ or liquid ratio measures the ability of a company to use its near cash or quick assets to immediately extinguish or retire its current liabilities. Quick assets include those current assets that presumably can be quickly converted to cash at close to their book values.

Generally, the acid test ratio should be 1:1 or better, however this varies widely by industry.

  a. Financial ratio   b. Net assets
  c. Quick ratio   d. P/E ratio

28. In accounting, _____ or *Carrying value* is the value of an asset according to its balance sheet account balance. For assets, the value is based on the original cost of the asset less any depreciation, amortization or impairment costs made against the asset. A company's _____ is its total assets minus intangible assets and liabilities.

  a. Current liabilities   b. Pro forma
  c. Retained earnings   d. Book value

29. In finance, _____ (or gearing) is borrowing money to supplement existing funds for investment in such a way that the potential positive or negative outcome is magnified and/or enhanced. It generally refers to using borrowed funds, or debt, so as to attempt to increase the returns to equity. Deleveraging is the action of reducing borrowings.

  a. Limited partnership   b. Leverage
  c. Financial endowment   d. Pension fund

30. The _____ percentage shows how profitable a company's assets are in generating revenue.

_____ can be computed as:

$$ROA = \frac{Net\ Income}{Total\ Assets}$$

This number tells you 'what the company can do with what it's got', i.e. how many dollars of earnings they derive from each dollar of assets they control. It's a useful number for comparing competing companies in the same industry.

a. Return on sales   b. P/E ratio

c. Return on assets   d. Receivables turnover ratio

31. _____ (or spoilage) refers to the process by which tissues of dead organisms break down into simpler forms of matter. Such a breakdown of dead organisms is essential for new growth and development of living organisms because it recycles the finite chemical constituents and frees up the limited physical space in the biome. Bodies of living organisms begin to decompose shortly after death.

a. 4-4-5 Calendar   b. 529 plan

c. Decomposition   d. 7-Eleven

32. _____ is the difference between price and the costs of bringing to market whatever it is that is accounted as an enterprise (whether by harvest, extraction, manufacture, or purchase) in terms of the component costs of delivered goods and/or services and any operating or other expenses.

A key difficulty in measuring profit is in defining costs. Pure economic monetary profits can be zero or negative even in competitive equilibrium when accounted monetized costs exceed monetized price.

a. Economic profit   b. A Random Walk Down Wall Street

c. AAB   d. Accounting profit

33. _____, Net Margin, Net _____ or Net Profit Ratio all refer to a measure of profitability. It is calculated using a formula and written as a percentage or a number.

$$\text{Net profit margin} = \frac{\text{Net profit after taxes}}{\text{Net Sales}}$$

The _____ is mostly used for internal comparison.

a. Net profit margin   b. Profit maximization

c. 4-4-5 Calendar   d. Profit margin

34. In business, operating margin, Operating Income Margin, Operating profit margin or _____ is the ratio of operating income (operating profit in the UK) divided by net sales, usually presented in percent.

$$\text{Operating margin} = \left(\frac{\text{Operating income}}{\text{Revenue}} \right)$$

(Relevant figures in italics)

$$\text{Operating margin} = \left(\frac{6,318}{24,088} \right) = \underline{\underline{26.23\%}}$$

It is a measurement of what proportion of a company's revenue is left over, before taxes and other indirect costs (such as rent, bonus, interest etc.), after paying for variable costs of production as wages, raw materials, etc. A good operating margin is needed for a company to be able to pay for its fixed costs, such as interest on debt.

a. Return on assets

b. Return on equity

c. Current ratio

d. Return on sales

35.   In finance, a _____ is collateral that the holder of a position in securities, options, or futures contracts has to deposit to cover the credit risk of his counterparty (most often his broker.) This risk can arise if the holder has done any of the following:

- borrowed cash from the counterparty to buy securities or options,
- sold securities or options short, or
- entered into a futures contract.

The collateral can be in the form of cash or securities, and it is deposited in a _____ account. On U.S. futures exchanges, '_____' was formally called performance bond.

_____ buying is buying securities with cash borrowed from a broker, using other securities as collateral.

a. Share

b. Margin

c. Procter ' Gamble

d. Credit

36.   _____ is a financial ratio that measures the efficiency of a company's use of its assets in generating sales revenue or sales income to the company.

$$Asset\ Turnover = \frac{Sales}{Average Total Assets}$$

- 'Sales' is the value of 'Net Sales' or 'Sales' from the company's income statement
- 'Average Total Assets' is the value of 'Total assets' from the company's balance sheet in the beginning and the end of the fiscal period divided by 2.

- Assets turnover

a. Inventory turnover

b. Earnings yield

c. Average accounting return

d. Asset turnover

37.   Times interest earned (TIE) or _____ is a measure of a company's ability to honor its debt payments. It may be calculated as either EBIT or EBITDA divided by the total interest payable.

$$\text{Times-Interest-Earned} = \frac{\text{EBIT or EBITDA}}{\text{Interest Charges}}$$

- Financial ratio
- Financial leverage
- EBIT
- EBITDA
- Debt service coverage ratio

Interest Charges = Traditionally 'charges' refers to interest expense found on the income statement.

Times Interest Earned or Interest Coverage is a great tool when measuring a company's ability to meet its debt obligations.

a. Interest coverage ratio   b. Earnings per share
c. Information ratio   d. Assets turnover

38. _____ or interest coverage ratio is a measure of a company's ability to honor its debt payments. It may be calculated as either EBIT or EBITDA divided by the total interest payable.

$$\text{Times-Interest-Earned} = \frac{\text{EBIT or EBITDA}}{\text{Interest Charges}}$$

- Financial ratio
- Financial leverage
- EBIT
- EBITDA
- Debt service coverage ratio

Interest Charges = Traditionally 'charges' refers to interest expense found on the income statement.

_____ or Interest Coverage is a great tool when measuring a company's ability to meet its debt obligations.

a. Return of capital   b. Times interest earned
c. Net assets   d. Cash conversion cycle

39. _____ is a list for goods and materials held available in stock by a business. It is also used for a list of the contents of a household and for a list for testamentary purposes of the possessions of someone who has died. In accounting _____ is considered an asset.

a. ABN Amro   b. A Random Walk Down Wall Street
c. Inventory   d. AAB

40. The _____ is an equation that equals the cost of goods sold divided by the average inventory. Average inventory equals beginning inventory plus ending inventory divided by 2.

The formula for _____:

$$\text{Inventory Turnover} = \frac{\text{Cost of Goods Sold}}{\text{Average Inventory}}$$

The formula for average inventory:

$$\text{Average Inventory} = \frac{\text{Beginning inventory} + \text{Ending inventory}}{2}$$

A low turnover rate may point to overstocking, obsolescence, or deficiencies in the product line or marketing effort.

a. Operating leverage
c. Earnings yield

b. Information ratio
d. Inventory turnover

41. _____ is one of the Accounting Liquidity ratios, a financial ratio. This ratio measures the number of times, on average, the inventory is sold during the period. Its purpose is to measure the liquidity of the inventory.
a. AAB
c. Inventory turnover ratio

b. ABN Amro
d. A Random Walk Down Wall Street

42. The _____ is a bank regulation that sets the minimum reserves each bank must hold to customer deposits and notes. These reserves are designed to satisfy withdrawal demands, and would normally be in the form of fiat currency stored in a bank vault (vault cash), or with a central bank.

The reserve ratio is sometimes used as a tool in the monetary policy, influencing the country's economy, borrowing, and interest rates.

a. Prime rate
c. Variable rate mortgage

b. Wall Street Journal prime rate
d. Reserve requirement

43. The _____ is a financial ratio that measures whether or not a firm has enough resources to pay its debts over the next 12 months. It compares a firm's current assets to its current liabilities. It is expressed as follows:

$$\text{Current ratio} = \frac{\text{Current Assets}}{\text{Current Liabilities}}$$

For example, if WXY Company's current assets are $50,000,000 and its current liabilities are $40,000,000, then its _____ would be $50,000,000 divided by $40,000,000, which equals 1.25.

a. PEG ratio

b. Current ratio

c. Sustainable growth rate

d. Debt service coverage ratio

44. _____ is a measure of the ability of a debtor to pay their debts as and when they fall due. It is usually expressed as a ratio or a percentage of current liabilities.

For a corporation with a published balance sheet there are various ratios used to calculate a measure of liquidity.

a. Accounting liquidity

b. Operating profit margin

c. Invested capital

d. Operating leverage

45. _____ is an economic concept with commonplace familiarity. It is the price that a good or service is offered at, or will fetch, in the marketplace. It is of interest mainly in the study of microeconomics.

a. Delta hedging

b. Convertible arbitrage

c. Market price

d. Central Securities Depository

46. The term _____ or economic cycle refers to the fluctuations of economic activity (business fluctuations) around a long-term growth trend. The cycle involves shifts over time between periods of relatively rapid growth of output (recovery and prosperity), and periods of relative stagnation or decline (contraction or recession.) These fluctuations are often measured using the real gross domestic product.

a. Deflation

b. Fixed exchange rate

c. Behavioral finance

d. Business cycle

47. _____ is the quotient of earnings per share divided by the share price. It is the reciprocal of the P/E ratio--the E/P or the EPS.

The _____ is quoted as a percentage, allowing an easy comparison to going bond rates.

a. Average accounting return

b. Assets turnover

c. Earnings yield

d. Asset turnover

48. The _____ of a stock is a measure of the price paid for a share relative to the annual income or profit earned by the firm per share. It is a financial ratio used for valuation: a higher _____ means that investors are paying more for each unit of income, so the stock is more expensive compared to one with lower _____.

The _____ has units of years, which can be interpreted as 'number of years of earnings to pay back purchase price'.

a. Return of capital

b. Sustainable growth rate

c. Quick ratio

d. P/E ratio

49. In business and finance, a _____ (also referred to as equity _____) of stock means a _____ of ownership in a corporation (company.) In the plural, stocks is often used as a synonym for _____s especially in the United States, but it is less commonly used that way outside of North America.

In the United Kingdom, South Africa, and Australia, stock can also refer to completely different financial instruments such as government bonds or, less commonly, to all kinds of marketable securities.

a. Procter ' Gamble   b. Share

c. Bucket shop   d. Margin

50. In finance, the term _____ describes the amount in cash that returns to the owners of a security. Normally it does not include the price variations, at the difference of the total return. _____ applies to various stated rates of return on stocks (common and preferred, and convertible), fixed income instruments (bonds, notes, bills, strips, zero coupon), and some other investment type insurance products (e.g. annuities.)

a. Yield to maturity   b. Macaulay duration

c. 4-4-5 Calendar   d. Yield

51. In finance, a _____ or accounting ratio is a ratio of two selected numerical values taken from an enterprise's financial statements. There are many standard ratios used to try to evaluate the overall financial condition of a corporation or other organization. They may be used by managers within a firm, by current and potential shareholders (owners) of a firm, and by a firm's creditors. Security analysts use these to compare the strengths and weaknesses in various companies.

a. Financial ratio   b. Sustainable growth rate

c. Price/cash flow ratio   d. Return on capital employed

52. In finance, _____ occurs when a debtor has not met its legal obligations according to the debt contract, e.g. it has not made a scheduled payment, or has violated a loan covenant (condition) of the debt contract. _____ may occur if the debtor is either unwilling or unable to pay their debt. This can occur with all debt obligations including bonds, mortgages, loans, and promissory notes.

a. Credit crunch   b. Vendor finance

c. Default   d. Debt validation

53. _____ is the risk of loss due to a debtor's non-payment of a loan or other line of credit (either the principal or interest (coupon) or both)

Most lenders employ their own models (credit scorecards) to rank potential and existing customers according to risk, and then apply appropriate strategies. With products such as unsecured personal loans or mortgages, lenders charge a higher price for higher risk customers and vice versa. With revolving products such as credit cards and overdrafts, risk is controlled through careful setting of credit limits.

a. Liquidity risk   b. Credit risk

c. Transaction risk   d. Market risk

54. In corporate finance, _____ is an estimate of true economic profit after making corrective adjustments to GAAP accounting, including deducting the opportunity cost of equity capital. GAAP is estimated to ignore US$300 billion in shareholder opportunity costs. _____ can be measured as Net Operating Profit After Taxes(or NOPAT) less the money cost of capital.

a. ABN Amro   b. Economic value added

c. AAB   d. A Random Walk Down Wall Street

55. _____ refers to the additional value of a commodity over the cost of commodities used to produce it from the previous stage of production. An example is the price of gasoline at the pump over the price of the oil in it. In national accounts used in macroeconomics, it refers to the contribution of the factors of production, i.e., land, labor, and capital goods, to raising the value of a product and corresponds to the incomes received by the owners of these factors.

a. Value added
b. Supply shock
c. Deregulation
d. Demand shock

56. _____ is a rent received on a regular basis, with little effort required to maintain it. It is advocated by some authors, especially by Robert Kiyosaki.

Some examples of _____ are:

- Repeated regular income, earned by a sales person, generated from the payment of a product or service that must be renewed on a regular basis, in order to continue receiving its benefits - also called residual income.
- Rental from property;
- Royalties from publishing a book or from licensing a patent or other form of intellectual property;
- Earnings from internet advertisement on your websites;
- Earnings from a business that does not require direct involvement from the owner or merchant;
- Dividend and interest income from owning securities, such as stocks and bonds, are usually referred to as portfolio income, which can be considered a form of _____;
- Pensions.

_____ is usually taxable. The American Internal Revenue Service defines _____ as 'any activity...

a. Horizontal merger
b. Passive income
c. 4-4-5 Calendar
d. Fixed exchange rate system

57. In economics, business, and accounting, a _____ is the value of money that has been used up to produce something, and hence is not available for use anymore. In business, the _____ may be one of acquisition, in which case the amount of money expended to acquire it is counted as _____. In this case, money is the input that is gone in order to acquire the thing.

a. Marginal cost
b. Fixed costs
c. Cost
d. Sliding scale fees

58. _____, _____ includes the direct costs attributable to the production of the goods sold by a company. This amount includes the materials cost used in creating the goods along with the direct labor costs used to produce the good. It excludes indirect expenses such as distribution costs and sales force costs.

a. Goodwill
b. Deferred financing costs
c. Net profit
d. Cost of goods sold

59. In economics and accounting, _____ is seen as the change in the market value of capital over a given period. It is calculated as the market price of the capital at the beginning of the period minus its market price at the end of the period.

Such a method in calculating depreciation differs from other methods, such as straight-line depreciation in that it is included in the calculation of implicit cost, and thus economic profit.

a. AAB
b. Economic depreciation
c. A Random Walk Down Wall Street
d. Index number

60.   Gross domestic product (GDP) is defined as the 'value of all final goods and services produced in a country in one year'. On the other hand, _____ is defined as the 'value of all (final) goods and services produced in a country in one year, plus income earned by its citizens abroad, minus income earned by foreigners in the country'. The key difference between the two is that GDP is the total output of a region, eg.

a. Gross national product
b. Purchasing power parity
c. 4-4-5 Calendar
d. TED spread

61.   An _____ allows a company to provide a monetary value for items that make up their inventory. Inventories are usually the largest current asset of a business, and proper measurement of them is necessary to assure accurate financial statements. If inventory is not properly measured, expenses and revenues cannot be properly matched and a company could make poor business decisions.

a. Inventory valuation
b. A Random Walk Down Wall Street
c. AAB
d. ABN Amro

62.   In finance, _____ is the process of estimating the potential market value of a financial asset or liability. they can be done on assets (for example, investments in marketable securities such as stocks, options, business enterprises, or intangible assets such as patents and trademarks) or on liabilities (e.g., Bonds issued by a company.) _____s are required in many contexts including investment analysis, capital budgeting, merger and acquisition transactions, financial reporting, taxable events to determine the proper tax liability, and in litigation.

a. Procter ' Gamble
b. Margin
c. Share
d. Valuation

63.   _____ refers to any one of several methods by which a company, for 'financial accounting' and/or tax purposes, depreciates a fixed asset in such a way that the amount of depreciation taken each year is higher during the earlier years of an asset's life. For financial accounting purposes, _____ is generally used when an asset is expected to be much more productive during its early years, so that depreciation expense will more accurately represent how much of an asset's usefulness is being used up each year. For tax purposes, _____ provides a way of deferring corporate income taxes by reducing taxable income in current years, in exchange for increased taxable income in future years.

a. ABN Amro
b. Accelerated depreciation
c. A Random Walk Down Wall Street
d. AAB

64.   In economics, _____ is a rise in the general level of prices of goods and services in an economy over a period of time. The term '_____' once referred to increases in the money supply (monetary _____); however, economic debates about the relationship between money supply and price levels have led to its primary use today in describing price _____. _____ can also be described as a decline in the real value of money--a loss of purchasing power in the medium of exchange which is also the monetary unit of account.

a. A Random Walk Down Wall Street
b. AAB
c. Inflation
d. ABN Amro

65.   The role of the _____ is to issue accounting standards in the United Kingdom. It is recognised for that purpose under the Companies Act 1985. It took over the task of setting accounting standards from the Accounting Standards Committee (ASC) in 1990.

a. ABN Amro   b. AAB
c. A Random Walk Down Wall Street   d. Accounting Standards Board

66.   In accounting and finance, _____ is the portion of receivables that can no longer be collected, typically from accounts receivable or loans. _____ in accounting is considered an expense.

There are two methods to account for _____:

1.   Direct write off method (Non - GAAP)

A receivable which is not considered collectible is charged directly to the income statement.

1.   Allowance method (GAAP)

An estimate is made at the end of each fiscal year of the amount of _____. This is then accumulated in a provision which is then used to reduce specific receivable accounts as and when necessary.

a. Bad debt   b. Tax expense
c. 529 plan   d. 4-4-5 Calendar

67.   _____ is the business practice where a company, or a sales force within a company, inflates its sales figures by forcing more products through a distribution channel than the channel is capable of selling to the world at large. Also known as 'trade loading', this can be the result of a company attempting to inflate its sales figures. Alternatively, it can be a consequence of a poorly managed sales force attempting to meet short term objectives and quotas in a way that is detrimental to the company in the long term.
a. Channel stuffing   b. False billing
c. Systematic risk   d. Peer group analysis

68.   _____ is the field of accountancy concerned with the preparation of financial statements for decision makers, such as stockholders, suppliers, banks, employees, government agencies, owners, and other stakeholders. The fundamental need for _____ is to reduce principal-agent problem by measuring and monitoring agents' performance and reporting the results to interested users.

_____ is used to prepare accounting information for people outside the organization or not involved in the day to day running of the company.

a. Financial Accounting   b. 529 plan
c. 7-Eleven   d. 4-4-5 Calendar

69.   The _____ is a private, not-for-profit organization whose primary purpose is to develop generally accepted accounting principles (GAAP) within the United States in the public's interest. The Securities and Exchange Commission (SEC) designated the _____ as the organization responsible for setting accounting standards for public companies in the U.S. It was created in 1973, replacing the Accounting Principles Board and the Committee on Accounting Procedure of the American Institute of Certified Public Accountants. The _____'s mission is 'to establish and improve standards of financial accounting and reporting for the guidance and education of the public, including issuers, auditors, and users of financial information.'

The _____ is not a governmental body.

a. Federal Deposit Insurance Corporation
c. Financial Accounting Standards Board

b. KPMG
d. World Congress of Accountants

70.   In financial accounting, the term _____ is most commonly used to describe any part of shareholders' equity, except for basic share capital. Sometimes, the term is used instead of the term provision; such a use, however, is inconsistent with the terminology suggested by International Accounting Standards Board. For more information about provisions, see provision (accounting.)

a. Closing entries
c. Treasury stock

b. Reserve
d. FIFO and LIFO accounting

71.   In business, _____ is income that a company receives from its normal business activities, usually from the sale of goods and services to customers. Some companies also receive _____ from interest, dividends or royalties paid to them by other companies. _____ may refer to business income in general, or it may refer to the amount, in a monetary unit, received during a period of time, as in 'Last year, Company X had _____ of $32 million.'

In many countries, including the UK, _____ is referred to as turnover.

a. Furniture, Fixtures and Equipment
c. Matching principle

b. Bottom line
d. Revenue

72.   The _____ principle is a cornerstone of accrual accounting together with matching principle. They both determine the accounting period, in which revenues and expenses are recognized. According to the principle, revenues are recognized when they are (1) realized or realizable, and are (2) earned (usually when goods are transferred or services rendered), no matter when cash is received.

a. Commodity Pool Operator
c. Tail risk

b. Revenue recognition
d. Regulation FD

73.   A _____ is a fungible, negotiable instrument representing financial value. They are broadly categorized into debt securities (such as banknotes, bonds and debentures), and equity securities; e.g., common stocks. The company or other entity issuing the _____ is called the issuer.

a. Book entry
c. Security

b. Tracking stock
d. Securities lending

74.   The U.S. _____ is an independent agency of the United States government which holds primary responsibility for enforcing the federal securities laws and regulating the securities industry, the nation's stock and options exchanges, and other electronic securities markets. The SEC was created by section 4 of the SEC of 1934 (now codified as 15 U.S.C. Â§ 78d and commonly referred to as the 1934 Act.)

a. 7-Eleven
c. 4-4-5 Calendar

b. 529 plan
d. Securities and Exchange Commission

75. An _____ is a contract written by a seller that conveys to the buyer the right -- but not the obligation -- to buy (in the case of a call _____) or to sell (in the case of a put _____) a particular asset, such as a piece of property such as, among others, a futures contract. In return for granting the _____, the seller collects a payment (the premium) from the buyer.

For example, buying a call _____ provides the right to buy a specified quantity of a security at a set strike price at some time on or before expiration, while buying a put _____ provides the right to sell.

a. Amortization
b. AT'T Mobility LLC
c. Option
d. Annuity

76. The _____ is the market for securities, where companies and governments can raise longterm funds. The _____ includes the stock market and the bond market. Financial regulators, such as the U.S. Securities and Exchange Commission, oversee the _____s in their designated countries to ensure that investors are protected against fraud.
a. Spot rate
b. Delta neutral
c. Forward market
d. Capital market

77. _____ are liabilities that may or may not be incurred by an entity depending on the outcome of a future event such as a court case. These liabilities are recorded in a company's accounts and shown in the balance sheet when both probable and reasonably estimable. A footnote to the balance sheet describes the nature and extent of the _____.
a. 529 plan
b. 4-4-5 Calendar
c. Contingent liabilities
d. Due-on-sale clause

78. _____ is the branch of economics that studies the dynamics of exchange rates, foreign investment, and how these affect international trade. It also studies international projects, international investments and capital flows, and trade deficits. It includes the study of futures, options and currency swaps.
a. ABN Amro
b. International finance
c. A Random Walk Down Wall Street
d. AAB

79. _____ are defined as identifiable non-monetary assets that cannot be seen, touched or physically measured, which are created through time and/or effort and that are identifiable as a separate asset. There are two primary forms of intangibles - legal intangibles (such as trade secrets (e.g., customer lists), copyrights, patents, trademarks, and goodwill) and competitive intangibles (such as knowledge activities (know-how, knowledge), collaboration activities, leverage activities, and structural activities.) Legal intangibles generate legal property rights defensible in a court of law.
a. AAB
b. A Random Walk Down Wall Street
c. ABN Amro
d. Intangible assets

80. Depreciation methods that provide for a higher depreciation charge in the first year of an asset's life and gradually decreasing charges in subsequent years are called accelerated depreciation methods. This may be a more realistic reflection of an asset's actual expected benefit from the use of the asset: many assets are most useful when they are new. One popular accelerated method is the declining-balance method. Under this method the Book Value is multiplied by a fixed rate.

The most common rate used is double the straight-line rate. For this reason, this technique is referred to as the _____. To illustrate, suppose a business has an asset with $1,000 Original Cost, $100 Salvage Value, and 5 years useful life. First, calculate straight-line depreciation rate. Since the asset has 5 years useful life, the straight-line depreciation rate equals (100% / 5) 20% per year. With _____, as the name suggests, double that rate, or 40% depreciation rate is used.

a. Double-declining-balance method
c. The Goodyear Tire ' Rubber Company

b. Doctrine of the Proper Law
d. Database auditing

81.   A _____ is a private or public market for the trading of company stock and derivatives of company stock at an agreed price; these are securities listed on a stock exchange as well as those only traded privately.

The size of the world _____ is estimated at about $36.6 trillion US at the beginning of October 2008 . The world derivatives market has been estimated at about $480 trillion face or nominal value, 12 times the size of the entire world economy.

a. Stock market
c. Adolph Coors

b. Anton Gelonkin
d. Andrew Tobias

82.   In the most general sense, a _____ is anything that is a hindrance, or puts individuals at a disadvantage.

Before we discuss the financial terms, we should note that a _____ can also have a much more important slang meaning.

This is best described in an example.

a. McFadden Act
c. Covenant

b. Limited liability
d. Liability

83.   The _____ founded on April 1, 2001 is the successor of the International Accounting Standards Committee (IASC) founded in June 1973 in London. It is responsible for developing the International Financial Reporting Standards (new name for the International Accounting Standards issued after 2001), and promoting the use and application of these standards.

The _____ is an independent, privately-funded accounting standard-setter based in London, UK.

a. International Federation of Accountants
c. American Accounting Association

b. Association of Certified Public Accountants
d. International Accounting Standards Board

84.   The _____ Options Exchange is a futures exchange based in London. _____ is now part of NYSE Euronext following its takeover by Euronext in January 2002 and Euronext's merger with New York Stock Exchange in April 2007.

The _____ started life on September 30, 1982, to take advantage of the removal of currency controls in the UK in 1979.

a. 4-4-5 Calendar   b. LIFFE

c. 7-Eleven   d. 529 plan

85. _____, authored by professors Benjamin Graham and David Dodd of Columbia Business School, laid the intellectual foundation for what would later be called value investing. The work was first published in 1934, following unprecedented losses on Wall Street. In summing up lessons learned, Graham and Dodd chided Wall Street for its myopic focus on a company's reported earnings per share, and were particularly harsh on the favored 'earnings trends.' They encouraged investors to take an entirely different approach by gauging the rough value of the operating business that lay behind the security.

a. 4-4-5 Calendar   b. Stock valuation

c. Growth stocks   d. Security Analysis

86. _____ is an investment paradigm that derives from the ideas on investment and speculation that Ben Graham ' David Dodd began teaching at Columbia Business School in 1928 and subsequently developed in their 1934 text Security Analysis. Although _____ has taken many forms since its inception, it generally involves buying securities whose shares appear underpriced by some form(s) of fundamental analysis. As examples, such securities may be stock in public companies that trade at discounts to book value or tangible book value, have high dividend yields, have low price-to-earning multiples or have low price-to-book ratios.

a. 4-4-5 Calendar   b. 529 plan

c. Value investing   d. Quality investing

87. A _____ is a financial contract whose value is derived from the value of something else (known as the underlying.) The underlying on which a _____ is based can be an asset, weather conditions bonds or other forms of credit.

a. 529 plan   b. 4-4-5 Calendar

c. 7-Eleven   d. Derivative

88. _____ is the discipline of identifying, monitoring and limiting risks. In some cases the acceptable risk may be near zero. Risks can come from accidents, natural causes and disasters as well as deliberate attacks from an adversary.

a. FIFO   b. Risk management

c. 4-4-5 Calendar   d. Penny stock

89. A _____ is an exchange of promises between two or more parties to do an act which is enforceable in a court of law. It is where an unqualified offer meets a qualified acceptance and the parties reach Consensus ad Idem. The parties must have the necessary capacity to _____ and the _____ must not be either trifling, indeterminate, impossible or illegal.

a. 529 plan   b. 7-Eleven

c. Contract   d. 4-4-5 Calendar

90. In finance, a _____ is a standardized contract, to buy or sell a specified commodity of standardized quality at a certain date in the future, at a market determined price (the futures price.)

The price is determined by the instantaneous equilibrium between the forces of supply and demand among competing buy and sell orders on the exchange at the time of the purchase or sale of the contract.

In many cases, the items may be such non-traditional 'commodities' as foreign currencies, commercial or government paper [e.g., bonds], or 'baskets' of corporate equity ['stock indices'] or other financial instruments.

a. Repurchase agreement

b. Heston model

c. Financial future

d. Futures contract

1.   An _____ is a contract written by a seller that conveys to the buyer the right -- but not the obligation -- to buy (in the case of a call _____) or to sell (in the case of a put _____) a particular asset, such as a piece of property such as, among others, a futures contract. In return for granting the _____, the seller collects a payment (the premium) from the buyer.

For example, buying a call _____ provides the right to buy a specified quantity of a security at a set strike price at some time on or before expiration, while buying a put _____ provides the right to sell.

   a. Option
   c. AT'T Mobility LLC

   b. Annuity
   d. Amortization

2.   A _____ is a financial contract between two parties, the buyer and the seller of this type of option. Often it is simply labeled a 'call'. The buyer of the option has the right, but not the obligation to buy an agreed quantity of a particular commodity or financial instrument (the underlying instrument) from the seller of the option at a certain time (the expiration date) for a certain price (the strike price.)

   a. Bull spread
   c. Bear spread

   b. Bear call spread
   d. Call option

3.   In options, the _____ is a key variable in a derivatives contract between two parties. Where the contract requires delivery of the underlying instrument, the trade will be at the _____, regardless of the spot price (market price) of the underlying instrument at that time.

Definition - The fixed price at which the owner of an option can purchase, in the case of a call in the case of a put, the underlying security or commodity.

   a. Moneyness
   c. Naked put

   b. Strike price
   d. Swaption

4.   In finance, a _____ is a standardized contract, to buy or sell a specified commodity of standardized quality at a certain date in the future, at a market determined price (the futures price.)

The price is determined by the instantaneous equilibrium between the forces of supply and demand among competing buy and sell orders on the exchange at the time of the purchase or sale of the contract.

In many cases, the items may be such non-traditional 'commodities' as foreign currencies, commercial or government paper [e.g., bonds], or 'baskets' of corporate equity ['stock indices'] or other financial instruments.

   a. Financial future
   c. Repurchase agreement

   b. Heston model
   d. Futures contract

5.   An _____ is defined as 'a promise which meets the requirements for the formation of a contract and limits the promisor's power to revoke an offer.' Restatement (Second) of Contracts Â§ 25 (1981.)

Quite simply, an _____ is a type of contract that protects an offeree from an offeror's ability to revoke the contract.

Consideration for the _____ is still required as it is still a form of contract.

a. AAB
c. A Random Walk Down Wall Street

b. ABN Amro
d. Option contract

6. In finance, a _____ is a derivative in which two counterparties agree to exchange one stream of cash flows against another stream. These streams are called the legs of the _____.

The cash flows are calculated over a notional principal amount, which is usually not exchanged between counterparties.

a. Volatility swap
c. Volatility arbitrage

b. Local volatility
d. Swap

7. A _____ is an exchange of promises between two or more parties to do an act which is enforceable in a court of law. It is where an unqualified offer meets a qualified acceptance and the parties reach Consensus ad Idem. The parties must have the necessary capacity to _____ and the _____ must not be either trifling, indeterminate, impossible or illegal.
a. Contract
c. 4-4-5 Calendar

b. 7-Eleven
d. 529 plan

8. The term _____ refers to three closely related concepts:

- The _____ model is a mathematical model of the market for an equity, in which the equity's price is a stochastic process.
- The _____ PDE is a partial differential equation which (in the model) must be satisfied by the price of a derivative on the equity.
- The _____ formula is the result obtained by solving the _____ PDE for a European call option.

Fischer Black and Myron Scholes first articulated the _____ formula in their 1973 paper, 'The Pricing of Options and Corporate Liabilities.' The foundation for their research relied on work developed by scholars such as Jack L. Treynor, Paul Samuelson, A. James Boness, Sheen T. Kassouf, and Edward O. Thorp. The fundamental insight of _____ is that the option is implicitly priced if the stock is traded.

Robert C. Merton was the first to publish a paper expanding the mathematical understanding of the options pricing model and coined the term '_____' options pricing model.

a. Perpetuity
c. Stochastic volatility

b. Modified Internal Rate of Return
d. Black-Scholes

9. A _____ is a financial contract between two parties, the seller (writer) and the buyer of the option. The put allows its buyer the right but not the obligation to sell a commodity or financial instrument (the underlying instrument) to the writer (seller) of the option at a certain time for a certain price (the strike price.) The writer (seller) has the obligation to purchase the underlying asset at that strike price, if the buyer exercises the option.
a. Bear spread
c. Bear call spread

b. Debit spread
d. Put option

10. In banking and finance, _____ denotes all activities from the time a commitment is made for a transaction until it is settled. _____ is necessary because the speed of trades is much faster than the cycle time for completing the underlying transaction.

In its widest sense _____ involves the management of post-trading, pre-settlement credit exposures, to ensure that trades are settled in accordance with market rules, even if a buyer or seller should become insolvent prior to settlement.

a. Clearing
c. Share

b. Clearing house
d. Procter ' Gamble

11. The institution most often referenced by the word '_____' is a public or publicly traded _____, the shares of which are traded on a public stock exchange (e.g., the New York Stock Exchange or Nasdaq in the United States) where shares of stock of _____s are bought and sold by and to the general public. Most of the largest businesses in the world are publicly traded _____s. However, the majority of _____s are said to be closely held, privately held or close _____s, meaning that no ready market exists for the trading of shares.

a. Corporation
c. Federal Home Loan Mortgage Corporation

b. Depository Trust Company
d. Protect

12. A _____ is a financial contract whose value is derived from the value of something else (known as the underlying.) The underlying on which a _____ is based can be an asset, weather conditions bonds or other forms of credit.

a. 529 plan
c. 4-4-5 Calendar

b. 7-Eleven
d. Derivative

13. _____ is a life of security. It may also refer to the final payment date of a loan or other financial instrument, at which point all remaining interest and principal is due to be paid.

1, 3, 6 months _____ band can be calculated by using 30-day per month periods.

a. Replacement cost
c. Primary market

b. False billing
d. Maturity

14. The _____ is a stock exchange based in New York City, New York. It is the largest stock exchange in the world by dollar value of its listed companies securities. As of October 2008, the combined capitalization of all domestic _____ listed companies was $10.1 trillion.

a. 529 plan
c. 4-4-5 Calendar

b. 7-Eleven
d. New York Stock Exchange

15. An _____ option has no intrinsic value. A call option is _____ when the strike price is above the spot price of the underlying security. A put option is _____ when the strike price is below the spot price.

a. Out-of-the-money
c. AAB

b. ABN Amro
d. A Random Walk Down Wall Street

16.   A _____ is a fungible, negotiable instrument representing financial value. They are broadly categorized into debt securities (such as banknotes, bonds and debentures), and equity securities; e.g., common stocks. The company or other entity issuing the _____ is called the issuer.
- a. Securities lending
- b. Book entry
- c. Tracking stock
- d. Security

17.   A _____, securities exchange or (in Europe) bourse is a corporation or mutual organization which provides 'trading' facilities for stock brokers and traders, to trade stocks and other securities. _____s also provide facilities for the issue and redemption of securities as well as other financial instruments and capital events including the payment of income and dividends. The securities traded on a _____ include: shares issued by companies, unit trusts and other pooled investment products and bonds.
- a. 4-4-5 Calendar
- b. 7-Eleven
- c. 529 plan
- d. Stock Exchange

18.   The _____ is an American financial and commodity derivative exchange based in Chicago. The _____ was founded in 1898 as the Chicago Butter and Egg Board. Originally, the exchange was a non-profit organization.
- a. Public Company Accounting Oversight Board
- b. Gamelan Council
- c. Chicago Mercantile Exchange
- d. Financial Crimes Enforcement Network

19.   The _____ is one of several stock market indices, created by nineteenth-century Wall Street Journal editor and Dow Jones ' Company co-founder Charles Dow. Dow compiled the index to gauge the performance of the industrial sector of the American stock market. It is the second-oldest U.S. market index, after the Dow Jones Transportation Average, which Dow also created.
- a. 7-Eleven
- b. 529 plan
- c. 4-4-5 Calendar
- d. Dow Jones Industrial Average

20.   A _____ is a method of measuring a section of the stock market. Many indices are cited by news or financial services firms and are used to benchmark the performance of portfolios such as mutual funds.
- a. Stop order
- b. Program trading
- c. Trading curb
- d. Stock market index

21.   In business and finance, a _____ (also referred to as equity _____) of stock means a _____ of ownership in a corporation (company.) In the plural, stocks is often used as a synonym for _____s especially in the United States, but it is less commonly used that way outside of North America.

In the United Kingdom, South Africa, and Australia, stock can also refer to completely different financial instruments such as government bonds or, less commonly, to all kinds of marketable securities.

- a. Procter ' Gamble
- b. Bucket shop
- c. Margin
- d. Share

22.   The _____ is a U.S. government-owned corporation within the Department of Housing and Urban Development

Ginnie Mae provides guarantees on mortgage-backed securities backed by federally insured or guaranteed loans, mainly loans issued by the Federal Housing Administration, Department of Veterans Affairs, Rural Housing Service, and Office of Public and Indian Housing. Ginnie Mae securities are the only MBS that are guaranteed by the United States government.

a. 4-4-5 Calendar   b. Jumbo mortgage
c. Government National Mortgage Association   d. Graduated payment mortgage

23.   _____ is a fee paid on borrowed assets. It is the price paid for the use of borrowed money , or, money earned by deposited funds . Assets that are sometimes lent with _____ include money, shares, consumer goods through hire purchase, major assets such as aircraft, and even entire factories in finance lease arrangements.
a. Interest   b. A Random Walk Down Wall Street
c. Insolvency   d. AAB

24.   An _____ is the price a borrower pays for the use of money they do not own, and the return a lender receives for deferring the use of funds, by lending it to the borrower. _____s are normally expressed as a percentage rate over the period of one year.

_____s targets are also a vital tool of monetary policy and are used to control variables like investment, inflation, and unemployment.

a. ABN Amro   b. AAB
c. Interest rate   d. A Random Walk Down Wall Street

25.   _____ is a derivative financial instrument.

The global market for exchange-traded _____s is notionally valued by the Bank for International Settlements at $3,075,400 million in 2005.

a. Eurobond   b. Education production function
c. Economic entity   d. Interest rate option

26.   In finance, a _____ is a debt security, in which the authorized issuer owes the holders a debt and, depending on the terms of the _____, is obliged to pay interest (the coupon) and/or to repay the principal at a later date, termed maturity.

Thus a _____ is a loan: the issuer is the borrower, the _____ holder is the lender, and the coupon is the interest. _____s provide the borrower with external funds to finance long-term investments, or, in the case of government _____s, to finance current expenditure.

a. Puttable bond   b. Bond
c. Convertible bond   d. Catastrophe bonds

27. A _____, also FX future or foreign exchange future, is a futures contract to exchange one currency for another at a specified date in the future at a price (exchange rate) that is fixed on the purchase date. Typically, one of the currencies is the US dollar. The price of a future is then in terms of US dollars per unit of other currency.

a. Non-deliverable forward
b. Currency future
c. Foreign exchange controls
d. Currency swap

28. In finance, _____ is the process of estimating the potential market value of a financial asset or liability. they can be done on assets (for example, investments in marketable securities such as stocks, options, business enterprises, or intangible assets such as patents and trademarks) or on liabilities (e.g., Bonds issued by a company.) _____s are required in many contexts including investment analysis, capital budgeting, merger and acquisition transactions, financial reporting, taxable events to determine the proper tax liability, and in litigation.

a. Share
b. Procter ' Gamble
c. Margin
d. Valuation

29. A put option is a right to sell a particular stock to the writer of the option at a certain price (the strike price) on or by the expiration date. If the contract writer does not have an offsetting short position in the stock that the contract is written on, the put writer is considered uncovered for the loss incurred if the current price of the stock is below the contract price. If the writer has enough cash in his brokerage account to pay for the stock at the strike price then, although he is still considered to be in a _____ position, he may also refer more specifically to his position as a cash-covered put.

a. Bear put spread
b. Debit spread
c. Moneyness
d. Naked put

30. In finance, _____ refers to Monday, October 19, 1987, when stock markets around the world crashed, shedding a huge value in a very short time. The crash began in Hong Kong, spread west through international time zones to Europe, hitting the United States after other markets had already declined by a significant margin. The Dow Jones Industrial Average (DJIA) dropped by 508 points to 1738.74 (22.61%).

a. 529 plan
b. 7-Eleven
c. Black Monday
d. 4-4-5 Calendar

31. An _____ is an individual or firm that advises clients on investment matters on a professional basis.

They tend to fall into two distinct categories:

- _____s offering direct financial advice to individuals or businesses, or
- _____s offering asset management for (typically) corporate clients, hedge funds and/or mutual funds.

Depending on the nature of the relationship, _____s charge fees calculated as a percentage (e.g., 1%) of assets under management , on an annual basis, an hourly or on a 'flat fee' basis.

In the United States whether a firm should be registered as an _____ with the SEC or a state is typically determined by the amount of assets receiving continuous and regular supervisory or management services (AUM.) In order for a firm to register with the SEC, the firm must have over $25 million of AUM at the time of registration or within 120 days of the effective date of the registration.

a. ABN Amro   b. AAB
c. A Random Walk Down Wall Street   d. Investment Advisor

32.   A _____ is a private or public market for the trading of company stock and derivatives of company stock at an agreed price; these are securities listed on a stock exchange as well as those only traded privately.

The size of the world _____ is estimated at about $36.6 trillion US at the beginning of October 2008 . The world derivatives market has been estimated at about $480 trillion face or nominal value, 12 times the size of the entire world economy.

a. Anton Gelonkin   b. Adolph Coors
c. Stock market   d. Andrew Tobias

33.   A _____ is a sudden dramatic decline of stock prices across a significant cross-section of a stock market. Crashes are driven by panic as much as by underlying economic factors. They often follow speculative stock market bubbles.
a. Stock market crash   b. 7-Eleven
c. 529 plan   d. 4-4-5 Calendar

34.   In finance, _____, also known as return on investment is the ratio of money gained or lost on an investment relative to the amount of money invested. The amount of money gained or lost may be referred to as interest, profit/loss, gain/loss, or net income/loss. The money invested may be referred to as the asset, capital, principal, or the cost basis of the investment.
a. Doctrine of the Proper Law   b. Composiition of Creditors
c. Stock or scrip dividends   d. Rate of return

35.   A _____ is a transaction in which the seller of call options already owns the corresponding amount of the underlying instrument, such as shares of a stock or other securities. These owned shares provide the 'cover' as they can be handed over to the buyer of the options when he decides to exercise them, instead of having to buy the optioned shares at unfavorable market prices in the case of 'uncovered' or short call. Thus, the _____ limits the (potentially unlimited) loss that results from a short call when the price of the underlying stock moves above the strike price of the option.
a. 4-4-5 Calendar   b. Covered call
c. 7-Eleven   d. 529 plan

36.   _____ is the discipline of identifying, monitoring and limiting risks. In some cases the acceptable risk may be near zero. Risks can come from accidents, natural causes and disasters as well as deliberate attacks from an adversary.
a. Risk management   b. 4-4-5 Calendar
c. Penny stock   d. FIFO

37.   A _____ is the price of a single share of a no. of saleable stocks of the company. Once the stock is purchased, the owner becomes a shareholder of the company that issued the share.
a. Stock split   b. Whisper numbers
c. Share price   d. Trading curb

38.   _____ is a term used to describe any option trading strategy that involves selling options. An option writer sells options to potentially profit from the decline of extrinsic value on options, sometimes referred to as time value.

_____ strategies include covered calls, naked calls and naked puts, bear call spreads, bull put spreads, ratio credit spreads, short strangles and short straddles.

a. ABN Amro

b. AAB

c. Options writing

d. A Random Walk Down Wall Street

39.   In finance, a _____ is an investment strategy involving the purchase or sale of particular option derivatives that allows the holder to profit based on how much the price of the underlying security moves, regardless of the direction of price movement. The purchase of particular option derivatives is known as a long _____, while the sale of the option derivatives is known as a short _____.

An option payoff diagram for a long _____ position

A long _____ involves going long, i.e., purchasing, both a call option and a put option on some stock, interest rate, index or other underlying.

a. Moneyness

b. Bear call spread

c. Straddle

d. Put option

40.   _____ are dollar-denominated bonds, issued mostly by Latin American countries in the 1980s, named after U.S. Treasury Secretary Nicholas Brady.

_____ were created in March 1989 in order to convert bonds issued by mostly Latin American countries into a variety or 'menu' of new bonds after many of those countries defaulted on their debt in the 1980's. At that time, the market for sovereign debt was small and illiquid, and the standardization of emerging-market debt facilitated risk-spreading and trading.

a. Coupon rate

b. Brady bonds

c. Municipal bond

d. Nominal yield

41.   _____ is a type of bond that allows the issuer of the bond to retain the privilege of redeeming the bond at some point before the bond reaches the date of maturity. In other words, on the call dates, the issuer has the right, but not the obligation, to buy back the bonds from the bond holders at the call price. Technically speaking, the bonds are not really bought and held by the issuer but cancelled immediately.

a. Bond fund

b. Gilts

c. Coupon rate

d. Callable bond

42.   A _____ is a bond issued by a corporation. The term is usually applied to longer-term debt instruments, generally with a maturity date falling at least a year after their issue date. (The term 'commercial paper' is sometimes used for instruments with a shorter maturity.)

a. Government bond

b. Brady bonds

c. Serial bond

d. Corporate bond

43. _____ is a risk-adjusted measure of the so-called active return on an investment. It is the return in excess of the compensation for the risk borne, and thus commonly used to assess active managers' performances. Often, the return of a benchmark is subtracted in order to consider relative performance, which yields Jensen's _____.
   a. Option   b. Annuity
   c. Amortization   d. Alpha

44. In finance, a _____ is a type of bond that can be converted into shares of stock in the issuing company, usually at some pre-announced ratio. It is a hybrid security with debt- and equity-like features. Although it typically has a low coupon rate, the holder is compensated with the ability to convert the bond to common stock, usually at a substantial discount to the stock's market value.
   a. Corporate bond   b. Bond fund
   c. Convertible bond   d. Gilts

45. _____ is typically a higher ranking stock than voting shares, and its terms are negotiated between the corporation and the investor.

_____ usually carry no voting rights, but may carry superior priority over common stock in the payment of dividends and upon liquidation. _____ may carry a dividend that is paid out prior to any dividends to common stock holders.

   a. Second lien loan   b. Follow-on offering
   c. Trade-off theory   d. Preferred stock

46. In finance, a _____ is a security that entitles the holder to buy stock of the company that issued it at a specified price, which is usually higher than the stock price at time of issue.

_____s are frequently attached to bonds or preferred stock as a sweetener, allowing the issuer to pay lower interest rates or dividends. They can be used to enhance the yield of the bond, and make them more attractive to potential buyers.

   a. Credit   b. Clearing
   c. Clearing house   d. Warrant

47. _____ is that which is owed; usually referencing assets owed, but the term can cover other obligations. In the case of assets, _____ is a means of using future purchasing power in the present before a summation has been earned. Some companies and corporations use _____ as a part of their overall corporate finance strategy.
   a. Credit cycle   b. Partial Payment
   c. Cross-collateralization   d. Debt

48. _____ are the earnings returned on the initial investment amount.

In the US, the Financial Accounting Standards Board (FASB) requires companies' income statements to report _____ for each of the major categories of the income statement: continuing operations, discontinued operations, extraordinary items, and net income.

The _____ formula does not include preferred dividends for categories outside of continued operations and net income.

a. Assets turnover   b. Average accounting return
c. Inventory turnover   d. Earnings per share

49.   In political science and economics, the _____ or agency dilemma treats the difficulties that arise under conditions of incomplete and asymmetric information when a principal hires an agent. Various mechanisms may be used to try to align the interests of the agent with those of the principal, such as piece rates/commissions, profit sharing, efficiency wages, performance measurement (including financial statements), the agent posting a bond, or fear of firing. The _____ is found in most employer/employee relationships, for example, when stockholders hire top executives of corporations.

a. Principal-agent problem   b. 529 plan
c. 7-Eleven   d. 4-4-5 Calendar

50.   _____ is a company's earnings per share (EPS) calculated using fully diluted shares outstanding (i.e. including the impact of stock option grants and convertible bonds.) Diluted EPS indicates a 'worst case' scenario, one in which everyone who could have received stock without purchasing it directly for the full market value did so.

To find diluted EPS, basic EPS is calculated for each of the categories on the income statement first.

a. Financial ratio   b. Net assets
c. Price/cash flow ratio   d. Diluted Earnings per share

51.   In the most general sense, a _____ is anything that is a hindrance, or puts individuals at a disadvantage.

Before we discuss the financial terms, we should note that a _____ can also have a much more important slang meaning.

This is best described in an example.

a. Limited liability   b. McFadden Act
c. Covenant   d. Liability

52.   _____ is a concept whereby a person's financial liability is limited to a fixed sum, most commonly the value of a person's investment in a company or partnership with _____. A shareholder in a limited company is not personally liable for any of the debts of the company, other than for the value of his investment in that company. The same is true for the members of a _____ partnership and the limited partners in a limited partnership.

a. Beneficial owner   b. Sarbanes-Oxley Act
c. Personal property   d. Limited liability

53.   A _____ in the law of the vast majority of United States jurisdictions is a legal form of business company that provides limited liability to its owners. It is a hybrid business entity having certain characteristics of both a corporation and a partnership or sole proprietorship (depending on how many owners there are.) The primary characteristic an _____ shares with a corporation is limited liability, and the primary characteristic it shares with a partnership is the availability of pass-through income taxation.

   a. Limited liability company   b. Pension fund

   c. Financial endowment   d. Fund of funds

54.   In finance, _____ occurs when a debtor has not met its legal obligations according to the debt contract, e.g. it has not made a scheduled payment, or has violated a loan covenant (condition) of the debt contract. _____ may occur if the debtor is either unwilling or unable to pay their debt. This can occur with all debt obligations including bonds, mortgages, loans, and promissory notes.

   a. Credit crunch   b. Debt validation

   c. Vendor finance   d. Default

55.   An _____ (or average value option) is a special type of option contract. For _____s the payoff is determined by the average underlying price over some pre-set period of time. This is different to the case of the usual European option, where the payoff of the option contract depends on the price of the underlying instrument at maturity.

   a. Option screener   b. Asian option

   c. Options arbitrage   d. Options spreads

56.   In finance, a _____ is a type of financial option where the option to exercise depends on the underlying crossing or reaching a given barrier level. _____s were created to provide the insurance value of an option without charging as much premium. For example, if you believe that IBM will go up this year, but are willing to bet that it won't go above $100, then you can buy the barrier and pay less premium than the vanilla option.

   a. Naked put   b. Binary option

   c. Barrier option   d. Net volatility

57.   The _____ are a type of exotic options with path dependency, among many other kind of options. The payoff depends on the optimal (maximum or minimum) underlying asset's price occurring over the life of the option. The option allows the holder to 'look back' over time to determine the payoff.

   a. Weighted mean   b. Database auditing

   c. Help desk and incident reporting auditing   d. Lookback options

58.   A _____ is a type of derivative in which the underlying is denominated in one currency, but the instrument itself is settled in another currency at some fixed rate. Such products are attractive for speculators and investors who wish to have exposure to a foreign asset, but without the corresponding exchange rate risk.

Common types of _____ include :

- _____ futures contracts, such as a futures contract on a European stock market index which is settled in US dollars.
- _____ options, in which the difference between the underlying and a fixed strike price is paid out in another currency.
- _____ swaps, in which one counterparty pays a non-local interest rate to the other, but the notional amount is in local currency. The second party may be paying a fixed or floating rate. For example, a swap in which the notional amount is denominated in Canadian dollars, but where the floating rate is set as USD LIBOR, would be considered a _____ swap.

a. Dollar roll

b. Credit default swap index

c. Quanto

d. Volatility arbitrage

59.   In finance, a _____ is a type of option where the payoff is either some fixed amount of some asset or nothing at all. The two main types of _____s are the cash-or-nothing _____ and the asset-or-nothing _____. The cash-or-nothing _____ pays some fixed amount of cash if the option expires in-the-money while the asset-or-nothing pays the value of the underlying security.

a. Calendar spread

b. Binary option

c. Naked put

d. Moneyness

1.   An _____ is a contract written by a seller that conveys to the buyer the right -- but not the obligation -- to buy (in the case of a call _____) or to sell (in the case of a put _____) a particular asset, such as a piece of property such as, among others, a futures contract. In return for granting the _____, the seller collects a payment (the premium) from the buyer.

For example, buying a call _____ provides the right to buy a specified quantity of a security at a set strike price at some time on or before expiration, while buying a put _____ provides the right to sell.

   a. Amortization   b. AT'T Mobility LLC
   c. Annuity   d. Option

2.   In finance, _____ is the process of estimating the potential market value of a financial asset or liability. they can be done on assets (for example, investments in marketable securities such as stocks, options, business enterprises, or intangible assets such as patents and trademarks) or on liabilities (e.g., Bonds issued by a company.) _____s are required in many contexts including investment analysis, capital budgeting, merger and acquisition transactions, financial reporting, taxable events to determine the proper tax liability, and in litigation.
   a. Valuation   b. Procter ' Gamble
   c. Margin   d. Share

3.   The term _____ refers to three closely related concepts:

   ● The _____ model is a mathematical model of the market for an equity, in which the equity's price is a stochastic process.
   ● The _____ PDE is a partial differential equation which (in the model) must be satisfied by the price of a derivative on the equity.
   ● The _____ formula is the result obtained by solving the _____ PDE for a European call option.

Fischer Black and Myron Scholes first articulated the _____ formula in their 1973 paper, 'The Pricing of Options and Corporate Liabilities.' The foundation for their research relied on work developed by scholars such as Jack L. Treynor, Paul Samuelson, A. James Boness, Sheen T. Kassouf, and Edward O. Thorp. The fundamental insight of _____ is that the option is implicitly priced if the stock is traded.

Robert C. Merton was the first to publish a paper expanding the mathematical understanding of the options pricing model and coined the term '_____' options pricing model.

   a. Perpetuity   b. Modified Internal Rate of Return
   c. Stochastic volatility   d. Black-Scholes

4.   The _____ is one of several stock market indices, created by nineteenth-century Wall Street Journal editor and Dow Jones ' Company co-founder Charles Dow. Dow compiled the index to gauge the performance of the industrial sector of the American stock market. It is the second-oldest U.S. market index, after the Dow Jones Transportation Average, which Dow also created.
   a. 7-Eleven   b. 529 plan
   c. 4-4-5 Calendar   d. Dow Jones Industrial Average

5. In finance, _____ refers to the value of a security which is intrinsic to or contained in the security itself. It is also frequently called fundamental value. It is ordinarily calculated by summing the future income generated by the asset, and discounting it to the present value.

a. Alpha
b. Amortization
c. Accretion
d. Intrinsic value

6. An _____ option has no intrinsic value. A call option is _____ when the strike price is above the spot price of the underlying security. A put option is _____ when the strike price is below the spot price.

a. ABN Amro
b. A Random Walk Down Wall Street
c. Out-of-the-money
d. AAB

7. In finance, the value of an option consists of two components, its intrinsic value and its _____. Time value is simply the difference between option value and intrinsic value. _____ is also known as theta, extrinsic value, or instrumental value.

a. Global Squeeze
b. Conservatism
c. Debt buyer
d. Time value

8. _____ most frequently refers to the standard deviation of the continuously compounded returns of a financial instrument with a specific time horizon. It is often used to quantify the risk of the instrument over that time period. _____ is typically expressed in annualized terms, and it may either be an absolute number ($5) or a fraction of the mean (5%).

a. Portfolio insurance
b. Seasoned equity offering
c. Currency swap
d. Volatility

9. A _____ is the price of a single share of a no. of saleable stocks of the company. Once the stock is purchased, the owner becomes a shareholder of the company that issued the share.

a. Stock split
b. Trading curb
c. Share price
d. Whisper numbers

10. A _____ is a payment made by a corporation to its shareholder members. When a corporation earns a profit or surplus, that money can be put to two uses: it can either be re-invested in the business (called retained earnings), or it can be paid to the shareholders as a _____. Many corporations retain a portion of their earnings and pay the remainder as a _____.

a. Dividend
b. Special dividend
c. Dividend puzzle
d. Dividend yield

11. _____ is a term used in accounting, economics and finance to spread the cost of an asset over the span of several years.

In simple words we can say that _____ is the reduction in the value of an asset due to usage, passage of time, wear and tear, technological outdating or obsolescence, depletion or other such factors.

In accounting, _____ is a term used to describe any method of attributing the historical or purchase cost of an asset across its useful life, roughly corresponding to normal wear and tear.

a. Depreciation   b. Bottom line
c. Deferred financing costs   d. Matching principle

12.   In economics and accounting, _____ is seen as the change in the market value of capital over a given period. It is calculated as the market price of the capital at the beginning of the period minus its market price at the end of the period.

Such a method in calculating depreciation differs from other methods, such as straight-line depreciation in that it is included in the calculation of implicit cost, and thus economic profit.

a. Economic depreciation   b. Index number
c. A Random Walk Down Wall Street   d. AAB

13.   In finance, a _____ is a position established in one market in an attempt to offset exposure to the price risk of an equal but opposite obligation or position in another market -- usually, but not always, in the context of one's commercial activity. Hedging is a strategy designed to minimize exposure to such business risks as a sharp contraction in demand for one's inventory, while still allowing the business to profit from producing and maintaining that inventory. A typical hedger might be a farmer with 2000 acres of unharvested wheat in the ground, who would rather tend his crop without the distraction of uncertain prices.
a. Hedge   b. 4-4-5 Calendar
c. 7-Eleven   d. 529 plan

14.   The _____ is the interest rate that it is assumed can be obtained by investing in financial instruments with no default risk. However, the financial instrument can carry other types of risk, e.g. market risk (the risk of changes in market interest rates), liquidity risk (the risk of being unable to sell the instrument for cash at short notice without significant costs) etc.

Though a truly risk-free asset exists only in theory, in practice most professionals and academics use short-dated government bonds of the currency in question.

a. London Interbank Bid Rate   b. Risk-free interest rate
c. London Interbank Offered Rate   d. Cash accumulation equation

15.   _____ is a fee paid on borrowed assets. It is the price paid for the use of borrowed money , or, money earned by deposited funds . Assets that are sometimes lent with _____ include money, shares, consumer goods through hire purchase, major assets such as aircraft, and even entire factories in finance lease arrangements.
a. AAB   b. A Random Walk Down Wall Street
c. Insolvency   d. Interest

16.   An _____ is the price a borrower pays for the use of money they do not own, and the return a lender receives for deferring the use of funds, by lending it to the borrower. _____s are normally expressed as a percentage rate over the period of one year.

_____s targets are also a vital tool of monetary policy and are used to control variables like investment, inflation, and unemployment.

a. AAB

b. ABN Amro

c. A Random Walk Down Wall Street

d. Interest rate

17.   In finance, the binomial options pricing model (BOPM) provides a generalisable numerical method for the valuation of options. The _____ was first proposed by Cox, Ross and Rubinstein (1979.) Essentially, the model uses a 'discrete-time' model of the varying price over time of the underlying financial instrument.

a. Modified Internal Rate of Return

b. Discount rate

c. Binomial model

d. Perpetuity

18.   In probability theory and statistics, a _____ identifies either the probability of each value of an unidentified random variable (when the variable is discrete), or the probability of the value falling within a particular interval (when the variable is continuous.) The _____ describes the range of possible values that a random variable can attain and the probability that the value of the random variable is within any (measurable) subset of that range. The Normal distribution, often called the 'bell curve'

When the random variable takes values in the set of real numbers, the _____ is completely described by the cumulative distribution function, whose value at each real x is the probability that the random variable is smaller than or equal to x.

a. P-value

b. Correlation

c. Probability distribution

d. Standard deviation

19.   In probability and statistics, the _____ is the single-tailed probability distribution of any random variable whose logarithm is normally distributed. If X is a random variable with a normal distribution, then Y = exp(X) has a _____; likewise, if Y is log-normally distributed, then log(Y) is normally distributed. (The base of the logarithmic function does not matter: if $\log_a$ (Y) is normally distributed, then so is $\log_b$(Y), for any two positive numbers a, b ≠ 1.)

a. 4-4-5 Calendar

b. Log-normal distribution

c. 7-Eleven

d. 529 plan

20.   _____ is one of the authors of the Black-Scholes equation. In 1997 he was awarded the Nobel Memorial Prize in Economic Sciences for 'a new method to determine the value of derivatives'. The model provides the fundamental conceptual framework for valuing options, such as calls or puts, and is referred to as the Black-Scholes model, which has become the standard in financial markets globally.

a. Robert James Shiller

b. Myron Samuel Scholes

c. Andrew Tobias

d. Adolph Coors

21.   In financial mathematics, the _____ of an option contract is the volatility implied by the market price of the option based on an option pricing model. In other words, it is the volatility that, given a particular pricing model, yields a theoretical value for the option equal to the current market price. Non-option financial instruments that have embedded optionality, such as an interest rate cap, can also have an _____.

a. Equity derivative

b. Interest rate derivative

c. Implied volatility

d. Interest rate future

22.   The _____ is an important family of continuous probability distributions, applicable in many fields. Each member of the family may be defined by two parameters, location and scale: the mean and variance respectively. The standard _____ is the _____ with a mean of zero and a variance of one

a. Normal distribution   b. Random variables
c. Probability distribution   d. Correlation

23.   In economics and finance, _____ is the practice of taking advantage of a price differential between two or more markets: striking a combination of matching deals that capitalize upon the imbalance, the profit being the difference between the market prices. When used by academics, an _____ is a transaction that involves no negative cash flow at any probabilistic or temporal state and a positive cash flow in at least one state; in simple terms, a risk-free profit.
a. Initial margin   b. Efficient-market hypothesis
c. Arbitrage   d. Issuer

24.   In finance, a _____ is a standardized contract, to buy or sell a specified commodity of standardized quality at a certain date in the future, at a market determined price (the futures price.)

The price is determined by the instantaneous equilibrium between the forces of supply and demand among competing buy and sell orders on the exchange at the time of the purchase or sale of the contract.

In many cases, the items may be such non-traditional 'commodities' as foreign currencies, commercial or government paper [e.g., bonds], or 'baskets' of corporate equity ['stock indices'] or other financial instruments.

a. Financial future   b. Repurchase agreement
c. Futures contract   d. Heston model

25.   In financial mathematics, _____ defines a relationship between the price of a call option and a put option--both with the identical strike price and expiry. To derive the _____ relationship, the assumption is that the options are not exercised before expiration day, which necessarily applies to European options. _____ can be derived in a manner that is largely model independent.
a. Hull-White model   b. Cox-Ingersoll-Ross model
c. Rendleman-Bartter model   d. Put-call parity

26.   A _____ is a financial contract between two parties, the seller (writer) and the buyer of the option. The put allows its buyer the right but not the obligation to sell a commodity or financial instrument (the underlying instrument) to the writer (seller) of the option at a certain time for a certain price (the strike price.) The writer (seller) has the obligation to purchase the underlying asset at that strike price, if the buyer exercises the option.
a. Bear call spread   b. Bear spread
c. Put option   d. Debit spread

27.   _____ is the process of setting or keeping the delta of a portfolio as close to zero as possible.

Mathematically, delta is the partial derivative ⌐×⌐> of the instrument or portfolio's fair value with respect to the price of the underlying security.

Therefore, if a position is delta neutral (or, instantaneously delta-hedged) its instantaneous change in value, for an infinitesimal change in the value of the underlying, will be zero; see Hedge (finance.)

a. Financial services
c. Delta Hedging

b. Convertible arbitrage
d. Central Securities Depository

28. _____ mature in one year or less. Like zero-coupon bonds, they do not pay interest prior to maturity; instead they are sold at a discount of the par value to create a positive yield to maturity. Many regard _____ as the least risky investment available to U.S. investors.

a. 4-4-5 Calendar
c. Treasury securities

b. Treasury Inflation Protected Securities
d. Treasury bills

29. In finance, _____, also known as return on investment is the ratio of money gained or lost on an investment relative to the amount of money invested. The amount of money gained or lost may be referred to as interest, profit/loss, gain/loss, or net income/loss. The money invested may be referred to as the asset, capital, principal, or the cost basis of the investment.

a. Rate of return
c. Stock or scrip dividends

b. Composiition of Creditors
d. Doctrine of the Proper Law

30. In economic models, the _____ time frame assumes no fixed factors of production. Firms can enter or leave the marketplace, and the cost (and availability) of land, labor, raw materials, and capital goods can be assumed to vary. In contrast, in the short-run time frame, certain factors are assumed to be fixed, because there is not sufficient time for them to change.

a. 529 plan
c. Short-run

b. 4-4-5 Calendar
d. Long-run

31. _____ is a method of hedging a portfolio of stocks against the market risk by short selling stock index futures.

This hedging technique is frequently used by institutional investors when the market direction is uncertain or volatile. Short selling index futures can offset any downturns, but it also hinders any gains.

a. Portfolio insurance
c. Delivery month

b. PAUG
d. Freight derivative

32. The institution most often referenced by the word '_____' is a public or publicly traded _____, the shares of which are traded on a public stock exchange (e.g., the New York Stock Exchange or Nasdaq in the United States) where shares of stock of _____s are bought and sold by and to the general public. Most of the largest businesses in the world are publicly traded _____s. However, the majority of _____s are said to be closely held, privately held or close _____s, meaning that no ready market exists for the trading of shares.

a. Protect
c. Federal Home Loan Mortgage Corporation

b. Depository Trust Company
d. Corporation

33. A _____, securities exchange or (in Europe) bourse is a corporation or mutual organization which provides 'trading' facilities for stock brokers and traders, to trade stocks and other securities. _____s also provide facilities for the issue and redemption of securities as well as other financial instruments and capital events including the payment of income and dividends. The securities traded on a _____ include: shares issued by companies, unit trusts and other pooled investment products and bonds.

a. 7-Eleven   b. 529 plan
c. 4-4-5 Calendar   d. Stock exchange

34.   A _____ is a method of measuring a section of the stock market. Many indices are cited by news or financial services firms and are used to benchmark the performance of portfolios such as mutual funds.

a. Stop order   b. Program trading
c. Trading curb   d. Stock market index

35.   In finance, _____ refers to Monday, October 19, 1987, when stock markets around the world crashed, shedding a huge value in a very short time. The crash began in Hong Kong, spread west through international time zones to Europe, hitting the United States after other markets had already declined by a significant margin. The Dow Jones Industrial Average (DJIA) dropped by 508 points to 1738.74 (22.61%).

a. 4-4-5 Calendar   b. Black Monday
c. 529 plan   d. 7-Eleven

1.   A _____ is a financial contract whose value is derived from the value of something else (known as the underlying.) The underlying on which a _____ is based can be an asset, weather conditions bonds or other forms of credit.
   a. 529 plan
                           b. 4-4-5 Calendar
   c. 7-Eleven
                           d. Derivative

2.   A _____ is an agreement between two parties to buy or sell an asset at a specified point of time in the future. The price of the underlying instrument, in whatever form, is paid before control of the instrument changes. This is one of the many forms of buy/sell orders where the time of trade is not the time where the securities themselves are exchanged.
   a. Loan Credit Default Swap Index
                           b. Forward contract
   c. Constant maturity credit default swap
                           d. Derivatives markets

3.   The _____ is the over-the-counter financial market in contracts for future delivery, so called forward contracts. Forward contracts are personalized between parties. The _____ is a general term used to describe the informal market by which these contracts are entered into.
   a. Limits to arbitrage
                           b. Forward market
   c. Spot rate
                           d. Delta hedging

4.   In finance, a _____ is a standardized contract, to buy or sell a specified commodity of standardized quality at a certain date in the future, at a market determined price (the futures price.)

The price is determined by the instantaneous equilibrium between the forces of supply and demand among competing buy and sell orders on the exchange at the time of the purchase or sale of the contract.

In many cases, the items may be such non-traditional 'commodities' as foreign currencies, commercial or government paper [e.g., bonds], or 'baskets' of corporate equity ['stock indices'] or other financial instruments.

   a. Repurchase agreement
                           b. Financial future
   c. Futures contract
                           d. Heston model

5.   An _____ is a contract written by a seller that conveys to the buyer the right -- but not the obligation -- to buy (in the case of a call _____) or to sell (in the case of a put _____) a particular asset, such as a piece of property such as, among others, a futures contract. In return for granting the _____, the seller collects a payment (the premium) from the buyer.

For example, buying a call _____ provides the right to buy a specified quantity of a security at a set strike price at some time on or before expiration, while buying a put _____ provides the right to sell.

   a. Amortization
                           b. Annuity
   c. AT'T Mobility LLC
                           d. Option

6.   An _____ is defined as 'a promise which meets the requirements for the formation of a contract and limits the promisor's power to revoke an offer.' Restatement (Second) of Contracts Â§ 25 (1981.)

Quite simply, an _____ is a type of contract that protects an offeree from an offeror's ability to revoke the contract.

Consideration for the _____ is still required as it is still a form of contract.

a. Option contract   b. ABN Amro

c. AAB   d. A Random Walk Down Wall Street

7.   A _____ is an exchange of promises between two or more parties to do an act which is enforceable in a court of law. It is where an unqualified offer meets a qualified acceptance and the parties reach Consensus ad Idem. The parties must have the necessary capacity to _____ and the _____ must not be either trifling, indeterminate, impossible or illegal.

a. 529 plan   b. Contract

c. 4-4-5 Calendar   d. 7-Eleven

8.   In finance, a _____ in a security, such as a stock or a bond means the holder of the position owns the security and will profit if the price of the security goes up.

Similarly, a _____ in a futures contract or similar derivative, means the holder of the position will profit if the price of the underlying security goes up. Going long is the more conventional practice of investing and is contrasted with going short

- Short (finance)

.

a. Central Securities Depository   b. Delta hedging

c. Long position   d. Forward market

9.   Days to Cover (DTC) is a numerical term that describes the relationship between the amount of shares in a given equity that have been short sold and the number of days of typical trading that it would require to 'cover' all _____ outstanding. For example, if there are ten million shares of XYZ Inc. that are currently short sold and the average daily volume of XYZ shares traded each day is one million, it would require ten days of trading for all _____ to be covered (10 million / 1 million.)

a. Cash budget   b. Guaranteed investment contracts

c. Stock or scrip dividends   d. Short positions

10.   The _____ is an American financial and commodity derivative exchange based in Chicago. The _____ was founded in 1898 as the Chicago Butter and Egg Board. Originally, the exchange was a non-profit organization.

a. Public Company Accounting Oversight Board   b. Financial Crimes Enforcement Network

c. Chicago Mercantile Exchange   d. Gamelan Council

11.   The concept was first developed in game theory and consequently zero-sum situations are often called _____s though this does not imply that the concept applies only to what are commonly referred to as games.

For 2-player finite _____s, the different game theoretic Solution concepts of Nash equilibrium, minimax, and maximin all give the same solution. In the solution, players play a mixed strategy.

a. 4-4-5 Calendar   b. 529 plan

c. 7-Eleven   d. Zero-sum game

12.   An _____ (or business indicator) is a statistic about the economy. _____s allow analysis of economic performance and predictions of future performance.

_____s include various indices, earnings reports, and economic summaries, such as unemployment, housing starts, Consumer Price Index (a measure for inflation), industrial production, bankruptcies, Gross Domestic Product, broadband internet penetration, retail sales, stock market prices, and money supply changes.

a. A Random Walk Down Wall Street   b. ABN Amro
c. AAB   d. Economic indicator

13.   A _____ is a financial services company that provides clearing and settlement services for financial transactions, usually on a futures exchange, and often acts as central counterparty (the payor actually pays the _____, which then pays the payee). A _____ may also offer novation, the substitution of a new contract or debt for an old, or other credit enhancement services to its members.

The term is also used for banks like Suffolk Bank that acted as a restraint on the over-issuance of private bank notes.

a. Warrant   b. Valuation
c. Bucket shop   d. Clearing house

14.   An _____ is the term used in financial circles for a type of computer system that facilitates trading of financial products outside of stock exchanges. The primary products that are traded on an _____ are stocks and currencies. They came into existence in 1998 when the SEC authorized their creation.
a. Open outcry   b. Insider trading
c. Intellidex   d. Electronic communication network

15.   _____ is a major futures and options exchange for European benchmark derivatives featuring open and low-cost electronic access globally. Its electronic trading and clearing platform offers a broad range of products and amongst other, operates the most liquid fixed income markets. _____ was established in 1998 with the merger of Deutsche Terminbörse and SOFFEX (Swiss Options and Financial Futures.)
a. ABN Amro   b. AAB
c. A Random Walk Down Wall Street   d. Eurex

16.   _____ N.V. is a pan-European stock exchange based in Paris and with subsidiaries in Belgium, France, Netherlands, Luxembourg, Portugal and the United Kingdom. In addition to equities and derivatives markets, the _____ group provides clearing and information services. As of 31 January 2006, markets run by _____ had a market capitalization of US$2.9 trillion, making it the 5th largest exchange on the planet.
a. Euronext   b. ABN Amro
c. A Random Walk Down Wall Street   d. AAB

17.   _____ denotes the total number of derivative contracts, like futures and options, that are currently active on a specific underlying security, having specific terms.

Namely, the total contracts for a specific strike price and expiration date, that have been traded, but have not yet expired, have not yet been closed through a closing transaction, or have not yet been terminated via early exercise. A closing transaction occurs when a counterparty that longs the contract sells, or, conversely, when a counterparty that shorts the contract buys.

a. International Swaps and Derivatives Association   b. Equity swap
c. Equity derivative   d. Open interest

18.   In banking and finance, _____ denotes all activities from the time a commitment is made for a transaction until it is settled. _____ is necessary because the speed of trades is much faster than the cycle time for completing the underlying transaction.

In its widest sense _____ involves the management of post-trading, pre-settlement credit exposures, to ensure that trades are settled in accordance with market rules, even if a buyer or seller should become insolvent prior to settlement.

a. Clearing house   b. Procter ' Gamble
c. Share   d. Clearing

19.   _____ is a fee paid on borrowed assets. It is the price paid for the use of borrowed money , or, money earned by deposited funds . Assets that are sometimes lent with _____ include money, shares, consumer goods through hire purchase, major assets such as aircraft, and even entire factories in finance lease arrangements.
a. A Random Walk Down Wall Street   b. AAB
c. Insolvency   d. Interest

20.   In finance, a _____ is collateral that the holder of a position in securities, options, or futures contracts has to deposit to cover the credit risk of his counterparty (most often his broker.) This risk can arise if the holder has done any of the following:

- borrowed cash from the counterparty to buy securities or options,
- sold securities or options short, or
- entered into a futures contract.

The collateral can be in the form of cash or securities, and it is deposited in a _____ account. On U.S. futures exchanges, '_____' was formally called performance bond.

_____ buying is buying securities with cash borrowed from a broker, using other securities as collateral.

a. Procter ' Gamble   b. Share
c. Credit   d. Margin

21.   The collateral can be in the form of cash or securities, and it is deposited in a _____. On U.S. futures exchanges, 'margin' was formally called performance bond.

Margin buying is buying securities with cash borrowed from a broker, using other securities as collateral.

a. Margin account   b. Dollar roll
c. Risk-neutral measure   d. Forward contract

22. _____, in bookkeeping, refers to assets, liabilities, income, and expenses recorded on individual pages of the so called book of final entry or ledger. Changes in _____ value are made by chronologically posting debit (DR) and credit (CR) entries to its page. Examples of _____s are cash, _____s receivable, mortgages, loans, land and buildings, common stock, sales, services provided, wages, and payroll overhead.
a. Option   b. Accretion
c. Alpha   d. Account

23. In economics and finance, _____ is the practice of taking advantage of a price differential between two or more markets: striking a combination of matching deals that capitalize upon the imbalance, the profit being the difference between the market prices. When used by academics, an _____ is a transaction that involves no negative cash flow at any probabilistic or temporal state and a positive cash flow in at least one state; in simple terms, a risk-free profit.
a. Issuer   b. Arbitrage
c. Initial margin   d. Efficient-market hypothesis

24. The variation margin or _____ is not collateral, but a daily offsetting of profits and losses. Futures are marked-to-market every day, so the current price is compared to the previous day's price. The profit or loss on the day of a position is then paid to or debited from the holder by the futures exchange.
a. Delivery month   b. Total return swap
c. Maintenance margin   d. SPI 200 futures contract

25. The _____ or spot rate of a commodity, a security or a currency is the price that is quoted for immediate (spot) settlement (payment and delivery.) Spot settlement is normally one or two business days from trade date. This is in contrast with the forward price established in a forward contract or futures contract, where contract terms (price) are set now, but delivery and payment will occur at a future date.
a. Market price   b. Spot price
c. Central Securities Depository   d. Cost of carry

26. In the original and simplified sense, _____ were things of value, of uniform quality, that were produced in large quantities by many different producers; the items from each different producer are considered equivalent. It is the contract and this underlying standard that define the commodity, not any quality inherent in the product.

_____ exchanges include:

- Chicago Board of Trade
- Kansas City Board of Trade
- Euronext.liffe
- Kuala Lumpur Futures Exchange
- Bhatinda Om ' Oil Exchange
- London Metal Exchange
- New York Mercantile Exchange
- Multi Commodity Exchange
- Dalian Commodity Exchange

Markets for trading _____ can be very efficient, particularly if the division into pools matches demand segments. These markets will quickly respond to changes in supply and demand to find an equilibrium price and quantity.

a. 7-Eleven   b. 4-4-5 Calendar
c. 529 plan   d. Commodities

27.   _____ (in a financial context) is the assumption of the risk of loss, in return for the uncertain possibility of a reward. Only if one may safely say that a particular position involves no risk may one say, strictly speaking, that such a position represents an 'investment.' Financial _____ involves the buying, holding, selling, and short-selling of stocks, bonds, commodities, currencies, collectibles, real estate, derivatives, or any valuable financial instrument to profit from fluctuations in its price as opposed to buying it for use or for income via methods such as dividends or interest. _____ represents one of four market roles in Western financial markets, distinct from hedging, long- or short-term investing, and arbitrage.
a. Market anomaly   b. Central Securities Depository
c. Speculation   d. Forward market

28.   In finance, a _____ is a debt security, in which the authorized issuer owes the holders a debt and, depending on the terms of the _____, is obliged to pay interest (the coupon) and/or to repay the principal at a later date, termed maturity.

Thus a _____ is a loan: the issuer is the borrower, the _____ holder is the lender, and the coupon is the interest. _____s provide the borrower with external funds to finance long-term investments, or, in the case of government _____s, to finance current expenditure.

a. Bond   b. Catastrophe bonds
c. Puttable bond   d. Convertible bond

29.   In finance, a _____ is a position established in one market in an attempt to offset exposure to the price risk of an equal but opposite obligation or position in another market -- usually, but not always, in the context of one's commercial activity. Hedging is a strategy designed to minimize exposure to such business risks as a sharp contraction in demand for one's inventory, while still allowing the business to profit from producing and maintaining that inventory. A typical hedger might be a farmer with 2000 acres of unharvested wheat in the ground, who would rather tend his crop without the distraction of uncertain prices.

a. 529 plan   b. 7-Eleven
c. 4-4-5 Calendar   d. Hedge

30.   In finance, _____ (or gearing) is borrowing money to supplement existing funds for investment in such a way that the potential positive or negative outcome is magnified and/or enhanced. It generally refers to using borrowed funds, or debt, so as to attempt to increase the returns to equity. Deleveraging is the action of reducing borrowings.

a. Financial endowment   b. Leverage
c. Pension fund   d. Limited partnership

31.   _____ in finance is the risk associated with imperfect hedging using futures. It could arise because of the difference between the asset whose price is to be hedged and the asset underlying the derivative, or because of a mismatch between the expiration date of the futures and the actual selling date of the asset.

Under these conditions, the spot price of the asset, and the futures price, do not converge on the expiration date of the future.

a. Currency risk   b. Liquidity risk
c. Credit risk   d. Basis risk

32.   _____ is the difference between price and the costs of bringing to market whatever it is that is accounted as an enterprise (whether by harvest, extraction, manufacture, or purchase) in terms of the component costs of delivered goods and/or services and any operating or other expenses.

A key difficulty in measuring profit is in defining costs. Pure economic monetary profits can be zero or negative even in competitive equilibrium when accounted monetized costs exceed monetized price.

a. AAB   b. A Random Walk Down Wall Street
c. Economic profit   d. Accounting profit

33.   _____ is a life of security. It may also refer to the final payment date of a loan or other financial instrument, at which point all remaining interest and principal is due to be paid.

1, 3, 6 months _____ band can be calculated by using 30-day per month periods.

a. Replacement cost   b. Primary market
c. False billing   d. Maturity

34.   In finance, _____, also known as return on investment is the ratio of money gained or lost on an investment relative to the amount of money invested. The amount of money gained or lost may be referred to as interest, profit/loss, gain/loss, or net income/loss. The money invested may be referred to as the asset, capital, principal, or the cost basis of the investment.
   a. Composiition of Creditors   b. Doctrine of the Proper Law
   c. Stock or scrip dividends   d. Rate of return

35.   A _____ is a method of measuring a section of the stock market. Many indices are cited by news or financial services firms and are used to benchmark the performance of portfolios such as mutual funds.
   a. Stop order   b. Program trading
   c. Stock market index   d. Trading curb

36.   _____ is a method of hedging a portfolio of stocks against the market risk by short selling stock index futures.

This hedging technique is frequently used by institutional investors when the market direction is uncertain or volatile. Short selling index futures can offset any downturns, but it also hinders any gains.

   a. Delivery month   b. Portfolio insurance
   c. PAUG   d. Freight derivative

37.   A _____ is a futures contract on a short term interest rate (STIR.) Contracts vary, but are often defined on an interest rate index such as 3-month sterling or US dollar LIBOR.

They are traded across a wide range of currencies, including the G12 country currencies and many others.

   a. Dual currency deposit   b. Notional amount
   c. Real estate derivatives   d. Financial future

38.   The _____ is one of several stock market indices, created by nineteenth-century Wall Street Journal editor and Dow Jones ' Company co-founder Charles Dow. Dow compiled the index to gauge the performance of the industrial sector of the American stock market. It is the second-oldest U.S. market index, after the Dow Jones Transportation Average, which Dow also created.
   a. 7-Eleven   b. 4-4-5 Calendar
   c. 529 plan   d. Dow Jones Industrial Average

39.   A _____ is a central financial exchange where people can trade standardized futures contracts; that is, a contract to buy specific quantities of a commodity or financial instrument at a specified price with delivery set at a specified time in the future.

Though the origins of futures trading can supposedly be traced to Ancient Greek or Phoenician times, the first modern organized _____ began in 1710 at the Dojima Rice Exchange in Osaka, Japan.

The United States followed in the early 1800s.

a. 529 plan

b. 4-4-5 Calendar

c. Futures Exchange

d. 7-Eleven

40.   The _____ started life on September 30, 1982, to take advantage of the removal of currency controls in the UK in 1979. The exchange modelled itself after the Chicago Board of Trade and the Chicago Mercantile Exchange. It initially offered futures contracts and options linked to short term interest rates.

a. 529 plan

b. 7-Eleven

c. 4-4-5 Calendar

d. London International Financial Futures Exchange

41.   The _____ is an American stock exchange. It is the largest electronic screen-based equity securities trading market in the United States. With approximately 3,200 companies, it has more trading volume per day than any other stock exchange in the world.

a. NASDAQ

b. 529 plan

c. 4-4-5 Calendar

d. 7-Eleven

42.   _____ are futures contracts with the underlying asset being one particular stock, usually in batches of 100. When purchased, no transmission of share rights or dividends occurs. Being futures contracts they are traded on margin, thus offering leverage, and they are not subject to the short selling limitations that stocks are.

a. Single-stock futures

b. Heston model

c. Weather derivatives

d. Volatility swap

43.   _____ is the strategy of making buy or sell decisions of financial assets (often stocks) by attempting to predict future market price movements. The prediction may be based on an outlook of market or economic conditions resulting from technical or fundamental analysis. This is an investment strategy based on the outlook for an aggregate market, rather than for a particular financial asset.

a. Divestment

b. Late trading

c. Portable alpha

d. Market timing

44.   _____ is casually defined as the use of computers in stock markets to engage in arbitrage and portfolio insurance strategies. However, the New York Stock Exchange (NYSE) defines the term as 'a wide range of portfolio trading strategies involving the purchase or sale of 15 or more stocks having a total market value of $1 million or more' without any direct reference to the use of computers. The word 'program' can be interpreted in its earlier, more general meaning of a defined and pre-arranged sequence of steps, rather than specifically a computer program.

a. Program trading

b. Share price

c. Stop order

d. Wash sale

45.   Behavioral economics and _____ are closely related fields that have evolved to be a separate branch of economic and financial analysis which applies scientific research on human and social, cognitive and emotional factors to better understand economic decisions by, say, consumers, borrowers, investors, and how they affect market prices, returns and the allocation of resources.

The field is primarily concerned with the bounds of rationality (selfishness, self-control) of economic agents. Behavioral models typically integrate insights from psychology with neo-classical economic theory.

a. Recession   b. Market structure
c. Medium of exchange   d. Behavioral finance

46.   In finance, the _____ between two currencies specifies how much one currency is worth in terms of the other. For example an _____ of 102 Japanese yen to the United States dollar means that JPY 102 is worth the same as USD 1. The foreign exchange market is one of the largest markets in the world.
a. Exchange rate   b. A Random Walk Down Wall Street
c. ABN Amro   d. AAB

47.   _____ are organizations which pool large sums of money and invest those sums in companies. They include banks, insurance companies, retirement or pension funds, hedge funds and mutual funds. Their role in the economy is to act as highly specialized investors on behalf of others.
a. ABN Amro   b. A Random Walk Down Wall Street
c. AAB   d. Institutional investors

48.   The _____ , largely the creation of Leo Melamed, is part of the Chicago Mercantile Exchange (CME), the largest futures exchange in the United States and the second largest in the world after Eurex, for the trading of futures contracts and options on futures. The _____ was started on May 16, 1972. Two of the more prevalent contracts traded are currency futures and interest rate futures.
a. AAB   b. International Monetary Market
c. A Random Walk Down Wall Street   d. ABN Amro

49.   An _____ is a company whose main business is holding securities of other companies purely for investment purposes. The _____ invests money on behalf of its shareholders who in turn share in the profits and losses.
a. AAB   b. Investment company
c. Unit investment trust   d. A Random Walk Down Wall Street

50.   The _____ or forward rate is the agreed upon price of an asset in a forward contract. Using the rational pricing assumption, we can express the _____ in terms of the spot price and any dividends etc., so that there is no possibility for arbitrage.

The _____ is given by:

$$\boxed{\times}$$

where

F is the _____ to be paid at time T
e^x is the exponential function
r is the risk-free interest rate
q is the cost-of-carry
S_0 is the spot price of the asset (i.e. what it would sell for at time 0)
D_i is a dividend which is guaranteed to be paid at time t_i where $0 < t_i < T$.

The two questions here are what price the short position (the seller of the asset) should offer to maximize his gain, and what price the long position (the buyer of the asset) should accept to maximize his gain?

At the very least we know that both do not want to lose any money in the deal.

a. Forward price
c. Financial Gerontology

b. Biweekly Mortgage
d. Security interest

51. An _____ is the price a borrower pays for the use of money they do not own, and the return a lender receives for deferring the use of funds, by lending it to the borrower. _____s are normally expressed as a percentage rate over the period of one year.

_____s targets are also a vital tool of monetary policy and are used to control variables like investment, inflation, and unemployment.

a. AAB
c. ABN Amro

b. A Random Walk Down Wall Street
d. Interest rate

52. An _____ is a futures contract with an interest-bearing instrument as the underlying asset.

Examples include Treasury-bill futures, Treasury-bond futures and Eurodollar futures.

The global market for exchange-traded _____s is notionally valued by the Bank for International Settlements at $5,794,200 million in 2005.

a. Interest rate future
c. Open interest

b. Interest rate derivative
d. Equity swap

53. The _____ of a commodity, a security or a currency is the price that is quoted for immediate (spot) settlement (payment and delivery.) Spot settlement is normally one or two business days from trade date. This is in contrast with the forward price established in a forward contract or futures contract, where contract terms (price) are set now, but delivery and payment will occur at a future date.

a. Market anomaly
c. Limits to arbitrage

b. Spot rate
d. Long position

54. _____ are government bonds issued by the United States Department of the Treasury through the Bureau of the Public Debt. They are the debt financing instruments of the U.S. Federal government, and they are often referred to simply as Treasuries or Treasurys. There are four types of marketable _____: Treasury bills, Treasury notes, Treasury bonds, and Treasury Inflation Protected Securities (TIPS.)

a. Treasury Inflation-Protected Securities
c. 4-4-5 Calendar

b. Treasury securities
d. Treasury Inflation Protected Securities

55. A _____ is a unit that is equal to 1/100th of a percentage point. It is frequently used to express percentage point changes of less than 1%. It avoids the ambiguity between relative and absolute discussions about rates.

a. 4-4-5 Calendar
c. 529 plan

b. Bond market
d. Basis point

56.   In financial accounting, a _____ or statement of financial position is a summary of a person's or organization's balances. Assets, liabilities and ownership equity are listed as of a specific date, such as the end of its financial year. A _____ is often described as a snapshot of a company's financial condition.

a. Financial statements

b. Statement of retained earnings

c. Balance sheet

d. Statement on Auditing Standards No. 70: Service Organizations

57.   An _____ is an exchange of tangible assets for intangible assets or vice versa. Since it is a swap of assets, the procedure takes place on the active side of the balance sheet and has no impact on the latter in regards to volume. As an example, a company may sell equity and receive the value in cash thus increasing liquidity.

a. AAB
c. A Random Walk Down Wall Street

b. ABN Amro
d. Asset swap

58.   _____ refers to any type of investment that yields a regular (or fixed) return.

For example, if you lend money to a borrower and the borrower has to pay interest once a month, you have been issued a fixed-income security. When a company does this, it is often called a bond or corporate bank debt (although preferred stock is also sometimes considered to be _____).

a. Bond market
c. 529 plan

b. 4-4-5 Calendar
d. Fixed income

59.   An _____ is a derivative in which one party exchanges a stream of interest payments for another party's stream of cash flows. _____s can be used by hedgers to manage their fixed or floating assets and liabilities. They can also be used by speculators to replicate unfunded bond exposures to profit from changes in interest rates.

a. International Swaps and Derivatives Association
c. Interest rate swap

b. Implied volatility
d. Equity swap

60.   In finance, a _____ is a derivative in which two counterparties agree to exchange one stream of cash flows against another stream. These streams are called the legs of the _____.

The cash flows are calculated over a notional principal amount, which is usually not exchanged between counterparties.

a. Volatility swap
c. Volatility arbitrage

b. Local volatility
d. Swap

61.   _____ is the corporate management term for the act of reorganizing the legal, ownership, operational, or other structures of a company for the purpose of making it more profitable or better organized for its present needs. Alternate reasons for restructing include a change of ownership or ownership structure, demerger repositioning debt _____ and financial _____.

a. Day trading

c. Cross-border leasing

b. Concentrated stock

d. Restructuring

62. _____ refers to a portfolio management strategy where the manager makes specific investments with the goal of outperforming an investment benchmark index. Investors or mutual funds that do not aspire to create a return in excess of a benchmark index will often invest in an index fund that replicates as closely as possible the investment weighting and returns of that index; this is called passive management. _____ is the opposite of passive management, because in passive management the manager does not seek to outperform the benchmark index.

a. Active management

c. AAB

b. A Random Walk Down Wall Street

d. ABN Amro

63. _____ is a security analysis discipline for forecasting the future direction of prices through the study of past market data, primarily price and volume. In its purest form, _____ considers only the actual price and volume behavior of the market or instrument. Technical analysts may employ models and trading rules based on price and volume transformations, such as the relative strength index, moving averages, regressions, inter-market and intra-market price correlations, cycles or, classically, through recognition of chart patterns.

a. Dow theory

c. Support and resistance

b. Point and figure

d. Technical analysis

1.   In finance, _____, also known as return on investment is the ratio of money gained or lost on an investment relative to the amount of money invested. The amount of money gained or lost may be referred to as interest, profit/loss, gain/loss, or net income/loss. The money invested may be referred to as the asset, capital, principal, or the cost basis of the investment.

   a. Composiition of Creditors   b. Rate of return

   c. Stock or scrip dividends   d. Doctrine of the Proper Law

2.   _____ is a form of corporation equity ownership represented in the securities. It is dangerous in comparison to preferred shares and some other investment options, in that in the event of bankruptcy, _____ investors receive their funds after preferred stockholders, bondholders, creditors, etc. On the other hand, common shares on average perform better than preferred shares or bonds over time.

   a. Stock split   b. Stop-limit order

   c. Stock market bubble   d. Common stock

3.   The _____ is a measure of the excess return (or Risk Premium) per unit of risk in an investment asset or a trading strategy it is defined as:

$$S = \frac{R - R_f}{\sigma} = \frac{E[R - R_f]}{\sqrt{\operatorname{var}[R - R_f]}},$$

where R is the asset return, R_f is the return on a benchmark asset, such as the risk free rate of return, $E[R - R_f]$ is the expected value of the excess of the asset return over the benchmark return, and σ is the standard deviation of the asset excess return.

Note, if R_f is a constant risk free return throughout the period,

$$\sqrt{\operatorname{var}[R - R_f]} = \sqrt{\operatorname{var}[R]}.$$

The _____ is used to characterize how well the return of an asset compensates the investor for the risk taken. When comparing two assets each with the expected return E[R] against the same benchmark with return R_f, the asset with the higher _____ gives more return for the same risk.

   a. Sharpe ratio   b. Current ratio

   c. P/E ratio   d. Receivables turnover ratio

4.   _____ means regulating, adapting or settling in a variety of contexts:

In commercial law, _____ means the settlement of a loss incurred on insured goods. The calculation of the amounts of compensation to be paid by or to the several interests is a complicated matter. It involves much detail and arithmetic, and requires a full and accurate knowledge of the principles of the subject.

   a. Intelligent investor   b. Asset recovery

   c. Equity method   d. Adjustment

5. _____ is a risk-adjusted measure of the so-called active return on an investment. It is the return in excess of the compensation for the risk borne, and thus commonly used to assess active managers' performances. Often, the return of a benchmark is subtracted in order to consider relative performance, which yields Jensen's _____.

    a. Amortization   b. Annuity

    c. Option   d. Alpha

6. The institution most often referenced by the word '_____' is a public or publicly traded _____, the shares of which are traded on a public stock exchange (e.g., the New York Stock Exchange or Nasdaq in the United States) where shares of stock of _____s are bought and sold by and to the general public. Most of the largest businesses in the world are publicly traded _____s. However, the majority of _____s are said to be closely held, privately held or close _____s, meaning that no ready market exists for the trading of shares.

    a. Corporation   b. Depository Trust Company

    c. Federal Home Loan Mortgage Corporation   d. Protect

7. An _____ or index tracker is a collective investment scheme (usually a mutual fund or exchange-traded fund) that aims to replicate the movements of an index of a specific financial market regardless of market conditions.

Tracking can be achieved by trying to hold all of the securities in the index, in the same proportions as the index. Other methods include statistically sampling the market and holding 'representative' securities.

    a. Investment company   b. Index fund

    c. AAB   d. A Random Walk Down Wall Street

8. _____ or Investment _____ is a set of techniques that performance analysts use to explain why a portfolio's performance differed from the benchmark. This difference between the portfolio return and the benchmark return is known as the active return. The active return is the component of a portfolio's performance that arises from the fact that the portfolio is actively managed.

    a. Convertible arbitrage   b. Central Securities Depository

    c. Delta neutral   d. Performance attribution

9. In business and accounting, _____s are everything of value that is owned by a person or company. The balance sheet of a firm records the monetary value of the _____s owned by the firm. The two major _____ classes are tangible _____s and intangible _____s.

    a. Accounts payable   b. Income

    c. Asset   d. EBITDA

10. _____ is a term used to refer to how an investor distributes his or her investments among various classes of investment vehicles (e.g., stocks and bonds.)

A large part of financial planning is finding an _____ that is appropriate for a given person in terms of their appetite for and ability to shoulder risk. This can depend on various factors; see investor profile.

    a. Investing online   b. Investment performance

    c. Asset allocation   d. Alternative investment

11.   A _____ is a fungible, negotiable instrument representing financial value. They are broadly categorized into debt securities (such as banknotes, bonds and debentures), and equity securities; e.g., common stocks. The company or other entity issuing the _____ is called the issuer.

   a. Security
               b. Securities lending
   c. Tracking stock
          d. Book entry

12.   _____ is a graph created by investors to measure the risk of risky and risk-free assets. The graph displays to the investors on the return they can make by taking on a certain level of risk. It is also known as a 'reward-to-variability ratio'.

   a. Portfolio investment
          b. Divestment
   c. Dollar cost averaging
      d. Capital allocation line

13.   The _____ is the relationship between the amount of return gained on an investment and the amount of risk undertaken in that investment. The more return sought, the more risk that must be undertaken.

There are various classes of possible investments, each with their own positions on the overall _____.

   a. Risk-return spectrum
        b. Blank endorsement
   c. Post earnings announcement drift
      d. Fiscal sponsorship

14.   _____ refers to a portfolio management strategy where the manager makes specific investments with the goal of outperforming an investment benchmark index. Investors or mutual funds that do not aspire to create a return in excess of a benchmark index will often invest in an index fund that replicates as closely as possible the investment weighting and returns of that index; this is called passive management. _____ is the opposite of passive management, because in passive management the manager does not seek to outperform the benchmark index.

   a. AAB
              b. ABN Amro
   c. Active management
      d. A Random Walk Down Wall Street

15.   A _____ is a situation that involves losing one quality or aspect of something in return for gaining another quality or aspect. It implies a decision to be made with full comprehension of both the upside and downside of a particular choice.

In economics the term is expressed as opportunity cost, referring the most preferred alternative given up.

   a. Trade-off
          b. Capital outflow
   c. Total revenue
      d. Break-even point

16.   The arithmetic _____ over n periods is defined as:

$$\boxed{\times} >$$

The geometric _____, also known as the time-weighted rate of return, over n periods is defined as:

$$\boxed{\times} >$$

The geometric _____ calculated over n years is also known as the annualized return.

The internal rate of return, also known as the dollar-weighted rate of return, is defined as the value(s) of > that satisfies the following equation:

>,

where:

- NPV = net present value of the investment

For both arithmetic returns and logarithmic returns, an investment is profitable when either > or > > 0, and unprofitable when either > or > < 0.

The value of an investment is doubled over a year if the annual ROR > or >. The value falls to zero when > or >.

a. Assets turnover

b. Inventory turnover

c. Average rate of return

d. Earnings yield

17. _____ is the strategy of making buy or sell decisions of financial assets (often stocks) by attempting to predict future market price movements. The prediction may be based on an outlook of market or economic conditions resulting from technical or fundamental analysis. This is an investment strategy based on the outlook for an aggregate market, rather than for a particular financial asset.

a. Portable alpha

b. Divestment

c. Late trading

d. Market timing

18. In statistics, _____ has two related meanings:

- the arithmetic _____
- the expected value of a random variable, which is also called the population _____.

It is sometimes stated that the '_____' is average. This is incorrect if '_____' is taken in the specific sense of 'arithmetic _____' as there are different types of averages: the _____, median, and mode. Other simple statistical analyses use measures of spread, such as range, interquartile range, or standard deviation. For a real-valued random variable X, the _____ is the expectation of X. Note that not every probability distribution has a defined _____; see the Cauchy distribution for an example.

a. Harmonic mean

b. Mean

c. Sample size

d. Probability distribution

19.   An _____ is a contract written by a seller that conveys to the buyer the right -- but not the obligation -- to buy (in the case of a call _____) or to sell (in the case of a put _____) a particular asset, such as a piece of property such as, among others, a futures contract. In return for granting the _____, the seller collects a payment (the premium) from the buyer.

For example, buying a call _____ provides the right to buy a specified quantity of a security at a set strike price at some time on or before expiration, while buying a put _____ provides the right to sell.

    a. Amortization   b. Annuity
    c. AT'T Mobility LLC   d. Option

20.   The term _____ refers to three closely related concepts:

- The _____ model is a mathematical model of the market for an equity, in which the equity's price is a stochastic process.
- The _____ PDE is a partial differential equation which (in the model) must be satisfied by the price of a derivative on the equity.
- The _____ formula is the result obtained by solving the _____ PDE for a European call option.

Fischer Black and Myron Scholes first articulated the _____ formula in their 1973 paper, 'The Pricing of Options and Corporate Liabilities.' The foundation for their research relied on work developed by scholars such as Jack L. Treynor, Paul Samuelson, A. James Boness, Sheen T. Kassouf, and Edward O. Thorp. The fundamental insight of _____ is that the option is implicitly priced if the stock is traded.

Robert C. Merton was the first to publish a paper expanding the mathematical understanding of the options pricing model and coined the term '_____' options pricing model.

    a. Modified Internal Rate of Return   b. Perpetuity
    c. Stochastic volatility   d. Black-Scholes

21.   In Finance the _____ is a mathematical model for security selection published by Fischer Black and Jack Treynor in 1973. The model assumes an investor who considers that most securities are priced efficiently, but who believes he has information that can be used to predict the abnormal performance (Alpha) of a few of them; the model finds the optimum portfolio to hold under such conditions.

In essence the optimal portfolio consists of two parts: an index fund containing all securities in proportion to their market value and an 'active portfolio' containing the securities for which the investor has made a prediction about alpha.

    a. LIBOR market model   b. Binomial model
    c. Modified Internal Rate of Return   d. Treynor-Black model

22.   In finance, an _____ is the difference between the expected return of a security and the actual return. _____s are sometimes triggered by 'events.' Events can include mergers, dividend announcements, company earning announcements, interest rate increases, lawsuits, etc. all which can contribute to an _____.

a. A Random Walk Down Wall Street

b. AAB

c. ABN Amro

d. Abnormal return

23.   Modern portfolio theory (MPT) proposes how rational investors will use diversification to optimize their portfolios, and how a risky asset should be priced. The basic concepts of the theory are Markowitz diversification, the _____, capital asset pricing model, the alpha and beta coefficients, the Capital Market Line and the Securities Market Line.

MPT models an asset's return as a random variable, and models a portfolio as a weighted combination of assets so that the return of a portfolio is the weighted combination of the assets' returns.

a. ABN Amro

b. Efficient frontier

c. A Random Walk Down Wall Street

d. AAB

1.   An _____ represents the ownership in the shares of a foreign company trading on US financial markets. The stock of many non-US companies trades on US exchanges through the use of _____s. _____s enable US investors to buy shares in foreign companies without undertaking cross-border transactions.
   a. American Depository Receipt   b. AAB
   c. ABN Amro   d. A Random Walk Down Wall Street

2.   _____ is the branch of economics that studies the dynamics of exchange rates, foreign investment, and how these affect international trade. It also studies international projects, international investments and capital flows, and trade deficits. It includes the study of futures, options and currency swaps.
   a. AAB   b. A Random Walk Down Wall Street
   c. ABN Amro   d. International finance

3.   _____ is a measurement of corporate or economic size equal to the share price times the number of shares outstanding of a public company. As owning stock represents owning the company, including all its equity, capitalization could represent the public opinion of a company's net worth and is a determining factor in stock valuation. Likewise, the capitalization of stock markets or economic regions may be compared to other economic indicators.
   a. Proxy fight   b. Market capitalization
   c. Just-in-time   d. Synthetic CDO

4.   The _____ is a bank that provides financial and technical assistance to developing countries for development programs (e.g. bridges, roads, schools, etc.) with the stated goal of reducing poverty.

The _____ differs from the _____ Group, in that the _____ comprises only two institutions:

   - International Bank for Reconstruction and Development (IBRD)
   - International Development Association (IDA)

Whereas the latter incorporates these two in addition to three more:

   - International Finance Corporation (IFC)
   - Multilateral Investment Guarantee Agency (MIGA)
   - International Centre for Settlement of Investment Disputes (ICSID)

John Maynard Keynes (right) represented the UK at the conference, and Harry Dexter White represented the US.

The _____ was created following the ratification of the United Nations Monetary and Financial Conference │ Bretton Woods agreement. The concept was originally conceived in July 1944 at the United Nations Monetary and Financial Conference.

   a. 529 plan   b. 4-4-5 Calendar
   c. 7-Eleven   d. World Bank

5.   A _____ is a private or public market for the trading of company stock and derivatives of company stock at an agreed price; these are securities listed on a stock exchange as well as those only traded privately.

The size of the world _____ is estimated at about $36.6 trillion US at the beginning of October 2008 . The world derivatives market has been estimated at about $480 trillion face or nominal value, 12 times the size of the entire world economy.

   a. Anton Gelonkin   b. Adolph Coors

   c. Stock market   d. Andrew Tobias

6.   A _____ is a fungible, negotiable instrument representing financial value. They are broadly categorized into debt securities (such as banknotes, bonds and debentures), and equity securities; e.g., common stocks. The company or other entity issuing the _____ is called the issuer.

   a. Book entry   b. Tracking stock

   c. Securities lending   d. Security

7.   A _____, securities exchange or (in Europe) bourse is a corporation or mutual organization which provides 'trading' facilities for stock brokers and traders, to trade stocks and other securities. _____s also provide facilities for the issue and redemption of securities as well as other financial instruments and capital events including the payment of income and dividends. The securities traded on a _____ include: shares issued by companies, unit trusts and other pooled investment products and bonds.

   a. 7-Eleven   b. 529 plan

   c. Stock exchange   d. 4-4-5 Calendar

8.   The term _____ is used to describe a nation's social, or business activity in the process of rapid industrialization. _____ are generally less-wealthy than the developed world, and are wealthier (or the wealthiest of) the developing world. According to The Economist many people find the term dated, but a new term has yet to gain much traction.

   a. AAB   b. Emerging markets

   c. A Random Walk Down Wall Street   d. ABN Amro

9.   The _____ is one of the measures of national income and input for a given country's economy. _____ is defined as the total cost of all finished goods and services produced within the country in a stipulated period of time (usually a 365-day year.) It is sometimes regarded as the sum of profits added at every level of production (the intermediate stages) of all final goods and services produced within a country in a stipulated timeframe, and it is rarely given a monetary value.

   a. Gross domestic product   b. Behavioral finance

   c. Macroeconomics   d. Recession

10.   The _____ is one of several stock market indices, created by nineteenth-century Wall Street Journal editor and Dow Jones ' Company co-founder Charles Dow. Dow compiled the index to gauge the performance of the industrial sector of the American stock market. It is the second-oldest U.S. market index, after the Dow Jones Transportation Average, which Dow also created.

   a. 4-4-5 Calendar   b. 529 plan

   c. 7-Eleven   d. Dow Jones Industrial Average

11.   A _____ is a method of measuring a section of the stock market. Many indices are cited by news or financial services firms and are used to benchmark the performance of portfolios such as mutual funds.

a. Program trading   b. Stop order
c. Trading curb   d. Stock market index

12.   The _____ is the market for securities, where companies and governments can raise longterm funds. The _____ includes the stock market and the bond market. Financial regulators, such as the U.S. Securities and Exchange Commission, oversee the _____s in their designated countries to ensure that investors are protected against fraud.
a. Delta neutral   b. Spot rate
c. Forward market   d. Capital market

13.   _____ proposes how rational investors will use diversification to optimize their portfolios, and how a risky asset should be priced. The basic concepts of the theory are Markowitz diversification, the efficient frontier, capital asset pricing model, the alpha and beta coefficients, the Capital Market Line and the Securities Market Line.

_____ models an asset's return as a random variable, and models a portfolio as a weighted combination of assets so that the return of a portfolio is the weighted combination of the assets' returns.

a. Market value   b. Modern portfolio theory
c. Consumer basket   d. Payback period

14.   In finance, the _____ between two currencies specifies how much one currency is worth in terms of the other. For example an _____ of 102 Japanese yen to the United States dollar means that JPY 102 is worth the same as USD 1. The foreign exchange market is one of the largest markets in the world.
a. ABN Amro   b. Exchange rate
c. A Random Walk Down Wall Street   d. AAB

15.   _____ is a form of risk that arises from the change in price of one currency against another. Whenever investors or companies have assets or business operations across national borders, they face _____ if their positions are not hedged.

- Transaction risk is the risk that exchange rates will change unfavourably over time. It can be hedged against using forward currency contracts;
- Translation risk is an accounting risk, proportional to the amount of assets held in foreign currencies. Changes in the exchange rate over time will render a report inaccurate, and so assets are usually balanced by borrowings in that currency.

The exchange risk associated with a foreign denominated instrument is a key element in foreign investment. This risk flows from differential monetary policy and growth in real productivity, which results in differential inflation rates.

a. Tracking error   b. Market risk
c. Credit risk   d. Currency risk

16.   In business and accounting, _____s are everything of value that is owned by a person or company. The balance sheet of a firm records the monetary value of the _____s owned by the firm. The two major _____ classes are tangible _____s and intangible _____s.

a. EBITDA

b. Accounts payable

c. Income

d. Asset

17. _____ is a term used to refer to how an investor distributes his or her investments among various classes of investment vehicles (e.g., stocks and bonds.)

A large part of financial planning is finding an _____ that is appropriate for a given person in terms of their appetite for and ability to shoulder risk. This can depend on various factors; see investor profile.

a. Investing online

b. Investment performance

c. Alternative investment

d. Asset allocation

18. In probability theory and statistics, _____ indicates the strength and direction of a linear relationship between two random variables. That is in contrast with the usage of the term in colloquial speech, which denotes any relationship, not necessarily linear. In general statistical usage, _____ or co-relation refers to the departure of two random variables from independence.

a. Geometric mean

b. Correlation

c. Probability distribution

d. Variance

19. _____ is a term used in accounting, economics and finance to spread the cost of an asset over the span of several years.

In simple words we can say that _____ is the reduction in the value of an asset due to usage, passage of time, wear and tear, technological outdating or obsolescence, depletion or other such factors.

In accounting, _____ is a term used to describe any method of attributing the historical or purchase cost of an asset across its useful life, roughly corresponding to normal wear and tear.

a. Matching principle

b. Deferred financing costs

c. Bottom line

d. Depreciation

20. _____ is the investment strategy where an investor buys a financial instrument denominated in a foreign currency, and hedges his foreign exchange risk by selling a forward contract in the amount of the proceeds of the investment back into his base currency. The proceeds of the investment are only known exactly if the financial instrument is risk-free and only pays interest once, on the date of the forward sale of foreign currency. Otherwise, some foreign exchange risk remains.

a. Triangular arbitrage

b. Covered interest arbitrage

c. Currency future

d. Floating exchange rate

21. _____ is a fee paid on borrowed assets. It is the price paid for the use of borrowed money , or, money earned by deposited funds . Assets that are sometimes lent with _____ include money, shares, consumer goods through hire purchase, major assets such as aircraft, and even entire factories in finance lease arrangements.

a. Insolvency

b. AAB

c. Interest

d. A Random Walk Down Wall Street

22. An _____ is the price a borrower pays for the use of money they do not own, and the return a lender receives for deferring the use of funds, by lending it to the borrower. _____s are normally expressed as a percentage rate over the period of one year.

_____s targets are also a vital tool of monetary policy and are used to control variables like investment, inflation, and unemployment.

a. A Random Walk Down Wall Street   b. AAB
c. ABN Amro   d. Interest rate

23. _____ is an economic concept, expressed as a basic algebraic identity that relates interest rates and exchange rates. The identity is theoretical, and usually follows from assumptions imposed in economics models. There is evidence to support as well as to refute the concept.

a. A Random Walk Down Wall Street   b. Unit price
c. Interest rate parity   d. AAB

24. In economics and finance, _____ is the practice of taking advantage of a price differential between two or more markets: striking a combination of matching deals that capitalize upon the imbalance, the profit being the difference between the market prices. When used by academics, an _____ is a transaction that involves no negative cash flow at any probabilistic or temporal state and a positive cash flow in at least one state; in simple terms, a risk-free profit.

a. Efficient-market hypothesis   b. Issuer
c. Initial margin   d. Arbitrage

25. In finance, a _____ is a position established in one market in an attempt to offset exposure to the price risk of an equal but opposite obligation or position in another market -- usually, but not always, in the context of one's commercial activity. Hedging is a strategy designed to minimize exposure to such business risks as a sharp contraction in demand for one's inventory, while still allowing the business to profit from producing and maintaining that inventory. A typical hedger might be a farmer with 2000 acres of unharvested wheat in the ground, who would rather tend his crop without the distraction of uncertain prices.

a. Hedge   b. 4-4-5 Calendar
c. 7-Eleven   d. 529 plan

26. _____ refers to the likelihood that changes in the business environment adversely affect operating profits or the value of assets in a specific country. For example, financial factors such as currency controls, devaluation or regulatory changes, or stability factors such as mass riots, civil war and other potential events contribute to companies' operational risks. This term is also sometimes referred to as political risk, however _____ is a more general term, which generally only refers to risks affecting all companies operating within a particular country.

a. Capital asset   b. Country Risk
c. Single-index model   d. Solvency

27. _____ of a business involves analyzing its financial statements and health, its management and competitive advantages, and its competitors and markets. The term is used to distinguish such analysis from other types of investment analysis, such as quantitative analysis and technical analysis.

_____ is performed on historical and present data, but with the goal of making financial forecasts.

a. 4-4-5 Calendar

b. Stock valuation

c. Fundamental analysis

d. Growth stocks

28. _____ is a type of risk faced by investors, corporations, and governments. It is a risk that can be understood and managed with proper aforethought and investment.

Broadly, _____ refers to the complications businesses and governments may face as a result of what are commonly referred to as political decisions--or 'any political change that alters the expected outcome and value of a given economic action by changing the probability of achieving business objectives.' .

a. Capital asset

b. Single-index model

c. Mid price

d. Political risk

29. _____ is a security analysis discipline for forecasting the future direction of prices through the study of past market data, primarily price and volume. In its purest form, _____ considers only the actual price and volume behavior of the market or instrument. Technical analysts may employ models and trading rules based on price and volume transformations, such as the relative strength index, moving averages, regressions, inter-market and intra-market price correlations, cycles or, classically, through recognition of chart patterns.

a. Dow theory

b. Technical analysis

c. Support and resistance

d. Point and figure

30. In finance, _____ is the process of estimating the potential market value of a financial asset or liability. they can be done on assets (for example, investments in marketable securities such as stocks, options, business enterprises, or intangible assets such as patents and trademarks) or on liabilities (e.g., Bonds issued by a company.) _____ s are required in many contexts including investment analysis, capital budgeting, merger and acquisition transactions, financial reporting, taxable events to determine the proper tax liability, and in litigation.

a. Procter ' Gamble

b. Margin

c. Share

d. Valuation

31. _____ in finance is a risk management technique, related to hedging, that mixes a wide variety of investments within a portfolio. Because the fluctuations of a single security have less impact on a diverse portfolio, _____ minimizes the risk from any one investment.

A simple example of _____ is the following: On a particular island the entire economy consists of two companies: one that sells umbrellas and another that sells sunscreen.

a. 529 plan

b. 7-Eleven

c. 4-4-5 Calendar

d. Diversification

32. In business and finance, a _____ (also referred to as equity _____) of stock means a _____ of ownership in a corporation (company.) In the plural, stocks is often used as a synonym for _____s especially in the United States, but it is less commonly used that way outside of North America.

In the United Kingdom, South Africa, and Australia, stock can also refer to completely different financial instruments such as government bonds or, less commonly, to all kinds of marketable securities.

a. Procter ' Gamble   b. Bucket shop

c. Margin   d. Share

33.   An _____ or index tracker is a collective investment scheme (usually a mutual fund or exchange-traded fund) that aims to replicate the movements of an index of a specific financial market regardless of market conditions.

Tracking can be achieved by trying to hold all of the securities in the index, in the same proportions as the index. Other methods include statistically sampling the market and holding 'representative' securities.

a. Investment company   b. A Random Walk Down Wall Street

c. AAB   d. Index fund

34.   Depending on the nature of the investment, the type of _____ will vary.

A common concern with any investment is that you may lose the money you invest - your capital. This risk is therefore often referred to as 'capital risk.'

If the assets you invest in are held in another currency there is a risk that currency movements alone may affect the value.

a. AAB   b. Investment risk

c. A Random Walk Down Wall Street   d. ABN Amro

35.   The _____, in terms of finance and investing, describes how the expected return of a stock or portfolio is correlated to the return of the financial market as a whole.

An asset with a beta of 0 means that its price is not at all correlated with the market; that asset is independent. A positive beta means that the asset generally follows the market.

a. Perpetuity   b. Beta coefficient

c. Current yield   d. LIBOR market model

36.   A _____ is the direction in which a financial market is moving. _____s can be classified as primary trends, secondary trends (short-term), and secular trends (long-term.) This principle incorporates the idea that market cycles occur with regularity and persistence.

a. 529 plan   b. 4-4-5 Calendar

c. 7-Eleven   d. Market trend

37.   _____ is a risk-adjusted measure of the so-called active return on an investment. It is the return in excess of the compensation for the risk borne, and thus commonly used to assess active managers' performances. Often, the return of a benchmark is subtracted in order to consider relative performance, which yields Jensen's _____.

a. Amortization   b. Annuity

c. Option   d. Alpha

38.   In probability theory and statistics, _____ is a measure of how much two variables change together (variance is a special case of the _____ when the two variables are identical.)

If two variables tend to vary together (that is, when one of them is above its expected value, then the other variable tends to be above its expected value too), then the _____ between the two variables will be positive. On the other hand, when one of them is above its expected value the other variable tends to be below its expected value, then the _____ between the two variables will be negative.

a. Covariance

b. Frequency distribution

c. Stratified sampling

d. Probability distribution

39.   In statistics and probability theory, the _____ is a matrix of covariances between elements of a vector. It is the natural generalization to higher dimensions of the concept of the variance of a scalar-valued random variable.

If entries in the column vector

$$X = \begin{bmatrix} X_1 \\ \vdots \\ X_n \end{bmatrix}$$

are random variables, each with finite variance, then the _____ Σ is the matrix whose (i, j) entry is the covariance

$$\Sigma_{ij} = \mathrm{cov}(X_i, X_j) = \mathrm{E}\big[(X_i - \mu_i)(X_j - \mu_j)\big]$$

where

$$\mu_i = \mathrm{E}(X_i)$$

is the expected value of the ith entry in the vector X.

a. 529 plan

b. 4-4-5 Calendar

c. 7-Eleven

d. Covariance matrix

40.   Modern portfolio theory (MPT) proposes how rational investors will use diversification to optimize their portfolios, and how a risky asset should be priced. The basic concepts of the theory are Markowitz diversification, the _____, capital asset pricing model, the alpha and beta coefficients, the Capital Market Line and the Securities Market Line.

MPT models an asset's return as a random variable, and models a portfolio as a weighted combination of assets so that the return of a portfolio is the weighted combination of the assets' returns.

a. AAB

b. ABN Amro

c. A Random Walk Down Wall Street

d. Efficient frontier

41.   The _____ is the weighted-average most likely outcome in gambling, probability theory, economics or finance.

In gambling and probability theory, there is usually a discrete set of possible outcomes. In this case, _____ is a measure of the relative balance of win or loss weighted by their chances of occurring.

a. A Random Walk Down Wall Street

b. AAB

c. ABN Amro

d. Expected return

42.   In finance, _____ refers to Monday, October 19, 1987, when stock markets around the world crashed, shedding a huge value in a very short time. The crash began in Hong Kong, spread west through international time zones to Europe, hitting the United States after other markets had already declined by a significant margin. The Dow Jones Industrial Average (DJIA) dropped by 508 points to 1738.74 (22.61%).

a. Black Monday

b. 7-Eleven

c. 4-4-5 Calendar

d. 529 plan

43.   A _____ is a variable associated with an increased risk of disease or infection. They are correlational and not necessarily causal, because correlation does not imply causation. For example, being young cannot be said to cause measles, but young people are more at risk as they are less likely to have developed immunity during a previous epidemic.

a. 529 plan

b. 7-Eleven

c. 4-4-5 Calendar

d. Risk factor

44.   In probability and statistics, the _____ of a collection of numbers is a measure of the dispersion of the numbers from their expected (mean) value. It can apply to a probability distribution, a random variable, a population or a data set. The _____ is usually denoted with the letter σ (lowercase sigma.)

a. Mean

b. Kurtosis

c. Sample size

d. Standard deviation

45.   _____ is the provision of resources (such as granting a loan) by one party to another party where that second party does not reimburse the first party immediately, thereby generating a debt, and instead arranges either to repay or return those resources (or material(s) of equal value) at a later date. The first party is called a creditor, also known as a lender, while the second party is called a debtor, also known as a borrower.

Movements of financial capital are normally dependent on either _____ or equity transfers.

a. Credit

b. Warrant

c. Comparable

d. Clearing house

46.   _____ or Investment _____ is a set of techniques that performance analysts use to explain why a portfolio's performance differed from the benchmark. This difference between the portfolio return and the benchmark return is known as the active return. The active return is the component of a portfolio's performance that arises from the fact that the portfolio is actively managed.

a. Central Securities Depository

b. Delta neutral

c. Performance attribution

d. Convertible arbitrage

47.   The institution most often referenced by the word '_____' is a public or publicly traded _____, the shares of which are traded on a public stock exchange (e.g., the New York Stock Exchange or Nasdaq in the United States) where shares of stock of _____s are bought and sold by and to the general public. Most of the largest businesses in the world are publicly traded _____s. However, the majority of _____s are said to be closely held, privately held or close _____s, meaning that no ready market exists for the trading of shares.

a. Depository Trust Company

b. Corporation

c. Protect

d. Federal Home Loan Mortgage Corporation

1. In economics and finance, _____ is the practice of taking advantage of a price differential between two or more markets: striking a combination of matching deals that capitalize upon the imbalance, the profit being the difference between the market prices. When used by academics, an _____ is a transaction that involves no negative cash flow at any probabilistic or temporal state and a positive cash flow in at least one state; in simple terms, a risk-free profit.

    a. Initial margin   b. Issuer
    c. Efficient-market hypothesis   d. Arbitrage

2. _____ , in finance, is a general theory of asset pricing, that has become influential in the pricing of stocks.

_____ holds that the expected return of a financial asset can be modeled as a linear function of various macro-economic factors or theoretical market indices, where sensitivity to changes in each factor is represented by a factor-specific beta coefficient. The model-derived rate of return will then be used to price the asset correctly - the asset price should equal the expected end of period price discounted at the rate implied by model.

    a. ABN Amro   b. AAB
    c. A Random Walk Down Wall Street   d. Arbitrage pricing theory

3. In business and accounting, _____s are everything of value that is owned by a person or company. The balance sheet of a firm records the monetary value of the _____s owned by the firm. The two major _____ classes are tangible _____s and intangible _____s.

    a. Asset   b. Income
    c. Accounts payable   d. EBITDA

4. Behavioral economics and _____ are closely related fields that have evolved to be a separate branch of economic and financial analysis which applies scientific research on human and social, cognitive and emotional factors to better understand economic decisions by, say, consumers, borrowers, investors, and how they affect market prices, returns and the allocation of resources.

The field is primarily concerned with the bounds of rationality (selfishness, self-control) of economic agents. Behavioral models typically integrate insights from psychology with neo-classical economic theory.

    a. Market structure   b. Recession
    c. Medium of exchange   d. Behavioral finance

5. The term _____ has three unrelated technical definitions, and is also used in a variety of non-technical ways.

- In financial economics, it refers to any asset used to make money, as opposed to assets used for personal enjoyment or consumption. This is an important distinction because two people can disagree sharply about the value of personal assets, one person might think a sports car is more valuable than a pickup truck, another person might have the opposite taste. But if an asset is held for the purpose of making money, taste has nothing to do with it, only differences of opinion about how much money the asset will produce. With the further assumption that people agree on the probability distribution of future cash flows, it is possible to have an objective _____ pricing model. Even without the assumption of agreement, it is possible to set rational limits on _____ value.
- In governmental accounting, it is defined as any asset used in operations with an initial useful life extending beyond one reporting period. Generally, government managers have a 'stewardship' duty to maintain _____s under their control. See International Public Sector Accounting Standards for details.
- In US tax accounting, it is defined as any property other than a list of exceptions. The main exceptions are anything held for sale, and any real estate or depreciable property used in business. Almost everything you own and use for personal purposes, pleasure or investment is a _____. If something is a _____ for tax purposes, gains or losses on sale or disposition are capital gains or capital losses. For individuals, however, capital losses on property held for personal use are generally not deductible. See the IRS publication Tax Facts about Capital Gains and Losses for details.

A well-known financial accounting textbook advises that the term be avoided except in tax accounting because it is used in so many different senses, not all of them well-defined. For example it is often used as a synonym for fixed assets or for investments in securities.

A common non-technical usage occurs when people ask that employees or the environment or something else be treated as a _____.

a. Political risk   b. Solvency
c. Capital asset   d. Settlement date

6. _____ is a security analysis discipline for forecasting the future direction of prices through the study of past market data, primarily price and volume. In its purest form, _____ considers only the actual price and volume behavior of the market or instrument. Technical analysts may employ models and trading rules based on price and volume transformations, such as the relative strength index, moving averages, regressions, inter-market and intra-market price correlations, cycles or, classically, through recognition of chart patterns.
a. Point and figure   b. Dow theory
c. Support and resistance   d. Technical analysis

7. In finance, _____ is the process of estimating the potential market value of a financial asset or liability. they can be done on assets (for example, investments in marketable securities such as stocks, options, business enterprises, or intangible assets such as patents and trademarks) or on liabilities (e.g., Bonds issued by a company.) _____s are required in many contexts including investment analysis, capital budgeting, merger and acquisition transactions, financial reporting, taxable events to determine the proper tax liability, and in litigation.
a. Procter ' Gamble   b. Share
c. Valuation   d. Margin

8. _____ is an Israeli-American psychologist and Nobel laureate, notable for his work on behavioral finance and hedonic psychology.

With Amos Tversky and others, he established a cognitive basis for common human errors using heuristics and biases and developed Prospect theory. He was awarded the 2002 Nobel Prize in Economics for his work in Prospect theory.

a. Andrew Tobias   b. Adolph Coors
c. Myron Samuel Scholes   d. Daniel Kahneman

9. The _____ is a hypothesis that people value a good or service more once their property right to it has been established. In other words, people place a higher value on objects they own than objects that they do not. In one experiment, people demanded a higher price for a coffee mug that had been given to them but put a lower price on one they did not yet own.
a. AAB   b. Endowment effect
c. ABN Amro   d. A Random Walk Down Wall Street

10. In prospect theory, _____ refers to the tendency for people to strongly prefer avoiding losses than acquiring gains. Some studies suggest that losses are twice as powerful, psychologically, as gains. _____ was first convincingly demonstrated by Amos Tversky and Daniel Kahneman.
a. Loss aversion   b. Herd behavior
c. Quantitative behavioral finance   d. Perth Leadership Outcome Model

11. _____ or net present worth (NPW) is defined as the total present value (PV) of a time series of cash flows. It is a standard method for using the time value of money to appraise long-term projects. Used for capital budgeting, and widely throughout economics, it measures the excess or shortfall of cash flows, in present value terms, once financing charges are met.
a. Negative gearing   b. Present value of costs
c. Tax shield   d. Net present value

12. The _____ is a cognitive bias for the status quo; in other words, people tend not to change an established behavior unless the incentive to change is compelling.

The finding has been observed in many fields, including political science and economics.

Kahneman, Thaler and Knetsch created experiments that could produce this effect reliably.

a. 529 plan   b. Status quo bias
c. 4-4-5 Calendar   d. 7-Eleven

13. _____ is the value on a given date of a future payment or series of future payments, discounted to reflect the time value of money and other factors such as investment risk. _____ calculations are widely used in business and economics to provide a means to compare cash flows at different times on a meaningful 'like to like' basis.

The most commonly applied model of the time value of money is compound interest.

a. Present value of benefits

b. Negative gearing

c. Net present value

d. Present value

14.   A _____ is a futures contract on a short term interest rate (STIR.) Contracts vary, but are often defined on an interest rate index such as 3-month sterling or US dollar LIBOR.

They are traded across a wide range of currencies, including the G12 country currencies and many others.

a. Real estate derivatives

b. Dual currency deposit

c. Notional amount

d. Financial Future

15.   In finance, a _____ is a standardized contract, to buy or sell a specified commodity of standardized quality at a certain date in the future, at a market determined price (the futures price.)

The price is determined by the instantaneous equilibrium between the forces of supply and demand among competing buy and sell orders on the exchange at the time of the purchase or sale of the contract.

In many cases, the items may be such non-traditional 'commodities' as foreign currencies, commercial or government paper [e.g., bonds], or 'baskets' of corporate equity ['stock indices'] or other financial instruments.

a. Heston model

b. Repurchase agreement

c. Futures contract

d. Financial future

16.   A _____ is a central financial exchange where people can trade standardized futures contracts; that is, a contract to buy specific quantities of a commodity or financial instrument at a specified price with delivery set at a specified time in the future.

Though the origins of futures trading can supposedly be traced to Ancient Greek or Phoenician times, the first modern organized _____ began in 1710 at the Dojima Rice Exchange in Osaka, Japan.

The United States followed in the early 1800s.

a. 7-Eleven

b. 529 plan

c. Futures Exchange

d. 4-4-5 Calendar

17.   In finance, an _____ is the difference between the expected return of a security and the actual return. _____s are sometimes triggered by 'events.' Events can include mergers, dividend announcements, company earning announcements, interest rate increases, lawsuits, etc. all which can contribute to an _____.

a. A Random Walk Down Wall Street

b. AAB

c. ABN Amro

d. Abnormal return

18.   A _____ is any actual or hypothesized stock market trend based on the calendar, such as rises and falls associated with particular days of the week or months of the year.

Examples include:

- Halloween indicator (or the 'Sell in May' principle)
- January effect
- Mark Twain effect
- Monday effect
- Weekend effect
- Turn-of-the-Month effect
- Holiday effect

a. Calendar effect   b. 7-Eleven
c. 4-4-5 Calendar   d. 529 plan

19.   The _____ is an anomaly discovered in behavioral finance. It relates to the tendency of investors to sell shares whose price has increased, while keeping assets that have dropped in value . Investors are unwilling to recognize losses (which they would be forced to do if they sold assets which had fallen in value), but are more willing to recognize gains.
a. Disposition effect   b. Psychological level
c. Herd behavior   d. Prospect theory

20.   A _____ is a payment made by a corporation to its shareholder members. When a corporation earns a profit or surplus, that money can be put to two uses: it can either be re-invested in the business (called retained earnings), or it can be paid to the shareholders as a _____. Many corporations retain a portion of their earnings and pay the remainder as a _____.

a. Dividend   b. Dividend yield
c. Dividend puzzle   d. Special dividend

21.   _____ are organizations which pool large sums of money and invest those sums in companies. They include banks, insurance companies, retirement or pension funds, hedge funds and mutual funds. Their role in the economy is to act as highly specialized investors on behalf of others.
a. Institutional investors   b. AAB
c. A Random Walk Down Wall Street   d. ABN Amro

22.   In finance, a _____ is a debt security, in which the authorized issuer owes the holders a debt and, depending on the terms of the _____, is obliged to pay interest (the coupon) and/or to repay the principal at a later date, termed maturity.

Thus a _____ is a loan: the issuer is the borrower, the _____ holder is the lender, and the coupon is the interest. _____s provide the borrower with external funds to finance long-term investments, or, in the case of government _____s, to finance current expenditure.

a. Puttable bond   b. Catastrophe bonds
c. Convertible bond   d. Bond

23. _____, refers to consumption opportunity gained by an entity within a specified time frame, which is generally expressed in monetary terms. However, for households and individuals, '_____ is the sum of all the wages, salaries, profits, interests payments, rents and other forms of earnings received... in a given period of time.' For firms, _____ generally refers to net-profit: what remains of revenue after expenses have been subtracted.

a. Income
b. OIBDA
c. Accrual
d. Annual report

24. An _____ is a tax levied on the financial income of people, corporations, or other legal entities. Various _____ systems exist, with varying degrees of tax incidence. Income taxation can be progressive, proportional, or regressive.

a. AAB
b. Income Tax
c. ABN Amro
d. A Random Walk Down Wall Street

25. A _____, is a collective investment scheme with a limited number of shares.

New shares are rarely issued after the fund is launched; shares are not normally redeemable for cash or securities until the fund liquidates. Typically an investor can acquire shares in a _____ by buying shares on a secondary market from a broker, market maker, or other investor as opposed to an open-end fund where all transactions eventually involve the fund company creating new shares on the fly (in exchange for either cash or securities) or redeeming shares (for cash or securities.)

a. Stock fund
b. Closed-end fund
c. Mutual fund fees and expenses
d. Money market funds

26. In statistics, _____ has two related meanings:

- the arithmetic _____
- the expected value of a random variable, which is also called the population _____.

It is sometimes stated that the '_____' is average. This is incorrect if '_____' is taken in the specific sense of 'arithmetic _____' as there are different types of averages: the _____, median, and mode. Other simple statistical analyses use measures of spread, such as range, interquartile range, or standard deviation. For a real-valued random variable X, the _____ is the expectation of X. Note that not every probability distribution has a defined _____; see the Cauchy distribution for an example.

a. Sample size
b. Harmonic mean
c. Probability distribution
d. Mean

27. The _____ is one of several stock market indices, created by nineteenth-century Wall Street Journal editor and Dow Jones ' Company co-founder Charles Dow. Dow compiled the index to gauge the performance of the industrial sector of the American stock market. It is the second-oldest U.S. market index, after the Dow Jones Transportation Average, which Dow also created.

a. 4-4-5 Calendar
b. Dow Jones Industrial Average
c. 7-Eleven
d. 529 plan

28. _____, is when a company issues common stock or shares to the public for the first time. They are often issued by smaller, younger companies seeking capital to expand, but can also be done by large privately-owned companies looking to become publicly traded.

In an _____ the issuer may obtain the assistance of an underwriting firm, which helps it determine what type of security to issue (common or preferred), best offering price and time to bring it to market.

 a. Asian Financial Crisis   b. Insolvency
 c. Initial public offering   d. Interest

29. _____ most frequently refers to the standard deviation of the continuously compounded returns of a financial instrument with a specific time horizon. It is often used to quantify the risk of the instrument over that time period. _____ is typically expressed in annualized terms, and it may either be an absolute number ($5) or a fraction of the mean (5%).
 a. Currency swap   b. Volatility
 c. Portfolio insurance   d. Seasoned equity offering

30. A _____ is the price of a single share of a no. of saleable stocks of the company. Once the stock is purchased, the owner becomes a shareholder of the company that issued the share.
 a. Whisper numbers   b. Stock split
 c. Trading curb   d. Share price

31. The institution most often referenced by the word '_____' is a public or publicly traded _____, the shares of which are traded on a public stock exchange (e.g., the New York Stock Exchange or Nasdaq in the United States) where shares of stock of _____s are bought and sold by and to the general public. Most of the largest businesses in the world are publicly traded _____s. However, the majority of _____s are said to be closely held, privately held or close _____s, meaning that no ready market exists for the trading of shares.
 a. Protect   b. Depository Trust Company
 c. Federal Home Loan Mortgage Corporation   d. Corporation

32. A '_____' is a 'Charge' that is paid to obtain the right to delay a payment. Essentially, the payer purchases the right to make a given payment in the future instead of in the Present. The '_____', or 'Charge' that must be paid to delay the payment, is simply the difference between what the payment amount would be if it were paid in the present and what the payment amount would be paid if it were paid in the future.
 a. Discount   b. Value at risk
 c. Risk modeling   d. Risk aversion

33. _____ of a business involves analyzing its financial statements and health, its management and competitive advantages, and its competitors and markets. The term is used to distinguish such analysis from other types of investment analysis, such as quantitative analysis and technical analysis.

_____ is performed on historical and present data, but with the goal of making financial forecasts.

 a. Stock valuation   b. Fundamental analysis
 c. Growth stocks   d. 4-4-5 Calendar

34. _____ is a heterodox theory on stock price movements that is used as the basis for technical analysis. The theory was derived from 255 Wall Street Journal editorials written by Charles H. Dow (1851-1902), journalist, founder and first editor of the Wall Street Journal and co-founder of Dow Jones and Company. Following Dow's death, William P. Hamilton, Robert Rhea and E. George Schaefer organized and collectively represented '_____,' based on Dow's editorials.

a. Technical analysis
b. Point and figure
c. Dow theory
d. Money flow

35. _____ is a concept in technical analysis that the movement of the price of a security will tend to stop and reverse at certain predetermined price levels.

A support level is a price level where the price tends to find support as it is going down. This means the price is more likely to 'bounce' off this level rather than break through it.

A resistance level is the opposite of a support level. It is where the price tends to find resistance as it is going up. This means the price is more likely to 'bounce' off this level rather than break through it.

a. Support and resistance
b. Technical analysis
c. Point and figure
d. Dow theory

36. _____ refers to a portfolio management strategy where the manager makes specific investments with the goal of outperforming an investment benchmark index. Investors or mutual funds that do not aspire to create a return in excess of a benchmark index will often invest in an index fund that replicates as closely as possible the investment weighting and returns of that index; this is called passive management. _____ is the opposite of passive management, because in passive management the manager does not seek to outperform the benchmark index.

a. ABN Amro
b. A Random Walk Down Wall Street
c. Active management
d. AAB

37. The _____ is a form of technical analysis that attempts to forecast trends in the financial markets and other collective activities. It is named after Ralph Nelson Elliott (1871-1948), an accountant who developed the concept in the 1930s: he proposed that market prices unfold in specific patterns, which practitioners today call Elliott waves. Elliott published his views of market behavior in the book The Wave Principle (1938), in a series of articles in Financial World magazine in 1939, and most fully in his final major work, Nature's Laws - The Secret of the Universe (1946.)

a. AAB
b. ABN Amro
c. A Random Walk Down Wall Street
d. Elliott wave principle

38. _____ is a charting technique used in technical analysis, a form of heterodox economics used to attempt to predict financial market prices. _____ charting is unique in that it does not plot price against time as all other techniques do. Instead in plots price against changes in direction by plotting a column of Xs as the price rises and a column of Os as the price falls.

a. Dow theory
b. Technical analysis
c. Money flow
d. Point and figure

39. _____ are the inflation-indexed bonds issued by the U.S. Treasury. The principal is adjusted to the Consumer Price Index, the commonly used measure of inflation. The coupon rate is constant, but generates a different amount of interest when multiplied by the inflation-adjusted principal, thus protecting the holder against inflation. _____ are currently offered in 5-year, 10-year and 20-year maturities.

a. Treasury securities   b. Treasury Inflation Protected Securities
c. 4-4-5 Calendar   d. Treasury Inflation-Protected Securities

40.   A _____ is a style of bar-chart used primarily to describe price movements of an equity over time.

It is a combination of a line-chart and a bar-chart, in that each bar represents the range of price movement over a given time interval. It is most often used in technical analysis of equity and currency price patterns.

a. 529 plan   b. 7-Eleven
c. 4-4-5 Calendar   d. Candlestick chart

41.   In economics, _____ describes the state of a market with respect to competition.

- Perfect competition, in which the market consists of a very large number of firms producing a homogeneous product.
- Monopolistic competition where there are a large number of independent firms which have a very small proportion of the market share.
- Oligopoly, in which a market is dominated by a small number of firms which own more than 40% of the market share.
- Oligopsony, a market dominated by many sellers and a few buyers.
- Monopoly, where there is only one provider of a product or service.
- Natural monopoly, a monopoly in which economies of scale cause efficiency to increase continuously with the size of the firm. A firm is a natural monopoly if it is able to serve the entire market demand at a lower cost than any combination of two or more smaller, more specialized firms.
- Monopsony, when there is only one buyer in a market.

The imperfectly competitive structure is quite identical to the realistic market conditions where some monopolistic competitors, monopolists, oligopolists, and duopolists exist and dominate the market conditions. The elements of _____ include the number and size distribution of firms, entry conditions, and the extent of differentiation.

These somewhat abstract concerns tend to determine some but not all details of a specific concrete market system where buyers and sellers actually meet and commit to trade.

a. Fixed exchange rate   b. Gross domestic product
c. Human capital   d. Market structure

42.   The _____ is an American stock exchange. It is the largest electronic screen-based equity securities trading market in the United States. With approximately 3,200 companies, it has more trading volume per day than any other stock exchange in the world.
a. 529 plan   b. 4-4-5 Calendar
c. 7-Eleven   d. NASDAQ

43.   An _____ represents the ownership in the shares of a foreign company trading on US financial markets. The stock of many non-US companies trades on US exchanges through the use of _____s. _____s enable US investors to buy shares in foreign companies without undertaking cross-border transactions.
a. A Random Walk Down Wall Street   b. ABN Amro
c. AAB   d. American Depository Receipt

44. A _____ is a financial contract between two parties, the buyer and the seller of this type of option. Often it is simply labeled a 'call'. The buyer of the option has the right, but not the obligation to buy an agreed quantity of a particular commodity or financial instrument (the underlying instrument) from the seller of the option at a certain time (the expiration date) for a certain price (the strike price.)

a. Bear spread

b. Call option

c. Bull spread

d. Bear call spread

45. In finance, a _____ is one who attempts to profit by investing in a manner that differs from the conventional wisdom, when the consensus opinion appears to be wrong.

A _____ believes that certain crowd behavior among investors can lead to exploitable mispricings in securities markets. For example, widespread pessimism about a stock can drive a price so low that it overstates the company's risks, and understates its prospects for returning to profitability.

a. Day trading

b. Contrarian

c. Secured debt

d. Direct access trading

46. A _____ is a bond issued by a corporation. The term is usually applied to longer-term debt instruments, generally with a maturity date falling at least a year after their issue date. (The term 'commercial paper' is sometimes used for instruments with a shorter maturity.)

a. Brady bonds

b. Serial bond

c. Government bond

d. Corporate bond

47. A _____ is a financial contract between two parties, the seller (writer) and the buyer of the option. The put allows its buyer the right but not the obligation to sell a commodity or financial instrument (the underlying instrument) to the writer (seller) of the option at a certain time for a certain price (the strike price.) The writer (seller) has the obligation to purchase the underlying asset at that strike price, if the buyer exercises the option.

a. Debit spread

b. Put option

c. Bear spread

d. Bear call spread

48. In finance, the Acid-test or _____ or liquid ratio measures the ability of a company to use its near cash or quick assets to immediately extinguish or retire its current liabilities. Quick assets include those current assets that presumably can be quickly converted to cash at close to their book values.

Generally, the acid test ratio should be 1:1 or better, however this varies widely by industry.

a. Quick ratio

b. Net assets

c. P/E ratio

d. Financial ratio

49. An _____ is a contract written by a seller that conveys to the buyer the right -- but not the obligation -- to buy (in the case of a call _____) or to sell (in the case of a put _____) a particular asset, such as a piece of property such as, among others, a futures contract. In return for granting the _____, the seller collects a payment (the premium) from the buyer.

For example, buying a call _____ provides the right to buy a specified quantity of a security at a set strike price at some time on or before expiration, while buying a put _____ provides the right to sell.

a. AT'T Mobility LLC   b. Option
c. Amortization   d. Annuity

50. _____ is the provision of resources (such as granting a loan) by one party to another party where that second party does not reimburse the first party immediately, thereby generating a debt, and instead arranges either to repay or return those resources (or material(s) of equal value) at a later date. The first party is called a creditor, also known as a lender, while the second party is called a debtor, also known as a borrower.

Movements of financial capital are normally dependent on either _____ or equity transfers.

a. Clearing house   b. Warrant
c. Comparable   d. Credit

51. In statistics, a _____, is a type of finite impulse response filter used to analyze a set of data points by creating a series of averages of different subsets of the full data set. A _____ is not a single number, but it is a set of numbers, each of which is the average of the corresponding subset of a larger set of data points. A _____ may also use unequal weights for each data value in the subset to emphasize particular values in the subset.

a. Voluntary Emissions Reductions   b. Gordon growth model
c. Moving average   d. Loans and interest, in Judaism

52. A _____ is a professionally managed type of collective investment scheme that pools money from many investors and invests it in stocks, bonds, short-term money market instruments, and/or other securities. The _____ will have a fund manager that trades the pooled money on a regular basis. Currently, the worldwide value of all _____s totals more than $26 trillion.

Since 1940, there have been three basic types of investment companies in the United States: open-end funds, also known in the US as _____s; unit investment trusts (UITs); and closed-end funds.

a. Trust company   b. Financial intermediary
c. Net asset value   d. Mutual fund

53. The _____ is usually the number of shares outstanding of a publicly traded company that is sold short, divided by the average daily trading volume (daily transaction).

It is one measure of the market's outlook on a given stock; a higher short interest ratio indicates more pessimism, because a higher proportion of a company's total float has already been sold short.

The short interest and _____ can be deceiving, however, when a company has many convertible securities outstanding and is perceived to be at risk, because convertible and options arbitrageurs will often sell the stock short to manage risk with their long positions in these other instruments.

a. 4-4-5 Calendar

b. 529 plan

c. Short selling

d. Short ratio

54. A _____ is a method of measuring a section of the stock market. Many indices are cited by news or financial services firms and are used to benchmark the performance of portfolios such as mutual funds.

a. Program trading

b. Trading curb

c. Stop order

d. Stock market index

55. _____, in bookkeeping, refers to assets, liabilities, income, and expenses recorded on individual pages of the so called book of final entry or ledger. Changes in _____ value are made by chronologically posting debit (DR) and credit (CR) entries to its page. Examples of _____s are cash, _____s receivable, mortgages, loans, land and buildings, common stock, sales, services provided, wages, and payroll overhead.

a. Account

b. Accretion

c. Alpha

d. Option

56. _____ is a fee paid on borrowed assets. It is the price paid for the use of borrowed money , or, money earned by deposited funds . Assets that are sometimes lent with _____ include money, shares, consumer goods through hire purchase, major assets such as aircraft, and even entire factories in finance lease arrangements.

a. A Random Walk Down Wall Street

b. AAB

c. Interest

d. Insolvency

57. The _____ is a financial technical analysis momentum oscillator measuring the velocity and magnitude of directional price movement by comparing upward and downward close-to-close movements.

The _____ was developed by J. Welles Wilder and published in Commodities magazine (now called Futures magazine) in June 1978, and in his New Concepts in Technical Trading Systems the same year.

a. Relative strength Index

b. Global depository receipt

c. Stock or scrip dividends

d. Database auditing

1.   The _____ is headquartered in the United States of America at Charlottesville, Virginia with offices in Hong Kong and London. Formerly known as the Association for Investment Management and Research (AIMR), the Institute awards the Chartered Financial Analyst (CFA) designation.

In 1925, an organization of investment analysts founded the Investment Analyst Society of Chicago.

  a. CFA Institute   b. Payback period
  c. Financial rand   d. Credit card balance transfer

2.   In economics, _____ is a rise in the general level of prices of goods and services in an economy over a period of time. The term '_____' once referred to increases in the money supply (monetary _____); however, economic debates about the relationship between money supply and price levels have led to its primary use today in describing price _____. _____ can also be described as a decline in the real value of money--a loss of purchasing power in the medium of exchange which is also the monetary unit of account.

  a. Inflation   b. A Random Walk Down Wall Street
  c. ABN Amro   d. AAB

3.   In finance, a _____ is a debt security, in which the authorized issuer owes the holders a debt and, depending on the terms of the _____, is obliged to pay interest (the coupon) and/or to repay the principal at a later date, termed maturity.

Thus a _____ is a loan: the issuer is the borrower, the _____ holder is the lender, and the coupon is the interest. _____s provide the borrower with external funds to finance long-term investments, or, in the case of government _____s, to finance current expenditure.

  a. Bond   b. Convertible bond
  c. Puttable bond   d. Catastrophe bonds

4.   In economics, business, and accounting, a _____ is the value of money that has been used up to produce something, and hence is not available for use anymore. In business, the _____ may be one of acquisition, in which case the amount of money expended to acquire it is counted as _____. In this case, money is the input that is gone in order to acquire the thing.

  a. Marginal cost   b. Sliding scale fees
  c. Cost   d. Fixed costs

5.   A _____ is a pool of assets forming an independent legal entity that are bought with the contributions to a pension plan for the exclusive purpose of financing pension plan benefits.

_____s are important shareholders of listed and private companies. They are especially important to the stock market where large institutional investors like the Ontario Teachers' Pension Plan dominate.

  a. Limited liability company   b. Leverage
  c. Leveraged buyout   d. Pension fund

6. In statistics and image processing, to smooth a data set is to create an approximating function that attempts to capture important patterns in the data, while leaving out noise or other fine-scale structures/rapid phenomena. Many different algorithms are used in _____. One of the most common algorithms is the 'moving average', often used to try to capture important trends in repeated statistical surveys.

a. 4-4-5 Calendar

b. Smoothing

c. 529 plan

d. 7-Eleven

7. An _____ can be defined as a contract which provides an income stream in return for an initial payment.

An immediate _____ is an _____ for which the time between the contract date and the date of the first payment is not longer than the time interval between payments. A common use for an immediate _____ is to provide a pension to a retired person or persons.

a. Amortization

b. AT'T Inc.

c. Intrinsic value

d. Annuity

8. In financial accounting, a _____ or statement of financial position is a summary of a person's or organization's balances. Assets, liabilities and ownership equity are listed as of a specific date, such as the end of its financial year. A _____ is often described as a snapshot of a company's financial condition.

a. Statement of retained earnings

b. Financial statements

c. Statement on Auditing Standards No. 70: Service Organizations

d. Balance sheet

9. _____, refers to consumption opportunity gained by an entity within a specified time frame, which is generally expressed in monetary terms. However, for households and individuals, '_____ is the sum of all the wages, salaries, profits, interests payments, rents and other forms of earnings received... in a given period of time.' For firms, _____ generally refers to net-profit: what remains of revenue after expenses have been subtracted.

a. Accrual

b. Annual report

c. OIBDA

d. Income

10. _____ is the income of individuals or nations after adjusting for inflation. It is calculated by subtracting inflation from the nominal income. Real variables, such as _____, real GDP, and real interest rate are variables that are measured in physical units, while nominal variables such as nominal income, nominal GDP, and nominal interest rate are measured in monetary units.

a. 4-4-5 Calendar

b. 529 plan

c. Real income

d. 7-Eleven

11. _____ is the imposition of two or more taxes on the same income (in the case of income taxes), asset (in the case of capital taxes), or financial transaction (in the case of sales taxes.) It refers to two distinct situations:

- taxation of dividend income without relief or credit for taxes paid by the company paying the dividend on the income from which the dividend is paid. This arises in the so-called 'classical' system of corporate taxation, used in the United States.
- taxation by two or more countries of the same income, asset or transaction, for example income paid by an entity of one country to a resident of a different country. The double liability is often mitigated by tax treaties between countries.

It is not unusual for a business or individual who is resident in one country to make a taxable gain (earnings, profits) in another. This person may find that he is obliged by domestic laws to pay tax on that gain locally and pay again in the country in which the gain was made. Since this is inequitable, many nations make bilateral _____ agreements with each other.

a. Double taxation

b. 529 plan

c. 4-4-5 Calendar

d. 7-Eleven

12. _____ is a term describing a range of accounting systems designed to correct problems arising from historical cost accounting in the presence of inflation. _____ is used in countries experiencing high inflation or hyperinflation. For example, in countries experiencing hyperinflation the International Accounting Standards Board requires corporate financial statements to be adjusted for changes in purchasing power using a price index.

a. Inflation accounting

b. AAB

c. Inflation targeting

d. A Random Walk Down Wall Street

13. _____, in bookkeeping, refers to assets, liabilities, income, and expenses recorded on individual pages of the so called book of final entry or ledger. Changes in _____ value are made by chronologically posting debit (DR) and credit (CR) entries to its page. Examples of _____s are cash, _____s receivable, mortgages, loans, land and buildings, common stock, sales, services provided, wages, and payroll overhead.

a. Option

b. Alpha

c. Accretion

d. Account

14. An _____ is a retirement plan account that provides some tax advantages for retirement savings in the United States.

a. A Random Walk Down Wall Street

b. Individual Retirement Arrangement

c. ABN Amro

d. AAB

15. A _____ is a profit that results from investments into a capital asset, such as stocks, bonds or real estate, which exceeds the purchase price. It is the difference between a higher selling price and a lower purchase price, resulting in a financial gain for the seller. Conversely, a capital loss arises if the proceeds from the sale of a capital asset are less than the purchase price.

a. Payroll tax

b. Capital gain

c. Tax brackets

d. Capital gains tax

16. A _____ is a tax charged on capital gains, the profit realized on the sale of a non-inventory asset that was purchased at a lower price. The most common capital gains are realized from the sale of stocks, bonds, precious metals and property. Not all countries implement a _____ and most have different rates of taxation for individuals and corporations.

a. Tax holiday

b. Withholding tax

c. Tax brackets

d. Capital gains tax

17. A _____ is a fungible, negotiable instrument representing financial value. They are broadly categorized into debt securities (such as banknotes, bonds and debentures), and equity securities; e.g., common stocks. The company or other entity issuing the _____ is called the issuer.

a. Tracking stock

b. Book entry

c. Securities lending

d. Security

18.   The _____ is a capital budgeting metric used by firms to decide whether they should make investments. It is an indicator of the efficiency or quality of an investment, as opposed to net present value (NPV), which indicates value or magnitude.

The IRR is the annualized effective compounded return rate which can be earned on the invested capital, i.e., the yield on the investment.

a. AAB

b. ABN Amro

c. A Random Walk Down Wall Street

d. Internal rate of return

19.   _____ is the incidence or process of transferring ownership of a business, enterprise, agency or public service from the public sector (government) to the private sector (business.) In a broader sense, _____ refers to transfer of any government function to the private sector including governmental functions like revenue collection and law enforcement.

The term '_____' also has been used to describe two unrelated transactions. The first is a buyout, by the majority owner, of all shares of a public corporation or holding company's stock, privatizing a publicly traded stock. The second is a demutualization of a mutual organization or cooperative to form a joint stock company.

a. 529 plan

b. 4-4-5 Calendar

c. 7-Eleven

d. Privatization

20.   In finance, _____, also known as return on investment is the ratio of money gained or lost on an investment relative to the amount of money invested. The amount of money gained or lost may be referred to as interest, profit/loss, gain/loss, or net income/loss. The money invested may be referred to as the asset, capital, principal, or the cost basis of the investment.

a. Composiition of Creditors

b. Doctrine of the Proper Law

c. Stock or scrip dividends

d. Rate of return

21.   In finance, _____ is the ability of an entity to pay its debts with available cash. _____ can also be described as the ability of a corporation to meet its long-term fixed expenses and to accomplish long-term expansion and growth. The better a company's _____, the better it is financially.

a. Capital asset

b. Solvency

c. Mid price

d. Political risk

22.   _____ refers to a business or organization attempting to acquire goods or services to accomplish the goals of the enterprise. Though there are several organizations that attempt to set standards in the _____ process, processes can vary greatly between organizations. Typically the word '_____' is not used interchangeably with the word 'procurement', since procurement typically includes Expediting, Supplier Quality, and Traffic and Logistics (T'L) in addition to _____.

a. 7-Eleven

b. Purchasing

c. 4-4-5 Calendar

d. 529 plan

23. A _____ or _____ is a tax designation for a corporation investing in real estate that reduces or eliminates corporate income taxes. In return, _____s are required to distribute 95% of their income, which may be taxable in the hands of the investors. The _____ structure was designed to provide a similar structure for investment in real estate as mutual funds provide for investment in stocks.

   a. Real estate investing   b. Tenancy

   c. Liquidation value   d. Real estate investment trust

24. An _____ represents the ownership in the shares of a foreign company trading on US financial markets. The stock of many non-US companies trades on US exchanges through the use of _____s. _____s enable US investors to buy shares in foreign companies without undertaking cross-border transactions.

   a. ABN Amro   b. A Random Walk Down Wall Street

   c. AAB   d. American Depository Receipt

1.   The _____ is headquartered in the United States of America at Charlottesville, Virginia with offices in Hong Kong and London. Formerly known as the Association for Investment Management and Research (AIMR), the Institute awards the Chartered Financial Analyst (CFA) designation.

In 1925, an organization of investment analysts founded the Investment Analyst Society of Chicago.

a. CFA Institute

b. Credit card balance transfer

c. Payback period

d. Financial rand

2.   _____ is an international professional designation offered by the _____ Institute (formerly known as AIMR) to financial analysts who complete a series of three examinations. In order to become a '_____ Charterholder' candidates must pass all three six-hour exams, possess a bachelor's degree (or equivalent, as assessed by the _____ institute) and have 48 months of work experience in an investment decision-making position. _____ charterholders are also obligated to adhere to a strict Code of Ethics and Standards governing their professional conduct.

a. 7-Eleven

b. 4-4-5 Calendar

c. Chartered Financial Analyst

d. 529 plan

3.   A _____, securities analyst, research analyst, equity analyst, or investment analyst is a person who performs financial analysis for external or internal clients as a core part of the job.

An analyst studies companies and other entities to arrive at the estimate of their financial value. It is normally done by analyzing financial reports, aided by follow-up interviews with company representatives and industry experts.

a. Financial Analyst

b. Purchasing manager

c. Stockbroker

d. Portfolio manager

4.   A _____ is a pool of assets forming an independent legal entity that are bought with the contributions to a pension plan for the exclusive purpose of financing pension plan benefits.

_____s are important shareholders of listed and private companies. They are especially important to the stock market where large institutional investors like the Ontario Teachers' Pension Plan dominate.

a. Leverage

b. Leveraged buyout

c. Limited liability company

d. Pension fund

5.   In statistics, _____ has two related meanings:

- the arithmetic _____
- the expected value of a random variable, which is also called the population _____.

It is sometimes stated that the '_____' is average. This is incorrect if '_____' is taken in the specific sense of 'arithmetic _____' as there are different types of averages: the _____, median, and mode. Other simple statistical analyses use measures of spread, such as range, interquartile range, or standard deviation. For a real-valued random variable X, the _____ is the expectation of X. Note that not every probability distribution has a defined _____; see the Cauchy distribution for an example.

a. Mean

b. Probability distribution

c. Sample size

d. Harmonic mean

6. _____ is a concept in economics, finance, and psychology related to the behaviour of consumers and investors under uncertainty. _____ is the reluctance of a person to accept a bargain with an uncertain payoff rather than another bargain with a more certain, but possibly lower, expected payoff.

The inverse of a person's _____ is sometimes called their risk tolerance

a. Discount factor

b. Risk premium

c. Risk adjusted return on capital

d. Risk aversion

7. _____ are organizations which pool large sums of money and invest those sums in companies. They include banks, insurance companies, retirement or pension funds, hedge funds and mutual funds. Their role in the economy is to act as highly specialized investors on behalf of others.

a. A Random Walk Down Wall Street

b. AAB

c. ABN Amro

d. Institutional investors

8. A _____ is an exchange of promises between two or more parties to do an act which is enforceable in a court of law. It is where an unqualified offer meets a qualified acceptance and the parties reach Consensus ad Idem. The parties must have the necessary capacity to _____ and the _____ must not be either trifling, indeterminate, impossible or illegal.

a. 4-4-5 Calendar

b. Contract

c. 7-Eleven

d. 529 plan

9. An _____ (or business indicator) is a statistic about the economy. _____s allow analysis of economic performance and predictions of future performance.

_____s include various indices, earnings reports, and economic summaries, such as unemployment, housing starts, Consumer Price Index (a measure for inflation), industrial production, bankruptcies, Gross Domestic Product, broadband internet penetration, retail sales, stock market prices, and money supply changes.

a. ABN Amro

b. A Random Walk Down Wall Street

c. AAB

d. Economic indicator

10. In finance, a _____ is a standardized contract, to buy or sell a specified commodity of standardized quality at a certain date in the future, at a market determined price (the futures price.)

The price is determined by the instantaneous equilibrium between the forces of supply and demand among competing buy and sell orders on the exchange at the time of the purchase or sale of the contract.

In many cases, the items may be such non-traditional 'commodities' as foreign currencies, commercial or government paper [e.g., bonds], or 'baskets' of corporate equity ['stock indices'] or other financial instruments.

a. Heston model

b. Futures contract

c. Financial future

d. Repurchase agreement

11.   A _____ is a professionally managed type of collective investment scheme that pools money from many investors and invests it in stocks, bonds, short-term money market instruments, and/or other securities. The _____ will have a fund manager that trades the pooled money on a regular basis. Currently, the worldwide value of all _____s totals more than $26 trillion.

Since 1940, there have been three basic types of investment companies in the United States: open-end funds, also known in the US as _____s; unit investment trusts (UITs); and closed-end funds.

a. Trust company

b. Financial intermediary

c. Net asset value

d. Mutual fund

12.   In economics, a _____ is a type of retirement plan in which the amount of the employer's annual contribution is specified.Individual accounts are set up for participants and benefits are based on the amounts credited to these accounts (through employer contributions and, if applicable, employee contributions) plus any investment earnings on the money in the account. Only employer contributions to the account are guaranteed, not the future benefits. In _____s, future benefits fluctuate on the basis of investment earnings.

a. Fixed asset turnover

b. Total revenue

c. Capital costs

d. Defined contribution plan

13.   In finance, _____, also known as return on investment is the ratio of money gained or lost on an investment relative to the amount of money invested. The amount of money gained or lost may be referred to as interest, profit/loss, gain/loss, or net income/loss. The money invested may be referred to as the asset, capital, principal, or the cost basis of the investment.

a. Doctrine of the Proper Law

b. Stock or scrip dividends

c. Composiition of Creditors

d. Rate of return

14.   An _____ or index tracker is a collective investment scheme (usually a mutual fund or exchange-traded fund) that aims to replicate the movements of an index of a specific financial market regardless of market conditions.

Tracking can be achieved by trying to hold all of the securities in the index, in the same proportions as the index. Other methods include statistically sampling the market and holding 'representative' securities.

a. Index fund

b. Investment company

c. A Random Walk Down Wall Street

d. AAB

15.   The _____ is one of the measures of national income and input for a given country's economy. _____ is defined as the total cost of all finished goods and services produced within the country in a stipulated period of time (usually a 365-day year.) It is sometimes regarded as the sum of profits added at every level of production (the intermediate stages) of all final goods and services produced within a country in a stipulated timeframe, and it is rarely given a monetary value.

a. Macroeconomics

b. Behavioral finance

c. Recession

d. Gross domestic product

16. _____ is a branch of economics that deals with the performance, structure, and behavior of a national or regional economy as a whole. Along with microeconomics, _____ is one of the two most general fields in economics. Macroeconomists study aggregated indicators such as GDP, unemployment rates, and price indices to understand how the whole economy functions.

a. Recession   b. Macroeconomics
c. Human capital   d. Behavioral finance

17. _____ is a type of permanent life insurance based on a cash value. That is, the policy is established with the insurer where premium payments above the cost of insurance are credited to the cash value. The cash value is credited each month with interest, and the policy is debited each month by a cost of insurance (COI) charge, and any other policy charges and fees which are drawn from the cash value if no premium payment is made that month.

a. ABN Amro   b. Universal life
c. A Random Walk Down Wall Street   d. AAB

18. In finance, a _____ is a debt security, in which the authorized issuer owes the holders a debt and, depending on the terms of the _____, is obliged to pay interest (the coupon) and/or to repay the principal at a later date, termed maturity.

Thus a _____ is a loan: the issuer is the borrower, the _____ holder is the lender, and the coupon is the interest. _____s provide the borrower with external funds to finance long-term investments, or, in the case of government _____s, to finance current expenditure.

a. Puttable bond   b. Catastrophe bonds
c. Bond   d. Convertible bond

19. Behavioral economics and _____ are closely related fields that have evolved to be a separate branch of economic and financial analysis which applies scientific research on human and social, cognitive and emotional factors to better understand economic decisions by, say, consumers, borrowers, investors, and how they affect market prices, returns and the allocation of resources.

The field is primarily concerned with the bounds of rationality (selfishness, self-control) of economic agents. Behavioral models typically integrate insights from psychology with neo-classical economic theory.

a. Market structure   b. Recession
c. Medium of exchange   d. Behavioral finance

20. A _____ s a time deposit, a financial product commonly offered to consumers by banks, thrift institutions, and credit unions.

They are similar to savings accounts in that they are insured and thus virtually risk-free; they are 'money in the bank'. They are different from savings accounts in that they have a specific, fixed term (often three months, six months, or one to five years), and, usually, a fixed interest rate.

a. Variable rate mortgage   b. Reserve requirement
c. Time deposit   d. Certificate of deposit

21.   The institution most often referenced by the word '_____' is a public or publicly traded _____, the shares of which are traded on a public stock exchange (e.g., the New York Stock Exchange or Nasdaq in the United States) where shares of stock of _____s are bought and sold by and to the general public. Most of the largest businesses in the world are publicly traded _____s. However, the majority of _____s are said to be closely held, privately held or close _____s, meaning that no ready market exists for the trading of shares.

a. Federal Home Loan Mortgage Corporation

b. Corporation

c. Protect

d. Depository Trust Company

22.   Explicit _____ is a measure implemented in many countries to protect bank depositors, in full or in part, from losses caused by a bank's inability to pay its debts when due. _____ systems are one component of a financial system safety net that promotes financial stability.

a. Deposit Insurance

b. Reserve requirement

c. Banking panic

d. Time deposit

23.   The _____ is a United States government corporation created by the Glass-Steagall Act of 1933. It provides deposit insurance, which guarantees the safety of checking and savings deposits in member banks, currently up to $250,000 per depositor per bank. Insured deposits are backed by the full faith and credit of the United States.

a. Ford Foundation

b. NYSE Group

c. FASB

d. Federal Deposit Insurance Corporation

24.   The _____ (FSLIC) was an institution that administered deposit insurance for savings and loan institutions in the United States. It was abolished in 1989 by the Financial Institutions Reform, Recovery and Enforcement Act, which passed responsibility for savings and loan deposit insurance to the Federal Deposit Insurance Corporation (FDIC.)

The FSLIC was created as part of the National Housing Act of 1934 in order to insure deposits in savings and loans, a year after the FDIC was created to insure deposits in commercial banks.

a. Securities Investor Protection Corporation

b. Prudent man rule

c. SIPC

d. Federal Savings and Loan Insurance Corporation

25.   A _____ is a financial institution that specializes in accepting savings deposits and making mortgage and other loans. The S'L or thrift term is mainly used in the United States; similar institutions in the United Kingdom, Ireland and some Commonwealth countries include building societies and trustee savings banks.

They are often mutually held, meaning that the depositors and borrowers are members with voting rights, and have the ability to direct the financial and managerial goals of the organization, not unlike the poliyholders of a mutual insurance company.

a. Savings and loan association

b. Mutual fund

c. Person-to-person lending

d. Net asset value

26.   The _____ is the over-the-counter financial market in contracts for future delivery, so called forward contracts. Forward contracts are personalized between parties. The _____ is a general term used to describe the informal market by which these contracts are entered into.

a. Limits to arbitrage   b. Spot rate
c. Delta hedging   d. Forward market

27.   A _____ is a fungible, negotiable instrument representing financial value. They are broadly categorized into debt securities (such as banknotes, bonds and debentures), and equity securities; e.g., common stocks. The company or other entity issuing the _____ is called the issuer.
a. Book entry   b. Security
c. Securities lending   d. Tracking stock

28.   In law, _____ refers to the process by which a company (or part of a company) is brought to an end, and the assets and property of the company redistributed. _____ can also be referred to as winding-up or dissolution, although dissolution technically refers to the last stage of _____. The process of _____ also arises when customs, an authority or agency in a country responsible for collecting and safeguarding customs duties, determines the final computation or ascertainment of the duties or drawback accruing on an entry.
a. 4-4-5 Calendar   b. Debt settlement
c. 529 plan   d. Liquidation

29.   _____ is a measure of the ability of a debtor to pay their debts as and when they fall due. It is usually expressed as a ratio or a percentage of current liabilities.

For a corporation with a published balance sheet there are various ratios used to calculate a measure of liquidity.

a. Invested capital   b. Operating profit margin
c. Operating leverage   d. Accounting liquidity

30.   In business and accounting, _____s are everything of value that is owned by a person or company. The balance sheet of a firm records the monetary value of the _____s owned by the firm. The two major _____ classes are tangible _____s and intangible _____s.
a. Accounts payable   b. Income
c. EBITDA   d. Asset

31.   _____ is a term used to refer to how an investor distributes his or her investments among various classes of investment vehicles (e.g., stocks and bonds.)

A large part of financial planning is finding an _____ that is appropriate for a given person in terms of their appetite for and ability to shoulder risk. This can depend on various factors; see investor profile.

a. Investing online   b. Investment performance
c. Alternative investment   d. Asset allocation

32.   An _____ is any government regulation or law that encourages or discourages foreign investment in the local economy, e.g. currency exchange limits.

As globalization integrates the economies of neighboring and of trading states, they are typically forced to trade off such rules as part of a common tax, tariff and trade regime, e.g. as defined by a free trade pact. _____ favoring local investors over global ones is typically discouraged in such pacts, and the idea of a separate _____ rapidly becomes a fiction or fantasy, as real decisions reflect the real need for nations to compete for investment, even from their own local investors.

a. Investment policy

b. AAB

c. A Random Walk Down Wall Street

d. ABN Amro

Chapter 1

1. d	2. d	3. b	4. d	5. a	6. b	7. a	8. b	9. d	10. d
11. b	12. b	13. c	14. b	15. d	16. d	17. b	18. a	19. d	20. a
21. c	22. d	23. d	24. d	25. d	26. a	27. d	28. d	29. c	30. b
31. d	32. d	33. d	34. c	35. a	36. d	37. d	38. b	39. d	40. d
41. d	42. a	43. d	44. a	45. d	46. d	47. c	48. d	49. b	50. c
51. d	52. b	53. a	54. c	55. b	56. a	57. b	58. b	59. d	60. b
61. b	62. b	63. d	64. d	65. d	66. c	67. c	68. d	69. d	70. c
71. c	72. b	73. d	74. d	75. d	76. a	77. b	78. a	79. d	80. d
81. c	82. b	83. a	84. d	85. c	86. d	87. d	88. a	89. d	90. d
91. a	92. a	93. d	94. d	95. d					

Chapter 2

1. b	2. a	3. b	4. d	5. d	6. d	7. c	8. c	9. c	10. a
11. b	12. b	13. d	14. d	15. a	16. d	17. d	18. b	19. d	20. b
21. b	22. c	23. d	24. d	25. d	26. b	27. d	28. b	29. d	30. d
31. d	32. d	33. d	34. b	35. a	36. d	37. c	38. b	39. d	40. d
41. a	42. c	43. c	44. d	45. b	46. d	47. d	48. d	49. d	50. c
51. d	52. d	53. b	54. d	55. d	56. a	57. d	58. a	59. c	60. b
61. a	62. d	63. d	64. b	65. d	66. d	67. a	68. d	69. b	70. d
71. d	72. a	73. a	74. d	75. d	76. d	77. d	78. d	79. b	80. a
81. a	82. b	83. d	84. c	85. a	86. d	87. d	88. a	89. c	90. d
91. d	92. d	93. d	94. d	95. b	96. a	97. c	98. d	99. a	100. d
101. d									

Chapter 3

1. d	2. d	3. b	4. c	5. d	6. c	7. c	8. d	9. d	10. a
11. a	12. d	13. d	14. d	15. d	16. d	17. d	18. d	19. b	20. a
21. d	22. d	23. d	24. a	25. a	26. c	27. d	28. d	29. d	30. d
31. a	32. c	33. d	34. b	35. d	36. d	37. a	38. b	39. d	40. c
41. a	42. d	43. d	44. c	45. b	46. a	47. d	48. d	49. b	50. a
51. d	52. a	53. c	54. d	55. a	56. b	57. d	58. d	59. c	60. d
61. d	62. d	63. a	64. c	65. b	66. d	67. d	68. c	69. d	70. a
71. b	72. d	73. a	74. d	75. d	76. d	77. a	78. c	79. b	80. c
81. c	82. b	83. d	84. a	85. d	86. d	87. c	88. b	89. d	90. a
91. d	92. b	93. d	94. a	95. c					

Chapter 4

1. b	2. a	3. b	4. b	5. d	6. d	7. a	8. b	9. a	10. b
11. d	12. d	13. d	14. d	15. d	16. a	17. a	18. a	19. a	20. b
21. b	22. b	23. b	24. d	25. d	26. d	27. d	28. d	29. d	30. d
31. c	32. d	33. d	34. d	35. d	36. a	37. a	38. a	39. d	40. d
41. d	42. a	43. a	44. d	45. d	46. a	47. a	48. a	49. a	50. d
51. a	52. d	53. a	54. d	55. c	56. b	57. b	58. c	59. b	60. d
61. c	62. d	63. d	64. a	65. a	66. d	67. d	68. a	69. b	70. c
71. d									

Chapter 5

1. d	2. d	3. a	4. d	5. d	6. b	7. c	8. c	9. d	10. a
11. d	12. d	13. d	14. d	15. a	16. a	17. a	18. b	19. a	20. d
21. c	22. b	23. d	24. c	25. a	26. c	27. d	28. c	29. d	30. d
31. a	32. d	33. d	34. c	35. d	36. b	37. d	38. b	39. d	40. d
41. b	42. c	43. b	44. c	45. a	46. a	47. d	48. d	49. d	50. d
51. c	52. d	53. c	54. c	55. d	56. d	57. d	58. c	59. d	60. c
61. d	62. c	63. a	64. d	65. b	66. d	67. d	68. d	69. a	70. d
71. b	72. d	73. c	74. d						

Chapter 6

1. d	2. d	3. d	4. b	5. d	6. c	7. b	8. a	9. d	10. d
11. d	12. d	13. d	14. b	15. b	16. d	17. d	18. b	19. d	20. b
21. d	22. d	23. d	24. d	25. d	26. b	27. d	28. d	29. c	30. d
31. d	32. a	33. d	34. b	35. d	36. a	37. d	38. d	39. a	40. d
41. a	42. a	43. d	44. b						

Chapter 7

1. a	2. a	3. b	4. b	5. d	6. d	7. c	8. d	9. d	10. d
11. d	12. d	13. b	14. d	15. c	16. a	17. c	18. b	19. a	20. c
21. a	22. d	23. a	24. c	25. b	26. d	27. a	28. d	29. d	30. b
31. b	32. a	33. d	34. a	35. d	36. b	37. a	38. a	39. a	40. d
41. d	42. c	43. c	44. d	45. a	46. c	47. d	48. d	49. d	50. d
51. d	52. a	53. d	54. d	55. c	56. b	57. b	58. c	59. d	60. c
61. a	62. b								

Chapter 8

1. b	2. c	3. d	4. d	5. b	6. d	7. d	8. c	9. d	10. a
11. b	12. d	13. b	14. d	15. d	16. d	17. a	18. d	19. d	20. d
21. d	22. c	23. b	24. a	25. d	26. b	27. d	28. d	29. a	30. d
31. d	32. c	33. a	34. d	35. d	36. b	37. b	38. d	39. b	40. a
41. a	42. a	43. a	44. b	45. d	46. c	47. d	48. c	49. d	50. a
51. d	52. d	53. a	54. a	55. d	56. d	57. d	58. a		

Chapter 9

1. c	2. d	3. d	4. d	5. d	6. d	7. b	8. d	9. b	10. d
11. d	12. b	13. d	14. d	15. d	16. d	17. a	18. b	19. c	20. d
21. d	22. b	23. d	24. c	25. d	26. d	27. c	28. c	29. c	30. d
31. d	32. d	33. d	34. d	35. c	36. a	37. d	38. d	39. c	40. d
41. d	42. a	43. d	44. d	45. b	46. b	47. d	48. b	49. d	50. d
51. c	52. d	53. d	54. d	55. a	56. d	57. d	58. d	59. c	60. c
61. d	62. d	63. d	64. d	65. c	66. b	67. d	68. b	69. d	70. b
71. a	72. d	73. b	74. c	75. a	76. d	77. d	78. d	79. c	80. d
81. d	82. d	83. c	84. d	85. c	86. b	87. d	88. d	89. b	90. d
91. d	92. b	93. a	94. b	95. d					

Chapter 10

1. c	2. a	3. c	4. d	5. c	6. d	7. c	8. d	9. d	10. d
11. b	12. d	13. d	14. b	15. d	16. d	17. a	18. d	19. c	20. a
21. d	22. a	23. b	24. d	25. c	26. d	27. b	28. d	29. a	30. d
31. b	32. b	33. c	34. c	35. a	36. c	37. d	38. d	39. d	40. d
41. b									

Chapter 11

1. c	2. d	3. d	4. c	5. a	6. a	7. d	8. c	9. c	10. b
11. d	12. d	13. d	14. b	15. d	16. b	17. d	18. c	19. a	20. b
21. d	22. d	23. a	24. d	25. b	26. a	27. d	28. d	29. c	30. d
31. b	32. b	33. c	34. a	35. d	36. b	37. d	38. c	39. c	40. a
41. a	42. d	43. b	44. d	45. d	46. d	47. d	48. d	49. a	50. b
51. d	52. b	53. d	54. c	55. d	56. d	57. d	58. c	59. a	60. d
61. d	62. d	63. b	64. c	65. c	66. c	67. c	68. a		

Chapter 12

1. a	2. d	3. d	4. d	5. d	6. a	7. d	8. a	9. a	10. d
11. a	12. c	13. a	14. a	15. d	16. a	17. b	18. c	19. d	20. d
21. d	22. c	23. d	24. d	25. a	26. a	27. a	28. d	29. d	30. a
31. c	32. d	33. d	34. d	35. d	36. d	37. d	38. a	39. c	40. a
41. d	42. a	43. d	44. a	45. d	46. c	47. b	48. a	49. b	50. d
51. c	52. a	53. d	54. d	55. d	56. a	57. b	58. b	59. c	60. d
61. b	62. a	63. d							

Chapter 13

1. a	2. c	3. d	4. c	5. b	6. c	7. d	8. d	9. c	10. b
11. c	12. b	13. b	14. d	15. c	16. b	17. c	18. c	19. d	20. d
21. d	22. b	23. d	24. c	25. d	26. d	27. c	28. d	29. b	30. c
31. c	32. d	33. d	34. d	35. b	36. d	37. a	38. b	39. c	40. d
41. c	42. d	43. b	44. a	45. c	46. d	47. c	48. d	49. b	50. d
51. a	52. c	53. b	54. b	55. a	56. b	57. c	58. d	59. b	60. a
61. a	62. d	63. b	64. c	65. d	66. a	67. a	68. a	69. c	70. b
71. d	72. b	73. c	74. d	75. c	76. d	77. c	78. b	79. d	80. a
81. a	82. d	83. d	84. b	85. d	86. c	87. d	88. b	89. c	90. d

Chapter 14

1. a	2. d	3. b	4. d	5. d	6. d	7. a	8. d	9. d	10. a
11. a	12. d	13. d	14. d	15. a	16. d	17. d	18. c	19. d	20. d
21. d	22. c	23. a	24. c	25. d	26. b	27. b	28. d	29. d	30. c
31. d	32. c	33. a	34. d	35. b	36. a	37. c	38. c	39. c	40. b
41. d	42. d	43. d	44. c	45. d	46. d	47. d	48. d	49. a	50. d
51. d	52. d	53. a	54. d	55. b	56. c	57. d	58. c	59. b	

Chapter 15

1. d	2. a	3. d	4. d	5. d	6. c	7. d	8. d	9. c	10. a
11. a	12. a	13. a	14. b	15. d	16. d	17. c	18. c	19. b	20. b
21. c	22. a	23. c	24. c	25. d	26. c	27. c	28. d	29. a	30. d
31. a	32. d	33. d	34. d	35. b					

Chapter 16

1. d	2. b	3. b	4. c	5. d	6. a	7. b	8. c	9. d	10. c
11. d	12. d	13. d	14. d	15. d	16. a	17. d	18. d	19. d	20. d
21. a	22. d	23. b	24. c	25. b	26. d	27. c	28. a	29. d	30. b
31. d	32. d	33. d	34. d	35. c	36. b	37. d	38. d	39. c	40. d
41. a	42. a	43. d	44. a	45. d	46. a	47. d	48. b	49. b	50. a
51. d	52. a	53. b	54. b	55. d	56. c	57. d	58. d	59. c	60. d
61. d	62. a	63. d							

Chapter 17

1. b	2. d	3. a	4. d	5. d	6. a	7. b	8. d	9. c	10. c
11. a	12. d	13. a	14. c	15. a	16. c	17. d	18. b	19. d	20. d
21. d	22. d	23. b							

Chapter 18

1. a	2. d	3. b	4. d	5. c	6. d	7. c	8. b	9. a	10. d
11. d	12. d	13. b	14. b	15. d	16. d	17. d	18. b	19. d	20. b
21. c	22. d	23. c	24. d	25. a	26. b	27. c	28. d	29. b	30. d
31. d	32. d	33. d	34. b	35. b	36. d	37. d	38. a	39. d	40. d
41. d	42. a	43. d	44. d	45. a	46. c	47. b			

Chapter 19

1. d	2. d	3. a	4. d	5. c	6. d	7. c	8. d	9. b	10. a
11. d	12. b	13. d	14. d	15. c	16. c	17. d	18. a	19. a	20. a
21. a	22. d	23. a	24. b	25. b	26. d	27. b	28. c	29. b	30. d
31. d	32. a	33. b	34. c	35. a	36. c	37. d	38. d	39. d	40. d
41. d	42. d	43. d	44. b	45. b	46. d	47. b	48. a	49. b	50. d
51. c	52. d	53. d	54. d	55. a	56. c	57. a			

Chapter 20

1. a	2. a	3. a	4. c	5. d	6. b	7. d	8. d	9. d	10. c
11. a	12. a	13. d	14. b	15. b	16. d	17. d	18. d	19. d	20. d
21. b	22. b	23. d	24. d						

Chapter 21

1. a	2. c	3. a	4. d	5. a	6. d	7. d	8. b	9. d	10. b
11. d	12. d	13. d	14. a	15. d	16. b	17. b	18. c	19. d	20. d
21. b	22. a	23. d	24. d	25. a	26. d	27. b	28. d	29. d	30. d
31. d	32. a								

Ingram Content Group UK Ltd.
Milton Keynes UK
UKHW050832200723
425492UK00005B/384